First Edition

PRESENTATIONS THAT MATTER

Melanie Morgan, Jennifer Hall & Lindsey B. Anderson

Presentations That Matter

Melanie Morgan, Jennifer Hall & Lindsey B. Anderson
First Edition

Copyright © by Melanie Morgan, Jennifer Hall & Lindsey B. Anderson
Copyright © by Van-Griner, LLC

Photos and other illustrations are owned by Van-Griner or used under license.

All products used herein are for identification purposes only, and may be trademarks or registered trademarks of their respective owners.

All rights reserved. No part of this book may be reproduced or transmitted in any form or by any means, electronic or mechanical, including photocopying, recording or by any information storage and retrieval system, without written permission from the author and publisher.

Printed in the United States of America
10 9 8 7 6 5 4 3 2 1
ISBN: 978-1-61740-438-2

Van-Griner Publishing
Cincinnati, Ohio
www.van-griner.com

CEO: Mike Griner
President: Dreis Van Landuyt
Project Manager: Maria Walterbusch
Customer Care Lead: Julie Reichert

Anderson 438-2 Sp18
183235
Copyright © 2019

Contents

Chapter 1 Introduction 1
Chapter 2 Presenting with Confidence 25
Chapter 3 Delivering with Skill 47
Chapter 4 Assessing the Speaking Situation 77
Chapter 5 Information Literacy. 105
Chapter 6 Presentation Preparation. 143
Chapter 7 Narratives and Storytelling 169
Chapter 8 Informative Presentations 203
Chapter 9 Visual Communication 225
Chapter 10 The Persuasive Process 259
Chapter 11 Persuasive Speaking 277
Chapter 12 Virtual Presentations. 315
Chapter 13 Presentation Situations 335

Chapter 1

Introduction

Objectives

After this chapter you will be able to:

- Articulate the importance of communication in your everyday life.
- Define communication.
- Understand the different communication models.
- Explain presentational speaking.
- Discuss various types of plagiarism.

Chapter 1   Introduction

In 2010, Brene Brown was working as an Associate Professor of Social Work at University of Houston. Few people outside of her department and those in the social work field knew who she was. Brown's work and research focused on how shame impacts people and their ability to be successful. That year, she was given the opportunity to talk about her research at a small, local TEDX event. She thought it was a good opportunity to share her ideas about shame and vulnerability with the audience who she assumed would mostly be other academics. Her main message was people needed to be willing to be vulnerable and admit their weaknesses in order to establish true connection with others. Feelings of shame prevent people from being vulnerable. For 20 minutes, Brown shared what she had learned from interviewing hundreds of people as well as insights into how shame and vulnerability had impacted her own life. After her talk, she worried about what people would think of her. She knew the talk would be posted online and assumed that as many as 500 people might watch her. Little did Brown know that her talk, entitled The Power of Vulnerability, would have more than 30 million views, making it one of the most watched and shared TED Talks of all time. Audiences connected with her message and widely shared the video with family, friends, and colleagues. The success of her talk helped catapult Brown into the national spotlight, and she is now the author of four best-selling books in which she further explores the ideas of shame, vulnerability, and courage. She now regularly speaks around the country to everyone from women's groups to collections of CEOs.

Let's Talk
1. Why do you think Brown's talk was so successful?
2. What does this example illustrate about the power of communication?

The Importance of Communication

Communication is a difficult concept to define because it is so pervasive and appears to be automatic. We constantly interact with others (both verbally and non-verbally); thus, there is an assumption that it is easy to communicate well. But this is not the case. In this chapter, we will discuss the importance of communication in your everyday life, define key terms like communication, presentational speaking, and plagiarism, and preview the remainder of the textbook.

Other people have recognized that it is difficult to communicate well and that it is critical to gain skills to help us become better communicators. For example, Warren Buffett, a successful American business tycoon, argued that learning to communicate well—specifically gaining the ability to speak in front of people—is the most important skill to master to help your career and increase your value in the workplace.[1]

While speaking to a class of business students at Columbia University, Buffett underscored the value of being able to communicate orally. He said:

Right now, I would pay a hundred thousand dollars for 10 percent of the future earnings of any of you ... If that's true, you're a million dollar asset right now, right? If 10 percent of you is worth a hundred thousand? [However] You could improve on that, many of you, and I certainly could have when I got out, just in terms of learning communication skills. ... It's not something that's taught, I actually went to a Dale Carnegie course later on in terms of public speaking. But if you improve your value 50 percent by having better communication skills, it's another 500-thousand dollars in terms of capital value. See me after the class and I'll pay you 150-thousand.

Through this quotation, Buffett put a monetary value on the process of learning and subsequently honing the skills needed to speak in public.

Chris Anderson, the head of TED Talks, also emphasized the importance of learning how to communicate well in a variety of situations in your everyday life. He explained, "As a leader—or as an advocate—public speaking is the key to unlocking empathy, stirring excitement, sharing knowledge and insights, and promoting a shared dream."[2]

As Buffett and Anderson noted through their comments, being able to speak well can help you effectively share your message with a variety of people (investors, customers, colleagues, managers, and friends) and will allow you to make your point in everyday life situations, such as those that take place at school, work, home, and your larger community.[3]

Definition of Communication

So what exactly is communication and how is it enacted? According to the National Communication Association (NCA), "communication focuses on how people use messages to generate meanings within and across various contexts, and is the discipline that studies all forms, modes, media, and consequences of communication through humanistic, social scientific, and aesthetic inquiry."[4]

At the heart of this definition of communication is the idea that people intentionally create messages. This means that communication is not accidental or automatic, but rather intentional and strategic.

The NCA definition also claims that these messages are used to create meanings that are plural rather than singular because they are context-specific. For instance, you could give the "okay" hand gesture in the United States to show approval, while the same gesture in Japan would signify money and in France would mean zero.[5]

Moreover, communication is enacted in a variety of ways. Think about how you communicate every day—in-person, electronically, text, and symbols. The variety of ways that communication can take place has also been noted. In fact, "communication involves transmission of verbal and non-verbal messages. It consists of a sender, a receiver and a channel of communication. In the process of transmitting messages, the clarity of the message may be interfered or distorted by what is often referred to as barriers."[6]

With that said, the actual communication process includes a variety of factors. The above definition that covers how communication is enacted highlights key aspects of the communication process—sender, receiver, channel, message, interference, encoding, and decoding. These factors lead us to the models of communication.

Communication Models

The process or enactment of communication is commonly conceptualized as either (1) linear, (2) interactive, or (3) transactional. These models are used to explain the act of communication using the factors previously discussed, like sender, receiver, and channel. These models will be presented in order of increasing complexity.

> **Communication Models**
> - Linear
> - Interactive
> - Transactional

Let's talk about each of the three types of communication models. The linear model[7] of communication is the most simplistic. It takes a transmission perspective, where the message is moved down a line until it reaches the intended audience. The model includes seven factors: (1) the **sender**/information source (this is the person who creates the message) (2) **encodes** a message, which is the act of taking abstract thoughts and turning them into a coherent message. (3) A **message** is the information or content that the sender wants to communicate to the receiver. This message is communicated through (4) a **channel** or the selected medium of communication (e.g., phone, email, television) to (5) a **receiver** who is the intended target/audience for the message. The receiver then (6) **decodes** or interprets the sent content in order to understand the sender's message. This process can be derailed by the presence of (7) **noise,** which is any interference with the transmission of the message (e.g., construction outside of a classroom or bustling traffic during a coffee date). Noise can also be more complex. For example, context and culture could impact encoding a message.

As you can imagine, the act of communication in the linear model is a one-way process that limits feedback and ultimately repeats itself until the interaction is complete.

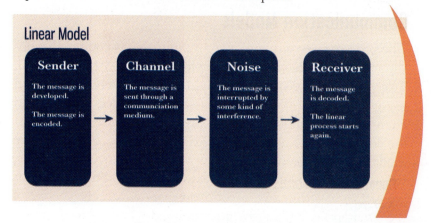

The interactive model extends the linear model by recognizing that in order for the communication process to be complete, the linear model has to be reversed. By this we mean that the receiver is expected to respond to the sender's message. As such, it allows for feedback, albeit in a procedural manner that is delayed. This model can be seen in communication that place over the phone, through emails, or via text-messages or other "lean" channels.[8] (See discussion on rich and lean mediums or channels below.)

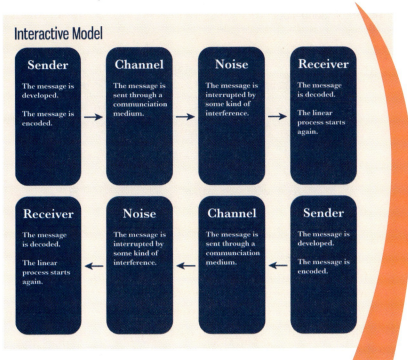

The transactional model builds on the linear and interactive models by recognizing that in many communicative interactions, the speaker and listener are simultaneously encoding and decoding messages within an environment that includes the context of the situation as well as the personal and cultural backgrounds of each communicator. Thus, there is not a delay in acting as a sender or receiver, but rather, both parties communicate (provide feedback, encode, and decode messages) simultaneously.

This model also accounts for a more nuanced understanding of noise, which can be environmental (the construction and traffic examples) as well as physiological (a sick audience member) and psychological (studying for a test in the next class).

As you can see, the transactional model has the most complex view of communication because it allows for overlapping feedback and, as such, is positioned as a two-way model of communication.[9]

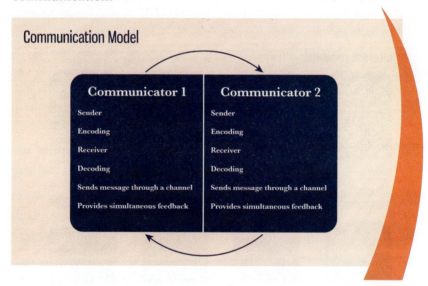

The models also introduce the idea of **"rich"** and **"lean"** communication mediums, which stems from the theory of media richness. This theory "advances the notion that communication richness (or leanness) is an objective property of communication media, and defines media richness as the ability to facilitate shared understanding within a time interval."[10] In other words, the theory examines how mediums can enhance or detract from an intended message/meaning as well as encourage or discourage two-way communication (feedback). For example, imagine the difference in communicating face-to-face vs. email. Sometimes when reading an email, we may think someone is angry with us because we can not interpret their nonverbal communication such as tone or facial expression. The medium of email constrains the type of communication that can occur.

The level of richness is determined by the following criteria:[11]

- **Capacity for immediate feedback:** A rich medium allows for quick/immediate feedback. For example, in face-to-face communication a conversational partner could express confusion by making a quizzical facial expression.
- **Capacity to transmit multiple cues:** A rich medium allows for multiple avenues to express understanding or provide nonverbal and/or verbal feedback. A text message does not allow you to insert tone into the content of the text.
- **Language variety:** A rich medium allows for multiple types of nonverbal and/or verbal language to be used. For example, a report about company profits may be written in a formal, precise style, but this does not allow for informal, common language that could enhance the reader's understanding.
- **Capacity of the medium to have a personal focus:** A rich medium allows for the expression of emotions and feelings by all communicative partners. For example, it is hard to convey emotion over email.

In addition to richness of the medium, the content of the message matters in terms of the appropriate channel. For example, you wouldn't break up with a romantic partner using a lean medium (like text messaging) because these channels do not allow for the expression of emotion or feeling. In fact, the selection of the wrong type of medium has been used in popular media for laughs, like Berger breaking up with Carrie through a Post-It note (a la *Sex and the City*). However, if you wanted to share a detailed list of tasks that one of your employees needed to complete by the end of the week, you would want to use a lean medium that conveys the information in a succinct and precise manner and does not allow for much ambiguity.

In addition to the richness of the medium and content of your message, think about how technology has influenced the importance of choosing the right medium (either lean or rich).[10] Also think about how technological advancements impact the effectiveness of the communication models (linear, interactive, and transactional). The information presented here matters as you choose mediums for the communication messages/narratives you want to share.

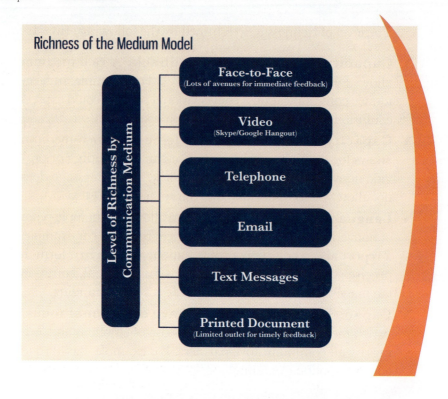

Presentational Speaking

This book is focused on a specific type of communication—**presentational speaking.** At this point you may be wondering what exactly presentational speaking is. We conceptualize presentational speaking as a form of communication that is used in daily interactions—from talking in class, to updating colleagues about a project, to speaking at a municipal meeting.

Presentational speaking is often confused with **public speaking,** but the two terms refer to different types of speaking. Presentational speaking is less formal than public speaking that takes place with a smaller audience and uses an extemporaneous style of delivery (see Chapter 3). It is useful to think of presentational speaking as "mini-presentations" that you will use more often than formal, public speaking events.[12] In other words, you will give a variety of informal presentations throughout a given day—away from "public," stiff, and overly formal settings. For example, you might provide an update at work/internship about a project you have been working on or attempt to persuade your roommate that it is his turn to clean the kitchen.

Most people assume any presentation you prepare for that has an audience is public speaking, but this is not the case. Public speaking is much more formal and often requires precise language using a memorized or manuscript style of delivery (see Chapter 3). Public speaking also does not allow for in-time audience feedback. When you think of public speaking, imagine one person presenting to a large, unknown audience without synchronous audience feedback. Examples of traditional public speaking include the president giving the State of the Union Address or a news anchor reading the day's top stories from a teleprompter. As you can see, these instances of communication are vastly different from what you are expected to do in this class, even during the larger presentation assignments.

However, both presentational and public speaking use the same basic skills including audience analysis, organization, and research.[12]

So why is presentational speaking an important skill to develop? As previously noted, it is a valuable skill that you will use throughout your lives in school, work, home, and community settings. In fact, the Association of American Colleges and Universities (AACU) has also recognized this imperative for college students and new graduates and echoes the importance of learning how to speak well while in college.[13]

Employer Priorities for Most Important College Learning Outcomes

Adapted from the Association of American Colleges and Universities 2015 National Survey of Business and Nonprofit Leaders and Current College Students.

Learning Outcome (LO) or Skill	Percent of Employers Rating the LO/Skill as Important
Oral communication skills	85%
Teamwork skills in diverse groups	83%
Written communication skills	82%
Critical thinking and analytic reasoning	81%
Ethical judgment and decision making	81%
Ability to apply knowledge to real-world settings	80%
Information literacy	68%

Over the course of the semester we will address each of the learning outcomes/skills that was recognized as important by employers and AACU using some of the following examples:

- Oral communication skills will be taught during daily class activities and larger speaking assignments.
- Teamwork skills in diverse groups will be developed as you work on the group presentation project.
- Written communication skills will be honed during the process of preparing and organizing your presentations (e.g., outlining).
- You will demonstrate critical thinking and analytical reasoning while developing your message and deciding on supporting evidence.
- Ethical judgment will be practiced as you decide how to present information accurately and honestly (e.g., plagiarism).

- Real-world applications will be emphasized as we show the practicality of the content covered in this course and ask you to think about how often you communicate and how important these skills are to your academic, professional, home, and community lives.
- Information literacy skills will be practiced as you learn how to research and select credible information that supports your message.

Ethical Communication

One of the key take-aways from the AACU report is that ethics are important. **Ethics** are the framework we use to determine what is morally right or wrong. However, this is a difficult term to define since ethical standards and perspectives vary among individuals, cultures, and contexts. This definition highlights how ethical standards can be interpreted differently based on culture and context, which is an important point to make since culture impacts communication choices.

Overview of Ethics

NCA has developed a more comprehensive definition of ethics using U.S. standards.[14]

This credo for ethical communication states,

Questions of right and wrong arise whenever people communicate. Ethical communication is fundamental to responsible thinking, decision-making, and the development of relationships and communities within and across contexts, cultures, channels, and media. Moreover, ethical communication enhances human worth and dignity by fostering truthfulness, fairness, responsibility, personal integrity, and respect for self and others. We believe that unethical communication threatens the quality of all communication and consequently the well being of individuals and the society in which we live. Therefore we, the members of the National Communication Association, endorse and are committed to practicing the following principles of ethical communication:

We advocate truthfulness, accuracy, honesty, and reason as essential to the integrity of communication.

- *We endorse freedom of expression, diversity of perspective, and tolerance of dissent to achieve the informed and responsible decision-making fundamental to a civil society.*
- *We strive to understand and respect other communicators before evaluating and responding to their messages.*
- *We promote access to communication resources and opportunities as necessary to fulfill human potential and contribute to the well being of families, communities, and society.*
- *We promote communication climates of caring and mutual understanding that respect the unique needs and characteristics of individual communicators.*
- *We condemn communication that degrades individuals and humanity through distortion, intimidation, coercion, violence, and through the expression of intolerance and hatred.*
- *We are committed to the courageous expression of personal convictions in pursuit of fairness and justice.*
- *We advocate sharing information, opinions, and feelings when facing significant choices while also respecting privacy and confidentiality.*
- *We accept responsibility for the short- and long-term consequences for our own communication and expect the same of others.*

The Role of Ethics in Presentational Speaking

Ethics is at the forefront of presentational speaking—from audience analysis and topic choice to research and the accurate presentation of information.

Audience analysis (see Chapter 4) involves ethical decision making as you start to evaluate who you will be speaking to during your presentation. It is important to be thoughtful about the information you collect and ethical in the way you use the information. For example, if you are preparing a presentation to support the idea that climate change is real and discover that only one of your audience members does not believe tin climate change, then you may want to rethink your presentation topic. If you decide to go forward with your climate change topic, then it is unfair to single that audience member out during your presentation.

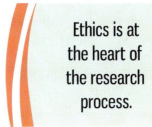

Ethics is at the heart of the research process.

Ethics is also at the heart of the research process (see Chapter 5). As a communicator you must be credible and unbiased. The onus is on the speaker to evaluate potential sources and determine their accuracy. Ethics in the research process also extends to presenting the gathered information correctly (not fudging the data, sharing the source of information, or citing the source correctly). This point leads us to the concept of plagiarism.

Plagiarism

Plagiarism is a vague concept that has multiple interpretations of what counts as plagiarized work.[15] A common definition of plagiarism states that it

> *is the act of using someone else's words, ideas, organization, drawings, designs, illustrations, statistical data, computer programs, inventions or any creative work as if it were new and original to you; this includes real and intellectual property and public domain material. It is the buying or procuring of papers, cutting and pasting from works on the internet, not using quotation marks around direct quotes, paraphrasing and not citing original works, and it is having someone else write your paper or a substantial part of your paper and turning it in as if it were new and original to you. To avoid plagiarism, one must internalize, understand and reorganize material and make it one's own.*[15]

As evidenced by this definition, the act of plagiarism takes many forms. For example, plagiarism includes (1) not using quotations correctly, (2) copying someone else's work, (3) forgetting to cite sources in your paper or on the reference page, (4) deliberately doing so, (5) helping someone on a paper, outline, or speech, or (6) recycling your old work.

When you are preparing for a presentation, it is important to know what the different types of plagiarism are so you can avoid the. The first type of plagiarism, **cloning,** is what typically think comes to mind when we think about plagiarism. Cloning is when a person takes another's work and claims it as his own. Turning in a friend's term paper from the previous semester or purchasing a term paper online are both examples of cloning. This type of plagiarism is most common in academic settings, it does occur in other situations. Mixed Martial Artist (MMA) fighter Kenny Florian found himself in trouble after it was discovered that the majority of an article he wrote for FoxSports.com had been taken word for word from another MMA analyst's YouTube video. Florian apologized to the public after the plagiarism was discovered and was quickly suspended from the network.[16]

Probably the most common type of plagiarism is known as **copy and paste** plagiarism. This is when a person takes parts of another's work or parts of multiple works and does not give appropriate credit for them. This can include not giving a citation for directly copied work or not putting quotation marks around a direct quote. When John Walsh, the former Junior Senator from Minnesota, was running for reelection in a hotly contested race, his opponents discovered that the majority of his Master's thesis had been plagiarized. In his thesis paper, he either failed to provide correct citations for material or did not put material he had copied word for word in quotation marks. The negative publicity this discovery generated forced Walsh to withdraw from the race and led his alma mater, the Army War College, to revoke his Master's degree.[17]

One way that people try to avoid copy and paste plagiarism is to paraphrase material rather than directly quoting it. **Ineffective paraphrasing** occurs when the paraphrase is too close to the original text and is not presented as a direct quote, or the paraphrase is not cited. Changing a few words, or the order of words, does not mean that you have now created original material. You must always give credit when you have taken another person's ideas or work. This issue of paraphrasing and plagiarism gained national attention in 2016 when Melania Trump addressed the Republican National Convention to support her husband and the Republican presidential nominee, Donald Trump. Shortly after her speech ended, footage of Michelle Obama's speech at the 2008 Democratic National Convention began to circulate and journalist identified several sections of Melania's speech that were nearly identical. These accusations of plagiarism both reflected poorly on the future first lady and were source of embarrassment to the Trump campaign.[18]

> Changing a few words, or the order of words, does not mean that you have now created original material.

Another form of plagiarism that people do not often consider is **excessive collaboration.** Excessive collaboration occurs when someone works collaboratively with another person, but then represents the work as his or her own. If you are assigned to prepare and deliver a final design presentation for class, it would not be acceptable for you to work with a student in a different section to prepare almost the same presentation and then each present it as your own. This does not mean that you cannot and should seek out feedback and advice from other classmates and colleagues. It does mean that any work you represent as your own should be a result of your own research, work, and ideas.

Another thing to be aware of is **copyright infringement.** Copyright infringement is different from plagiarism and is often unintentional, but it can have steep financial consequences. "Copyright is the right of authors to control the use of their work for a limited period of time."[19] The work must be original to the author and a "tangible medium of expression."[20] In presentations, copyright infringement is often related to the use of graphics and videos in a slide show. Most of the uses of graphics and videos in this course will fall under the fair use category, meaning that you can use the work without paying for it. However, the creative work (photo, video, etc.) must be appropriately cited.

> ### Academic Integrity and Plagiarism Policies
> Each university has its own policy regarding plagiarism. Search your university's website for academic integrity and plagiarism policies.

Another type of plagiarism is **self-plagiarism.** It may sound counterintuitive, but it is possible to plagiarize yourself. Self-plagiarism occurs when you turn in work that was previously used for the same course or another course. For example, if you gave a presentation about the benefits of adopting a vegetarian diet for a nutrition class and then you use the same presentation in this class, then you just plagiarized yourself. You need to make sure to always create new work for each of your classes or to give background about how the material you are submitting was previously used.

With all types of plagiarism, it is important to remember that you do not have to intentionally misrepresent other's work as you own to plagiarize something. **Accidental plagiarism** occurs when someone unintentionally improperly or forgets to cite work taken from another source. This is why it is important to know how to cite direct quotes and how to properly cite work that has been paraphrased. Just because you did not mean to plagiarize, does not mean that you did not do it. If you ever have a question about whether or not something needs to be cited, it is always a good idea to error on the side of caution.

Preview of the Remainder of the Textbook

We will be discussing a variety of topics needed to communicate well in this textbook. In the remainder of the chapter, we will preview what you have to look forward to learning about this semester.

Chapter 2: Presenting with Confidence—This chapter will also introduce the concept of communication apprehension and offer suggestions for keeping it at bay while you deliver formal and informal presentations.

Chapter 3: Delivering with Skill—In Chapter 3 we will discuss aspects of verbal and nonverbal delivery, such as vocal fry, up speak, rapport, movement, and posture.

Chapter 4: Assessing the Speaking Situation—Chapter 4 will help you understand who you are speaking to so you can choose an interesting topic, collect appropriate information, and frame your message. We will also talk about environmental analysis, so you can be prepared for the setting in which you are presenting (time of day, seating, and length of class).

Chapter 5: Information Literacy—This chapter introduces the research process. This includes finding supporting evidence, evaluating sources, and choosing a variety of data (e.g., statistics, interviews).

Chapter 6: Presentation Preparation—In Chapter 6 we will discuss ways for you to prepare your presentation. Specifically, we will talk about main and supporting ideas, organizational structures, and the major parts of a presentation (introduction, body, and conclusion).

Chapter 7: Narratives and Storytelling—Chapter 7 introduces the idea that narratives are an important part of presentational speaking. Here we talk about how narratives can be used to structure your message as well as how storytelling can serve as evidence for your presentation.

Chapter 8: Informative Presentations—In Chapter 8 we will share the characteristics of informative presentations and review the various types, which include how-to speeches, technical communication, and scientific communication.

Chapter 9: Visual Communication—Chapter 9 will provide best practices for integrating visual aids into your presentation. We will discuss types of visual information (infographics), slide design concepts, and visual aid templates (PowerPoint, Prezi).

Chapter 10: The Persuasive Process—Chapter 10 examines the persuasive process and highlights some basic persuasive and argumentation strategies.

Chapter 11: Persuasive Speaking—Chapter 11 continues to discuss persuasive speaking and focuses on how to organize different types of persuasive presentations.

Chapter 12: Virtual Presentations—In Chapter 12 we will discuss the increasing need to learn how to present online and will share best practices for presenting in virtual formats.

Chapter 13: Presentation Situations—We conclude the textbook by discussing various types of presentation situations. Often called special occasion speaking, we will talk about briefings, poster sessions, lightening presentations, elevator pitches, speeches of introductions, and toasts.

Chapter Summary

In this chapter we introduced the general purpose of this book. Specifically, we discussed the importance of communication in your everyday life, defined key terms like communication, presentational speaking, and plagiarism, and previewed the remainder of the textbook. After reading this chapter, you should be more aware of the important and complex role that communication, generally, and presentational speaking, specifically, play in your everyday life.

Case Study Conclusion

Brene Brown's story illustrates how powerful a presentation can be. By agreeing to give a TEDX Talk, Brown provided people across the globe the opportunity to hear her message. Her story also illustrates two of the key factors that make a presentation successful: content and delivery. The information that Brown shared was interesting and relevant to her audience. One of your primary goals in giving a presentation is to provide your audience with information that they want or need. Her delivery also helped her audience to connect with the message. Rather than reading from her notes, Brown looked directly at her audience and spoke to them. Her voice was confident and unhesitating, a signal to the audience that she was knowledgeable and credible. Our goal with this book is to help you learn how to communicate in ways that will enable you to reach your communication goals.

References

1. Buffet, W. 2009. "Speech to Students" (speech). From "Warren Buffet and Bill Gates: Keeping America Great." *CNBC*. Video retrieved from: http://www.cnbc.com/id/33891448.
2. Anderson, C. 2016. *TED Talks: The Official TED Guide to Public Speaking*. New York: Houghton Mifflin Harcourt.
3. Gallo, C. 2017. "Billionaire Warren Buffett Says This 1 Skill Will Boost Your Career Value by 50 Percent." *Inc.* January 5, 2017. http://www.inc.com/carmine-gallo/the-one-skill-warren-buffett-says-will-raise-your-value-by-50.html.
4. "What Is Communication?" 2016. National Communication Association. https://www.natcom.org/about-nca/what-communication.
5. Cotton, G. 2013. "Gestures to Avoid in Cross-Cultural Business: In Other Words, 'Keep Your Fingers to Yourself!'" *HUFFPOST* (blog), June 13, 2013. http://www.huffingtonpost.com/gayle-cotton/cross-cultural-gestures_b_3437653.html.
6. Munodawafa, D. 2008. "Communication: Concepts, Practice, and Challenges." *Health Education Research* 23(3): 369–370. https://doi.org/10.1093/her/cyn024.
7. Shannon, C. E., and W. Weaver. 1949. "The Mathematical Theory of Information." *The Bell System Technical Journal* 27: 379–423.
8. "Communication Process." n.d. *Communication Studies*. http://www.communicationstudies.com/communication-process.
9. "The Models of Communication." n.d. *The Communication Process*. http://thecommunicationprocess.com/models-of-communication/for interactive.
10. Sun, P-C, and H. K. Cheng. 2005. "The Design of Instructional Multimedia in e-Learning: A Media Richness Theory-Based Approach." *Computers and Education* 49(3): 662–676. http://dx.doi.org/10.1016/j.compedu.2005.11.016.
11. Daft. R. I., R. H. Lengel, and L. K. Trevino. 1987. "Message Equivocality, Media Selection, and Manager Performance: Implications for Information Systems." *MIS Quarterly* 11(3): 355–366.
12. Foss, S. K., and K. A. Foss. 2012. *Inviting Transformation: Presentational Speaking for a Changing World* (3rd ed.). Long Grove, IL: Waveland Press.
13. "Falling Short: College Learning and Career Success." 2015. *AACU*. https://www.aacu.org/leap/public-opinion-research/2015-survey-falling-short.
14. "Credo for Ethical Communication." 2016. *NCA*. http://www.natcom.org/ethicalstatements/.

15. Liddell, J. 2003. "A Comprehensive Definition of Plagiarism." *Community & Junior College Libraries* 11: 43–52. doi: 10.1300/J107v11n03_07.
16. Thomas, L. 2016. "Fox Sports Suspends Kenny Florian for Plagiarizing Portions of Preview Article." *MMA Fighting* (blog), Jan. 16, 2016. https://www.mmafighting.com/2016/1/16/10779846/fox-sports-suspends-kenny-florian-for-plagiarizing-portions-of
17. Martin, J. 2014. "Plagiarism Costs Degree for Senator John Walsh." *New York Times*, Oct. 10, 2014. https://www.nytimes.com/2014/10/11/us/politics/plagiarism-costs-degree-for-senator-john-walsh.html.
18. McCarthy, T., and B. Jacobs. 2016. "Melania Trump Convention Speech Seems to Plagiarise Michelle Obama." *The Guardian*, July 19, 2016. https://www.theguardian.com/us-news/2016/jul/19/melania-trump-republican-convention-plagiarism-michelle-obama.
19. "University Copyright Office," accessed March 6, 2018, https://www.lib.purdue.edu/uco/
20. "University Copyright Office."
21. Clair, R. P., L. B. Anderson, and D. Torres. November 2016. "Extending Narrative Empathy and 'Facing' Ethical Challenges in Non-profit Organizations: The Case of Kiva." Paper to be presented at the annual meeting of the National Communication Association, Philadelphia, PA.

Chapter 2

Presenting with Confidence

Objectives

After this chapter you will be able to:

- Identify the reasons for and symptoms of public speaking anxiety.
- Apply strategies for managing public speaking anxiety.
- Assess your level of public speaking anxiety.
- Identify symptoms of public speaking anxiety.

Pastor Joel Osteen has made a career out of public speaking. Not only does he preach to a congregation of over 25,000 each Sunday, but his sermons are also broadcast on television to a global audience each week. He regularly sells out entire stadiums with fans eager to hear his message. Nicknamed the "smiling preacher," one could easily assume that Osteen was born with a natural gift for speaking in public, but the reality is that Osteen spent most of his life terrified by the thought of speaking in front of a group. The son of a successful preacher, Osteen showed no inclination to follow in his father's footsteps as doing something as simple as standing up to make an announcement in church filled him with extreme anxiety. Instead of taking an active speaking role in the family ministry, he was content to work behind the scenes running the audio visual equipment.

Things changed though, in 1999, when Osteen's father became seriously ill and asked Osteen to deliver the sermon for him that Sunday. At first he declined, too nervous to address the entire congregation, but as his father's health continued to decline, Osteen decided that he needed to help his father. That Sunday he stood up and delivered his first ever public sermon at the age of 35. He was so nervous he was almost physically sick. He is the first to tell you that there was nothing great about that sermon, but he at least made it through the service. Osteen's father died just days later, and while Osteen still had a tremendous fear of public speaking, he continued to preach believing he was called to do so. This did not stop him, however, from feeling sick each time he knew that he was going to have to preach or address a crowd.

Let's Talk
1. What strategies could Osteen use to help cope with his extreme fear of public speaking?
2. Can you relate to Osteen's fear of public speaking?

Introduction

Like Joel Osteen, for many people, the mere thought of giving a presentation is anxiety provoking. Getting up and speaking in front of a group makes people nervous. Public speaking anxiety often manifests itself in poor delivery techniques such as nervous movements, poor eye contact, or rapid speech rate. In this chapter you will learn more about what communion public speaking anxiety is, why people experience public speaking anxiety, types of anxiety, and techniques for managing your anxiety and nerves.

Public Speaking Anxiety

If you are someone with a fear of public speaking, you are not alone. Each year, Chapman University conducts a survey to learn about people's fears. In 2016, public speaking was the most commonly identified personal fear, outranking snakes, heights, bugs, and drowning.[1] It is estimated that up to 75 percent of people suffer from some level of communication apprehension.[2] Other famous people who you might be surprised to learn suffered from an almost debilitating fear of public speaking include Warren Buffet, Ghandi, Harrison Ford, Barbra Streisand, and Leonardo DiCaprio. Interestingly, DiCaprio once admitted in an interview that he used to hope he would not win any awards for his acting because he did not want to get up and give an acceptance speech.

This fear is so common that comedian Jerry Seinfeld once did a bit about the fear of public speaking outranking death, meaning that many people would rather be in the casket than delivering the eulogy at a funeral. The reality is that for many people, maybe even you, the thought of speaking in a front of a group is a terrifying prospect as you have **glossophobia,** the official term for a fear of public speaking which comes from the Greek words meaning "glass tongue."

Communication apprehension is the formal term used to describe the anxiety one experiences as the result of actual or anticipated communication. Communication apprehension includes the anxiety one experiences not just while in a speaking situation, but as well as thinking about being in a situation. In 1970, James McCroskey, a communication professor, introduced the Personal Report of Public Speaking Anxiety (PRPSA) which is a scale that measures the level of anxiety associated with public speaking.

> Stage fright is not the only form of communication-related anxiety people experience.

This scale contains items designed to assess how much anxiety a person experiences when facing public speaking situations.

McCroskey recognized, though, that public speaking or "stage fright" is not the only form of communication-related anxiety people experience, and he and his colleagues worked to develop a broader Personal Report of Communication Apprehension Scale (PRCA).[3] Over the years this scale has been refined; the 24-item scale (PRCA-24) measures an individual's level of anxiety when it comes to four communication situations: interpersonal, small group, meetings, and public speaking. One of the key things to note about communication apprehension is that people have varying levels of comfort and anxiety associated with different speaking situations. For example, a student named Jose may be perfectly comfortable in a public speaking situation but experiences a lot of anxiety when in a meeting. Another student, Renee, may enjoy having one-on-one conversations, but dreads the thought of giving a presentation to a group.

When talking about any type of communication apprehension, it is important to recognize two distinct types of anxiety:

trait and **situational,** sometimes referred to as "trait and state." **Trait anxiety** refers to anxiety that is caused by an individual's personality or physical makeup. For example, people who have been diagnosed with Social Anxiety Disorder often have a high level of communication apprehension. Trait anxiety is a result of the chemical makeup of the brain and involves the biological response to a perceived or actual speaking situation. Because of individual differences, some people are more likely to be anxious before a public speaking situation than others.[4] In contrast, **situational anxiety** is anxiety that results because of situational factors such as having an audience, being in a high-pressure situation such as a job interview, or being unprepared for a speaking situation. Even the most outgoing and extroverted person will likely experience some anxiety before a major presentation at work that the boss is attending, and that could affect a performance review. Depending on the type of anxiety trait or state, the strategies for managing that anxiety will differ.

Another interesting distinction among those who experience public speaking anxiety is whether their anxiety falls into a habituation pattern or sensitization pattern. **Habituation** is when there is a decrease in anxiety level after beginning to engage in the feared activity whereas **sensitization** is an increase in anxiety while engaging in the activity. For a speaker who leans towards habituation, there might be a lot of nerves and anxiety leading up to the speaking situation, but as the presentation begins, the speaker becomes less anxious and more comfortable. In contrast, those who lean toward sensitization have anxiety leading up to the speaking situation that increases as the speaking begins and continues to rise until the presentation is ending. The theory is that sensitizers are more sensitive to changes in their bodies, and stress symptoms such as increased heart rate or sweaty palms lead to even more anxiety.[5] The majority of people are habituators; once they stand up and start speaking, their anxiety levels will decrease.[5]

Personal Report of Public Speaking Anxiety (PRPSA)

Directions: This instrument is composed of 34 statements concerning feelings about communicating with other people. Indicate the degree to which the statements apply to you by marking whether you (1) strongly disagree, (2) disagree, (3) are undecided, (4) agree, or (5) strongly agree with each statement. Work quickly; just record your first impression.

1. ____ While preparing for giving a speech, I feel tense and nervous.
2. ____ I feel tense when I see the words "speech" and "public speech" on a course outline when studying.
3. ____ My thoughts become confused and jumbled when I am giving a speech.
4. ____ Right after giving a speech, I feel that I have had a pleasant experience.
5. ____ I get anxious when I think about a speech coming up.
6. ____ I have no fear of giving a speech.
7. ____ Although I am nervous just before starting a speech, I soon settle down after starting and feel calm and comfortable.
8. ____ I look forward to giving a speech.
9. ____ When the instructor announces a speaking assignment in class, I can feel myself getting tense.
10. ____ My hands tremble when I am giving a speech.
11. ____ I feel relaxed while giving a speech.
12. ____ I enjoy preparing for a speech.
13. ____ I am in constant fear of forgetting what I prepared to say.
14. ____ I get anxious if someone asks me something about my topic that I do not know.
15. ____ I face the prospect of giving a speech with confidence.
16. ____ I feel that I am in complete possession of myself while giving a speech.
17. ____ My mind is clear when giving a speech.
18. ____ I do not dread giving a speech.
19. ____ I perspire just before starting a speech.
20. ____ My heart beats very fast just as I start a speech.
21. ____ I experience considerable anxiety while sitting in the room just before my speech starts.
22. ____ Certain parts of my body feel very tense and rigid while giving a speech.
23. ____ Realizing that only a little time remains in a speech makes me very tense and anxious.

Personal Report of Public Speaking Anxiety (PRPSA) Continued

24. ____ While giving a speech, I know I can control my feelings of tension and stress.
25. ____ I breathe faster just before starting a speech.
26. ____ I feel comfortable and relaxed in the hour or so just before giving a speech.
27. ____ I do poorer on speeches because I am anxious.
28. ____ I feel anxious when the teacher announces the date of a speaking assignment.
29. ____ When I make a mistake while giving a speech, I find it hard to concentrate on the parts that follow.
30. ____ During an important speech, I experience a feeling of helplessness building up inside me.
31. ____ I have trouble falling asleep the night before a speech.
32. ____ My heart beats very fast while I present a speech.
33. ____ I feel anxious while waiting to give my speech.
34. ____ While giving a speech, I get so nervous I forget facts I really know.

To determine your score on the PRPSA, complete the following steps:

- **Step 1:** Add the scores for items 1, 2, 3, 5, 9, 10, 13, 14, 19, 20, 21, 22, 23, 25, 27, 28, 29, 30, 31, 32, 33, and 34.
- **Step 2:** Add the scores for items 4, 6, 7, 8, 11, 12, 15, 16, 17, 18, 24, and 26.

Complete the following formula: PRPSA = 72 − Total from Step 2 + Total from Step 1. Your score on the PRPSA can range between 34 and 170:

- 34–84   indicates a very low anxiety about public speaking.
- 85–92   indicates a moderately low level of anxiety about public speaking.
- 93–110   suggests moderate anxiety in most public speaking situations but not so severe that the individual cannot cope and be a successful speaker.
- 111–119   suggests a moderately high anxiety about public speaking. People with such scores will tend to avoid public speaking.
- 120–170   indicates a very high anxiety about public speaking. People with these scores will go to considerable lengths to avoid all types of public speaking situations.

You can also take the assessment online at: http://www.wadsworth.com/communication_d/templates/student_resources/053455170X_sellnow/psa/main_frame.htm.

You may have noticed that the previous section mentions managing public speaking anxiety, not curing or overcoming it. The reality is that many people do get nervous about public speaking, and many occasions that require public speaking have situational factors that provoke anxiety. Imagine, for example, that you are giving a sales pitch at work to a potential client. The high-stakes nature of this situation may lead to anxiety even if you typically have no problem with public speaking. Because of trait and situational anxiety, it is likely that you will continue to experience some level of anxiety at one time or another. This is why we focus on managing your anxiety so that it does not become debilitating.

Situational Causes of Public Speaking Anxiety

In addition to personality and trait reasons for anxiety, there are several situational factors that can lead to increased public speaking anxiety. By recognizing what these situational factors are and when you are facing them, you can develop better strategies for either minimizing or making the best of these factors. The following are some of the major reasons people may experience public speaking anxiety.

- **Fear of failure:** When asked why they are nervous to speak in public, many people will respond that they are afraid they will do a terrible job and fail miserably. Asked to describe their worst case scenario for public speaking, people are quick to describe scenes of completely forgetting what to say, tripping on stage, or making absolutely no sense. Because presentational speaking occurs in public, not only is there a fear of not doing well, but the failure will be visible to the entire audience. When the stakes of a presentation are high, people will often experience an increased level of anxiety.

- **Fear of judgment:** This fear is similar to that of fear of failure but arises from anxiety over what people in the audience will think of you as a speaker. One of the common things that students express when asked to describe why a public speaking class such as this one makes them nervous is that they are being graded and assessed by the instructor.[6] Some worry that audience members will deem them as incompetent, boring, or unskilled. The fear of judgment often correlates with who is the audience. A presentation for superiors at work might cause more anxiety than a presentation to a group of peers, or a toast at a wedding where several of your close friends and family are in attendance might be more nerve-wracking than a toast at an event full of strangers. In both of these cases, the judgment of certain audience members has greater weight than others.

- **Lack of preparation:** Imagine that you are taking guitar lessons and you are scheduled to perform in your first recital. Rather than spending the weeks leading up to the recital practicing and perfecting your piece, you wait until the night before and try to learn the song as quickly as you can. There is a high likelihood that when you walk on stage to perform the next day, you will be even more nervous than you normally would be because you do not know your song well. If you had spent the weeks before practicing diligently and had mastery over the song, you would most likely still be nervous about playing for an audience, but at least you will have confidence that you have practiced and know your piece. Public speaking is no different. If you do not adequately prepare and give yourself enough time to plan a compelling message and practice it until you know the content well, you are going to be more anxious when you stand up to present.

- **Lack of experience:** When we are just learning how to do something or are doing it for the first time, we are often anxious. We are hyper-aware of the limitations of our skills. If you do not have a lot of experience in standing up in front of people or in delivering formal presentations, you are more likely to be anxious when you are asked to do so. Going back to our guitar example, someone who has been playing for over 15 years is much less likely to have anxiety about performing than someone who has only been taking lessons for six months.

Symptoms of Public Speaking Anxiety

When you start to feel nervous about a presentation, speaking anxiety is often accompanied by physical symptoms. This is because of the phenomena known as **fight-or-flight** response, or heightened arousal. When humans are confronted with a perceived threat, the brain floods the body with stress hormones including adrenaline and cortisol that increase a person's heart rate and blood pressure, and provide a burst of energy to smooth muscle tissues. These hormones prepare the body to either flee from the threat or confront it head on. As a person springs into action to alleviate the threat, the hormones are used to get the person to engage in the activity that will be most beneficial. Once the threat is gone, he or she is able to return to a calmer state of being because the hormone levels return to normal.

From an evolutionary perspective, this is a great adaptation. When a caveman faced a threat, it was most likely something life threatening such as a wild animal, and the only options for survival were to either escape the threat or to fight it. In modern times, the threats we face are rarely life threatening, such as giving a speech in public, but the body's reaction is the same. This means that if you are getting ready to give a presentation, your flight-or-fight response kicks in. Your body is literally preparing to either run away or engage in a physical altercation. Because neither of these is an option in the case of giving a presentation, you are left with a lot of stress hormones surging through your body, and you are not doing anything to physically alleviate the effect of those hormones, which can lead to jitteriness, shortness of breath, and dry mouth.

Common Physical Symptoms of Public Speaking Anxiety

- Dry mouth
- Red face
- Sweating
- Feeling jittery
- Upset stomach
- Shaking
- Shortness of breath
- Increased heart rate

It is important to note that symptoms may start to arise as soon as one starts to think about an upcoming speaking event, and symptoms may intensify up until and during the actual presentation. In addition to the physical symptoms listed in the call-out above, some mental symptoms may include feelings of panic, an increase of negative thoughts, or difficulty in focusing. Because blood is rushing to your limbs to help you physically avert the threat, your brain may not feel like it is operating optimally.

Strategies for Coping with Public Speaking Anxiety

The good news is that even though public speaking anxiety is a very real and common thing, there are numerous strategies and techniques that have been proven to reduce overall feelings of anxiety.

The first set of strategies focuses on alleviating or minimizing some of the specific symptoms. Since the majority of the symptoms are caused by having too many stress hormones in the blood stream, any sort of physical activity you can do to use them up is helpful. Before your presentation, a quick walk down the hall or standing up to get a drink can release some of your built up energy. If you are feeling jittery when you stand up to present, be sure that you are not holding a sheet of paper or pen that will magnify the movement of your hands. Incorporating movement into your presentation, if appropriate, is another way to release energy while speaking.

When we are stressed, we tend to take short, rapid breaths. This is your body's attempt to actually take in more air than it needs, and this can leave you feeling lightheaded. If you feel yourself getting short of breath, you can consciously slow down your breathing by counting to five as you inhale, holding your breath for a count of seven, and then slowly exhaling. Be sure as you are breathing that you can feel your stomach expanding as this indicates you are taking full breaths. Not only is deep breathing calming and proven to reduce physical symptoms of arousal, including an increased heartrate, but a fully oxygenated brain will function better.

During a period of extreme stress, your body diverts blood flow from your digestive system, as these are considered less essential survival functions. This is why you may experience dry mouth or an upset stomach when you are nervous. If you know you are prone to dry mouth when you get nervous, be sure to keep a bottle of water nearby, and take small sips throughout your presentation.

The next set of strategies goes beyond just dealing with specific symptoms and is designed to combat the underlying communication apprehension you feel and to make you more comfortable when faced with a public speaking situation. Utilizing one or a combination of the following strategies can help you manage both your trait and situational anxiety.

Prepare and Practice

This strategy is so simple and straightforward that you might wonder why it is even included. It is included because, as we learned earlier, even though lack of preparation is one of the leading causes of public speaking anxiety, many people do not give themselves the time they need to prepare and practice their presentation or speech. A 2006 study of college students found that the majority of students procrastinated when it came to prepping for a presentation for speech class, and many reported cramming the night before to try and learn the material. This same study found that there was a direct correlation between the amount of time students spent preparing for their presentations and their grades.[7] Preparation can be especially helpful in dealing with the anxiety that arises when there is a lot riding on a presentation, such as earning a grade in class or trying to secure a new client at work. If you wait until the night before a big presentation to write and practice, it is likely that you will not know your material as well as you should, and this can lead to additional stress and anxiety.

> Many people do not give themselves the time they need to prepare and practice their presentation or speech.

When it comes to practice, though, not all practice is the same. The most effective practice sessions are those where you most closely simulate the actual speaking situation. Sitting at your desk reading through your presentation silently may help you to learn your message, but giving a great presentation involves far more than simply being able to remember the words you want to say. The more you can simulate the actual speaking situation, the more comfortable you will be when it is time to present, as your body and mind will feel as if you have been there before. In sports, trainers often talk about muscle memory which is the concept that the more your body engages in a physical activity, the more easily it can do that activity, as your muscles remember the training and can do the required movements almost mindlessly. Similarly, in speaking situations, if you have physically walked through your presentation, your body will be more likely to remember what it should do.[8]

When practicing for a presentation, there are a few best practices to keep in mind. Practice saying your speech aloud so that you can practice your tone and speaking rate. Rather than sitting in a chair, stand like you would during a presentation and practice using your visual aids to help you remember when to use them. Practice with the notecards you plan to use during your presentation instead of practicing with your full outline or manuscript. This will help you to more effectively learn your presentation and your note cards will serve as adequate reminders while you are speaking. Consider practicing where you are giving your presentation if possible, so you are familiar with the space. If at all possible, it is always good to practice before a small audience. Even if it is just a roommate or friend, practicing in front of people is the best way to help you get comfortable having an audience look at you and allows you to practice things such as eye contact. Again, even though this is a simple strategy, it is incredibly effective at not only reducing speech anxiety, but in elevating the quality of your presentation.[9,10]

Skills Training

A primary reason that people feel anxious about public speaking is they fear that they will not be good at it and will fail at their attempts. **Skills training** in the form of workshops, coaching, and courses like the one you are in now have been proven to reduce speakers' overall anxiety as well as improve their public speaking abilities. By developing the skills required to give an effective presentation such as message composition and delivery skills, speakers can feel more confident and less fearful of failure and negative judgment.[11,12] Skills training is so valuable that many people will spend a lot of money and time for it. In 2016, executives could enroll in a two day workshop offered by the Dale Carnegie Training Center for $1,800. Toastmasters, a nonprofit where members join and develop their communication and speaking skills, is a global organization with chapters in over 142 countries. Professionals who recognize the importance of excellent speaking skills often join Toastmasters to gain the knowledge and skills needed to succeed in their career fields. This requires a weekly commitment to attend meetings and includes a hefty membership fee.

Systematic Desensitization/Exposure

A common technique therapist and psychologists use when patients have an extreme fear of something, such as flying or spiders, is exposure therapy, or **systematic desensitization.** Patients are slowly exposed to low levels of the threat with the first exposures being as non-threatening as possible. A person terrified of flying for example, might first watch videos of people flying or even just view pictures of airplanes. As the patient gets better able to cope with the threat, the exposure level increases until the person is able to get on a plane and fly. Similarly, people with a high level of public speaking anxiety can slowly work their way up to a public presentation. Take, for example, Damion, a student enrolled in a public speaking class who feels sick to his stomach at the thought of being asked to answer a question in front of the class. First, he might be asked to just imagine himself giving a presentation and be encouraged to try calming techniques such as deep breathing while doing so. The next step might be answering questions in class while seated at his desk. Exposure would progress to standing up in a front of a group and introducing himself and then to presenting to a smaller group of two to three classmates rather than the entire class. Eventually, with repeated exposure to the threat and the recognition that he survived the threat, Damion will be able to get up and give a formal presentation to an audience. Studies have repeatedly found that systematic desensitization is a highly effective treatment for public speaking anxiety[13,14,15] which lends credence to the advice that the more you do it, the easier it will become.

A recent development in treating public speaking anxiety with systematic desensitization is the use of virtual reality and virtual audiences. Instead of practicing or presenting in front of an actual audience, speakers present in front of video footage of an audience or to computer-generated avatars. Some audience simulators are so advanced that the computer-generated avatars will change their reactions based on what the speaker is saying and how the speaker is saying it. Studies have found that virtual audiences can arouse similar stress reactions to an actual audience, and practicing in front of a virtual audience can greatly reduce the anxiety speakers feel when later addressing a live audience.[16,17]

Visualization

Visualization is a technique used by many elite performers, from athletes to musicians, in which they repeatedly imagine themselves going through a performance successfully. Three-time Olympic gold medal winners, Misty May-Treanor and Kerri Walsh Jennings, who have dominated the beach volleyball scene, credit visualization as a key factor in their success as visualization helps them to be calm in the moment and stay focused on their play.[18] The secret to successful visualization is imagining yourself going through all of the steps for your presentation, from approaching the front of the room, to going through all of the main points of your presentation, to your presentation ending well. The second key is to visualize yourself

> The secret to successful visualization is imagining yourself going through all of the steps for your presentation.

being successful. When nerves kick in, it is easy to visualize yourself making a mistake, but effective visualization focuses on seeing yourself at peak performance.[9,19,20]

Cognitive Restructuring

Cognitive restructuring is similar to visualization in that it relies on positive thoughts, but instead of visualizing the speaking situation, this technique involves replacing the negative thoughts a person has about public speaking and his or her public speaking skills with more positive thoughts. For example, Chen knows that she will be giving an update on her team's marketing plan at the next staff meeting. Chen is very nervous about public speaking in general and especially presentations like this one where her superiors and coworkers are present. In the days leading up to the presentation, she repeatedly says things to herself like, "I hate giving presentations," "I am sure I will screw this up," and "I am a terrible speaker." When using cognitive restructuring, she would replace those negative thoughts with more positive ones such as, "Presentations are an important part of my job," "I will do a good job," and "I know what I am talking about and will give a great presentation." The theory behind this method is that the way we think and talk to ourselves has a large influence on our mental state and our behavior.[21,22]

Another useful trick is to reframe the way you think about your public speaking anxiety. In general, we tend to perceive public speaking anxiety as a negative thing, and the desire is often to rid ourselves of that anxiety. As we learned earlier in our discussion of fight-or-flight syndrome, your body's response to a perceived threat is intended to make you more capable of effectively handling that threat. The increased adrenaline can be used to your advantage when you are anxious before giving a presentation by giving you a boost of energy that can make your delivery more intense and engaging. Many athletes and performers will tell you that if they are not feeling anxious before a game or show, something is off, and their subsequent performance will be flat and not up to par. One way to frame your anxiety is as excitement rather than nerves.[23] Although many of the symptoms of excitement, such as jitteriness, increased heart rate, and butterflies in the stomach, are similar to anxiety, excitement has positive rather than negative connotations.

Present More Frequently

If speaking in public makes you nervous, this tip may not be your favorite, but it is a great way to get more comfortable. As we discussed earlier in the section on systematic desensitization, repeated exposure to a perceived threat can minimize your anxiety. The more opportunities you have to speak in a front of a group, the more opportunities you have to develop your skills and to recognize that you can survive presenting to people. Instead of trying to avoid presentations, look for ways that you can practice your presentational skills.

Using any or a combination of the above techniques is a great way to manage your public speaking anxiety whether it is pervasive and you have trait anxiety or you occasionally feel anxious when faced with certain speaking situations. If you are feeling anxious when you have to speak, it is important to deliver your presentation in a way that conveys confidence and comfort to the audience even if you are not feeling entirely confident and at ease. In the next chapter, we will look at the many factors that comprise speech delivery and tips for optimizing these components.

Chapter Summary

In this chapter we look at the prominence of the fear of public speaking, some reasons for this fear, and more importantly, several strategies for managing this fear so that it does not interfere with your ability to deliver a great presentation.

Case Study Conclusion

What were some of the suggestions you made to help the younger Joel Osteen overcome his paralyzing fear of public speaking so he could preach publicly? Osteen was not instantly cured of public speaking anxiety but instead used several techniques to help manage his, at times, overwhelming fear. One of the most effective strategies he credits with his ability to manage his anxiety was positive self-talk. While it was easy to beat up on himself for his perceived faults and lack of communication skills, he found that by consciously telling himself that he could preach and was able to deliver a solid message, his overall mindset began to change. Additionally, he continued to get up each Sunday and speak to the congregation, and as time went on, he became more and more comfortable speaking in front of a group. Even though he still characterizes himself as shy, he is able to stand and speak to stadiums full of people to share his message.

References

[1] "America's Top Fears 2016." *Chapman University* (blog), October 30, 2016. https://blogs.chapman.edu/wilkinson/2016/10/11/americas-top-fears-2016/.

[2] Pull, C. B. 2012. "Current Status of Knowledge on Public-Speaking Anxiety." *Current Opinion in Psychology* 25(1): 32–38. doi: 10.1097/YCO.0b013e32834e06dc.

[3] McCroskey, J. C. 1978. "Validity of the PRCA as an Index of Oral Communication Apprehension." *Communication Monographs* 45(3): 192–203. doi: 10.1080/03637757809375965.

[4] Hindo, C. S., and A. A. Gonzáles-Prendes. 2011. "One Session Exposure Treatment for Social Anxiety with Specific Fear of Public Speaking." *Research on Social Work Practice* 21(5): 528–538. http://10.0.4.153/1049731510393984.

[5] Behnke, R. R., and C. R. Sawyer. 2004. "Public Speaking Anxiety as a Function of Sensitization and Habituation Processes." *Communication Education* 53(2): 164–173. http://10.0.0.10/03634520410001682429.

[6] Singh, M. K. M., A. R. David, and J. C. S. Choo. 2011. "Communication Apprehension Among International Undergraduates: The Impact on Their Communicative Skills." *Modern Journal of Language Teaching Methods* 1(2): 18–30. http://www.search.proquest.com/docview/1146163263?accountid=13360.

7. Pearson, J. C., J. T. Child, and D. H. Kahl, Jr. 2010. "Preparation Meeting Opportunity: How Do College Students Prepare for Public Speeches?" *Communication Quarterly* 54(3): 351. https://doi.org/10.1080/0146337060087321.

8. Reshawn, R. 2015. "Present Like a Pro: Public Speaking Skills for Newbies." *U.S. News & World Report*, December 16, 2016. http://money.usnews.com/money/blogs/outside-voices-careers/2015/11/16/present-like-a-pro-public-speaking-skills-for-newbies.

9. Choi, C. W., J. M. Honeycutt, and G. D. Bodie. 2015. "Effects of Imagined Interactions and Rehearsal on Speaking Performance." *Common Education* 64(1): 25–44. http://10.0.4.56/03634523.2014.978795.

10. Sterling, E., A. Bravo, A. L. Porzecanski, et al. 2016. "Research and Teaching: Think before (and after) You Speak: Practice and Self-Reflection Bolster Oral Communication Skills." *Journal of College Science Teaching* 46(6). doi: 10.2505/4/jcst16_045_06_87.

11. Ellingson, L. L. 2016. "Embodied Knowledge: Writing Researchers' Bodies into Qualitative Health Research." *Qualitative Health Research* 16(2): 298–310. doi: 10.1177/1049732305281944.

12. Pribyl, C. B., J. Keaten, and M. Sakamoto. 2001. "The Effectiveness of a Skills-Based Program in Reducing Public Speaking Anxiety." *Japanese Psychology Research* 43(3): 148. http://search.ebscohost.com/loging.aspx?direct=true&db=aph&ANA=4859579&site=ehost-live.

13. Ayres, J., T. Hopf, and Anthony Will. 2009. "Are Reductions in CA an Experimental Artifact? A Solomon four-group answer." *Communication Quarterly* 48(1): 19-26. http://search.ebscohost.com/login.aspx?direct=true&db=aph&AN=3966451&site=ehost-live.

14. Nash, G., G. Crimmins, and F. Oprescu. 2016. "If First Year Students Are Afraid of Public Speaking Assessments What Can Teachers Do to Alleviate Such Anxiety?" *Assessment & Evaluation in Higher Education* 41(4): 586–600. http://10.0.4.56/02602938.2015.103.

15. Bodie, G. D. 2010. "A Racing Heart, Rattling, Knees, and Ruminative Thoughts: Defining, Explaining, and Treating Public-Speaking Anxiety." *Communication Education* 59(1): 70–105. http://10.0.4.56/03634520903443849.

16. Pertaub, D-P, M. Slater, and C. Barker. 2002. "An Experiment on Public Speaking Anxiety in Response to Three Different Types of Virtual Audience." *Presence: Teleoperators Virtual Environments* 11(1): 68–78. http://search.ebscohost.com/login.aspx?direct=true&db=aph&AN=6472508&site=ehost-live.

17. Slater, M., D-P Pertaub, C. Barker, and D. M. Clark. 2006. "An Experimental Study on Fear of Public Speaking Using a Virtual Environment." *CyberPsychology & Behavior* 9(5): 627–633. http://10.0.4.65/cpb.2006.9.627.

18. Stone, A. 2015. "Kerri Walsh Says No Pressure for Rio Olympics." *USA Today*, December 17, 2016. http://usatoday.com/story/sports/olympics/2015/02/23/kerri-walsh-jennings-april-ross-rio-olympics/23913015/.

19. Ayres, J., and T. A. Ayres. 2003. "Using Images to Enhance the Impact of Visualization." *Communication Reports* 16(1): 47. http://search.ebscohost.com/login.aspx?direct=true&db=aph&AN=9350244&site=ehost-live.

20. Ayres, J., and T. Hopf. 1999. "Vividness and Control: Factors in the Effectiveness of Performance Visualization" *Communication Education* 48(4): 287. http://search.ebscohost.com/login.aspx?direct=true&db=aph&AN=2381034&site=ehost-live.

21. Shi, X., T. M. Brinthaupt, and M. McCree. 2015. "The Relationship of Self-talk Frequency to Communication Apprehension and Public Speaking Anxiety." *Personality and Individual Differences* 75: 125–129. doi:10.1016/j.paid.2014.11.023.

22. Sánchez, F., F. Carvajal, and C. Saggiomo. 2016. "Self-talk and Academic Performance in Undergraduate Students." *Autodiálogos y Rend académ en Estud Univ.* 32(1): 139–147. http://10.0.23.130/analesps.32.1.188441.

23. Brooks, A. W. 2014. "Get Excited: Reappraising Pre-Performance Anxiety as Excitement." *Journal of Experimental Psychology: General* 143(3): 1144–1158. http://10.0.4.13/a0035325.

Chapter **3**

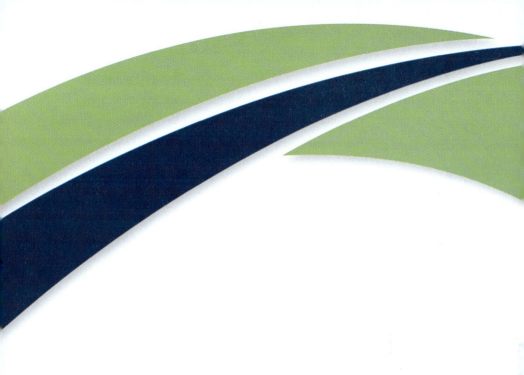

Delivering with Skill

Objectives

After this chapter you will be able to:

- Identify the key elements of effective speech delivery.
- Explain the four main delivery styles.
- Demonstrate effective delivery techniques for presentational speaking.
- Understanding verbal and nonverbal aspects of delivery.

Chapter 3   Delivering with Skill

In 2016, Hillary Clinton gave a historic address when she delivered her acceptance speech at the Democratic National Convention after winning the Democratic nomination for president. After a long and hard fought primary season, Clinton was the first woman to be a major party's presidential candidate. While her nomination earned her praise, her speaking style did not. As she spoke, viewers across the country, as well as several noted political pundits took to Twitter to criticize her, saying she lacked excitement and passion about her nomination. They commented that she appeared cold and robotic. During the almost hour long speech, Clinton outlined several of her policy plans in a direct and businesslike tone. Critics slammed her for this, believing that she should have used this opportunity to make a more emotional appeal to the American public and used her own energy to inspire energy among her potential voters.[1] Clinton went on to lose the presidential election with her lack of likeability being one of the persistent criticisms lobbied against her. While this is not the only reason she lost the election, this is an excellent illustration of how important not only what you say is, but also how you say it. (Image to right: Calebrw at English Wikipedia [CC BY-SA 3.0 (https://creativecommons.org/licenses/by-sa/3.0) or GFDL (http://www.gnu.org/copyleft/fdl.html)], from Wikimedia Commons.)

Let's Talk

1. Why do you think Clinton's delivery style was more important to many people than the content of her presentation?
2. What strategies could Clinton use to help her appear more passionate and enthusiastic?

Introduction

Whenever you are in a speaking situation, whether it is a formal presentation in class, a project update at work, or a story about something funny that happened at last week's football game that you want to tell your friends, the ultimate goal is to tell your story in a way that connects with your audience. As important as the words you use are, in some ways, the way you tell your story is even more important. The delivery of your message, the tone of your voice, the gestures you use, and even the way you stand influence your audience's perception of your credibility, your likeability, and your trustworthiness.

When you consider figures throughout history who have been considered great orators, in addition to their skill in crafting messages that resonated with the audience, they also were extremely skilled at presenting their messages in a way that was engaging and captivating. Former President Ronald Regan, nicknamed the "great communicator," was able to use his acting skills to speak to large crowds in a way that both entertained and conveyed confidence and skill. Renowned civil rights activist, Reverend Martin Luther King Jr., is remembered not only for his poetic and inspiring words but his distinct delivery style which included a southern rhythm and cadence that connected him to his audience.[2] Former President Barrack Obama was catapulted to the national spotlight after giving a public address at the Democratic National Convention when he was a new Senator from Illinois. Like other great speakers, he was considered a wordsmith, but additionally, his delivery style was one that connected him with the audience and helped the nation feel hopeful and encouraged[3] at a time when many Americans were struggling.

Even if you never become a famous orator or address a nation or a crowd of thousands, the way you deliver a speech or presentation is critical because your language choice is only one component of communication. You may have the most interesting story to share, but if you stumble as you tell it, sound bored, or use distracting hand gestures, your story will lose its impact. Nonverbal messages including tone, facial expressions, gestures, and posture are essential for helping message receivers fully understand what is being communicated. One often cited statistic is that over 90 percent of a message is conveyed nonverbally.[4] While the number has been somewhat debunked as it is difficult to quantify the impact of nonverbal messages, communication scholars agree that nonverbal communication serves several functions in the communication situation. Because nonverbal communication serves so many functions, your delivery skills can influence audience perceptions of your credibility, help you develop rapport with your audience, and impact the assessment of your overall message.[5,6]

Before we look at the specific elements of speech delivery, we will first discuss the four primary delivery styles used for presentations: memorized, manuscript, impromptu, and extemporaneous. Each of these styles has its own strengths, challenges, and limitations, and the situation in which you are speaking will often dictate which style you will use.

Memorized

When using **memorized delivery,** you use the same techniques you would use if you were in a play and had to memorize your lines. Although it may be tempting to memorize your presentation so you can be sure to include all of your wanted points and not have to worry about looking at notes that would interfere with your eye contact, speaking from memory is very challenging, and the negatives of this style usually outweigh the benefits. Memorized speeches lack spontaneity and adaptability, which makes them sound rehearsed rather

> Memorized speeches lack spontaneity and adaptability.

than conversational. One of the major risks of memorizing a presentation is forgetting a line and not being able to regain your place in the presentation. Because of these drawbacks, this technique is rarely recommended, but when you are giving a short toast or introduction, this style can be useful.

Manuscript

Manuscript delivery is when you write out your presentation word for word and read from this script when giving your presentation. This style is most commonly used for formal speeches when it is important for a speaker to say the exact words that were written. When a politician gives a public address such as the State of the Union or the State of the State, he or she will use a teleprompter and read the speech that has been prepared. Other occasions that might call for a manuscript include commencement addresses, official testimony in front of a legislative body, or any time that your words will be recorded as part of an official record. While it might be tempting to use this style, as many people are nervous about forgetting a part of the presentation, it is very challenging to read from a script without sounding like you are reading to the audience rather than speaking to them. Eye contact is also challenging for those who do not have the benefit of a teleprompter. When using a paper manuscript, the speaker needs to look down to read the text. With limited eye contact and vocal tone that does not sound like genuine conversation, it can be difficult for speakers to connect with the audience. If you are in a situation where you will be delivering from a manuscript, here are a few tips to improve your presentation:

- Make sure your manuscript is easy to read.
- Use a large font and extra spacing between lines.
- Use wider side margins so your eyes do not have to travel as far when you move to the next line.

- Practice varying your tone and rhythm.
- Look up at the audience at the end of sentences and between paragraphs.
- Mark your spot in the manuscript when you look up so you do not lose your place.

Impromptu

In many ways, impromptu speaking is the complete opposite of speaking from a manuscript. **Impromptu speaking** is when you are asked to speak before a group without any notice and time to prepare. Take, for example, a recent reception for a group of graduate students from the communication department. Each graduate was asked to introduce themselves to the group and share a little bit about their research interests. It was not a high-pressure presentation, but it did require each person to stand up and talk for a minute to a group of about 50 people. Other situations where your impromptu speaking skills might be called upon include giving a project update at work, sharing a story at a family gathering, or discussing your experiences on a relevant topic at a community meeting. For many people, impromptu situations are especially nerve-wracking as they do not like being put on the spot. Their nerves often make it difficult to put together their thoughts and can lead to a disorganized and rambling presentation or make it hard to think of something to say.

Here are some tips for successfully delivering an impromptu presentation:

- Anticipate situations when you might be asked to speak such as staff meetings or at organization meetings.
- Take a minute to breathe and gather your thoughts before you speak.
- Determine two or three key points you want to convey.
- Keep it short.
- Have a clear conclusion even if it is as simple as saying thank you.

Extemporaneous

This last delivery style, **extemporaneous speaking,** is when you spend time practicing, but you have not memorized what you are going to say, and you do not speak from a manuscript. Instead, you prepare an outline or notes with your main ideas and supporting examples and work from that to develop and practice your presentation. Because you are not speaking from memory or a script, your presentation is more flexible, and you will sound more conversational and natural while presenting. Because you are not bound to a set script, you can respond to audience feedback and adapt your message as needed. This is a very common delivery style, and it is frequently used in business presentations, where you prepare your material and message but do not go into the meeting with a word-for-word script or a memorized monologue. The way that many of your instructors lecture during class is another example of extemporaneous speaking.

Here are some tips for successfully delivering an extemporaneous presentation:

- Organize your thoughts and ideas ahead of time.
- Limit the amount of writing on your notes so you are not tempted to read.
- Practice so you are familiar and comfortable with your material.

No matter what delivery style you are using, there are common elements of delivery that will either enhance or detract from your message. These elements can be broken down into three categories: physical, verbal, and general delivery. In the following section we will look at the components of each of these categories and discover tricks and tips for using these components to enhance your presentation.

Physical Delivery

When you present in front of an audience or tell a story to a group of friends over dinner, there is a high likelihood that the people you are speaking to can see you, which is why the way you stand, your facial expressions, and your gestures are such a critical component of your delivery style. Imagine for a moment that you are attending a workshop focused on developing your leadership skills. As you sit waiting for the session to begin, you notice the session leader is at the front of the room wearing clothes that are slightly wrinkled, has a frown on her face, repeatedly twirls her hair with her finger, and shuffles through a messy stack of papers with her other hand. Before she has even spoken a word and before you have had a chance to read her bio, you have started to form an impression of her based on her nonverbal communication, and it is quite likely that your impression is less than positive. Maybe you think she is unorganized, unprofessional, anxious, or unfriendly. Your impression may be completely wrong, but it is important to remember that your nonverbals start communicating as soon as people can see you, even if you haven't uttered a word. This means you need to be aware of what your body and face are doing as soon as you enter the speaking situation.

Eye Contact

A traditional English proverb states, "The eyes are the windows to the soul." In many Western cultures including the United States, a high value is placed on looking people in the eye when speaking. When a person avoids eye contact, it can be perceived as being dishonest, rude, or uncomfortable.[5,7] Additionally, eye contact is a way to indicate to a person that you are engaged in the conversation. A study from the University of Miami found that when we are listening to someone, 43.4 percent of our attention is focused on the eyes. Researchers at Cornell University found that shoppers were much more likely to purchase a box of Trix cereal when the rabbit on the box was drawn with the eyes looking directly at the consumer than when the eyes were drawn looking down. Clearly, eye contact is important in communicating with your audience.

Therefore, when you are speaking to a Western audience, it is essential that you not only look at your audience but that you engage in meaningful eye contact with them. There are, however, some barriers to making eye contact. If you are relying too heavily on your notes and have to read the majority of your presentation, it will be difficult to look at your audience. Another barrier is nerves. Making eye contact also makes you more aware of your audience. To overcome these barriers, you may have been given the advice to pick a spot on the wall and stare at it or to look at people's foreheads instead of their eyes. This advice, while well intentioned, is not effective. People are very aware of eye contact, and if you are staring at their foreheads instead of looking into their eyes, they will know. Another strategy people will use is to pick one person in the audience, usually someone they know, and look at that person throughout the presentation. Again, this is not a great strategy as other members of the audience will feel as if you are ignoring them. When speaking to a group, you need to scan the room and be sure you are looking at all places in the room. For a very large group it will be impossible to actually look each individual person in the eye, but you can spend extended time looking at each area around the room. Former President Bill Clinton explained that whenever he is addressing a large crowd, he does not think about talking to hundreds or thousands but instead focuses on talking to one person at a time. For each thought or sentence he says, he picks one person in the room, talks to him or her for that thought, and

> **A traditional English proverb states, "The eyes are the windows to the soul."**

then moves to the next person. This strategy allows him to have meaningful and extended eye contact around the room and, as a bonus, alleviates some of the stress that comes with trying to speak to such a large group.

It is important to recognize that the norms and expectations regarding eye contact are culturally based. In many Hispanic, Native American, Asian, and African cultures, direct eye contact is perceived as being rude or disrespectful, especially when someone with less power is addressing a superior. If you are giving a presentation in another country or to a group from another culture, you should be aware of these norms. Additionally, if you are listening to a speaker from a different culture, be careful about making judgments about his or her honesty, credibility, and trustworthiness based on his or her eye contact.

Posture

Good **posture** is not only good for your spine and alignment, but the way you stand can convey confidence, power, or lack thereof. If you are slouching with your hands in your pockets, you can come across as being disinterested or bored whereas if you stand up with your legs spread widely apart with your arms crossed, you might be perceived as angry or aggressive. One thing to consider when you are standing and speaking is whether you are using **open posture** or **closed posture.** The two previous examples of slouching and crossed arms are both closed poses; closed poses cut off your connection to the audience. Open postures, on the other hand, are those with your arms at your sides, your shoulders back and relaxed, and your head held high. Whether or not you realize it, the way that you stand influences how people perceive your capability and credibility, and your posture can send a subtle message to others about your approachability and your willingness to engage in conversation. If you were lost when visiting a new city, who would you approach to ask for directions: A man waiting at the bus stop who is leaning forward with his arms crossed and staring at his feet, or the man sitting next to him on the bench with his hands resting in his lap looking at the passing cars? You would probably choose the second man because his overall posture is more open and more inviting.

So you may be wondering how you should stand in a way that is both open and professional. The first thing to consider is your spine. You want to hold your backbone as straight as possible extending from your lower back up through your head. Push your shoulders slightly back while keeping them relaxed. When feeling anxious or uncomfortable, many people hunch their shoulders inward. By pushing your shoulders back, it will open up your chest, and it prevents you from closing yourself off or looking like you are trying to hide yourself from the audience. Another important thing to consider is how you are distributing your weight on your feet. Avoid resting all of your weight on one leg and standing with your hip cocked or standing with your legs crossed. Instead, stand with your feet slightly apart and your weight evenly distributed. Be sure not to lock your knees as this can cut off your blood flow and lead to feeling light-headed.

Another interesting idea about posture that has become more popular in the last few years is the work of social psychologist Amy Cuddy on what she terms *power poses*. Her work posits that there are certain poses, including what she calls the *superman pose* where you stand tall with your arms straight in front of you, that actually increase your confidence and calm your nerves.[8] She does not recommend using these poses on stage—it might look strange to your audience if you were to stand with your arms and legs out in an X shape—but instead stand in a power pose for a minute or two prior to your presentation to help you feel more confident. Her original research found that standing in power poses actually increased levels of testosterone in the body, thus boosting confidence. More recently, additional research has failed to replicate this finding, but even without the hormonal changes, those who use power poses report a positive mental change in their levels of confidence and a reduction in anxiety. In addition to striking a power pose before you speak, you can apply these concepts to the way you stand on stage. One similarity among the power poses is that the body is standing tall and taking up a large amount of space. By standing tall as you are speaking, keeping your shoulders open and broad, and gesturing widely, you can help increase your physical feelings of confidence.

Movement

Depending on the speaking situation, specifically the physical environment in which you are speaking, movement may be more or less a part of your delivery style. Movement is another way to convey your confidence and power when used correctly. One reason that movement works as a delivery tool is because in many situations, the people who have the most power or control in a situation are those who are able to move. Think about a traditional classroom. Who is free to get up and move, the instructor or the students? The answer is the instructor. When you are speaking in front of a group, you can use movement to demonstrate your power, to take up space in the room, and to add visual interest. Not all movement is positive, however. Many people will pace back and forth, cross and uncross their legs, or sway from side to side when speaking because of nerves. This type of movement is distracting and annoying to the audience. So how can you use movement to your advantage? One strategy is to walk or move as you transition from point to point. When you are making a key point, moving towards the audience can add emphasis. Moving to explain and highlight key features of your visual aids is another way to incorporate movement that is purposeful into your presentation.

> Movement is a way to convey your confidence and power when used correctly.

Gestures

When you are speaking, you may find that you naturally move your hands without even thinking about it. This is because gestures are a fundamental way that we communicate. Gestures are beneficial in conversation and presentations because they are a visual component and engage the audience with the message both auditorily and visually.[9] In 2015, a behavior consultancy firm, the Science of People, conducted a study to determine what factors of delivery style contributed to a TED Talk going viral. After analyzing the different communication factors used by the speakers, both verbal and nonverbal, the consultants found that talks in which the speakers used more hand gestures were rated more highly by observers and were more likely to have more views. One of the theories for this connection is that use of hand gestures makes a speaker seem more charismatic and engaged. In addition, gestures help us think. In fact, the use of gestures has been shown to improve memory since they serve as a connection between physical movements and words—making recall easier.[10]

The categories of gestures used in communication include the following:

- **Emblems:** These are gestures that have a specific meaning such as thumbs up for good or thumbs down for bad. It is important to note that emblematic gestures are culturally based, and some gestures have different meanings around the world.
- **Adaptors:** These are gestures that people use when they feel anxious or uncomfortable such as fiddling with a pencil, rubbing an arm, or tapping a finger.
- **Descriptors:** These gestures are used to visually convey the words that are being spoken such as indicating the size of something with your hands or holding up fingers to illustrate numbers.
- **Emphatics:** These are gestures that add emphasis to your message or convey an emotion or mood such as shaking your fist when you are angry or hitting the table to emphasize a point.

Like many of the elements of physical delivery, the effective use of gestures can enhance your presentation by adding visual interest and increasing understanding, but the ineffective use, or lack of use, can harm your overall evaluation by the audience.

One challenge that many people face when standing up to speak or give a presentation is not knowing what to do with their hands, so they clasp them together behind their backs, shove them in their pockets, or hold their arms rigidly by their sides. The downfall to this strategy is that it limits your ability to gesture naturally, and the audience may perceive you as being stiff or robotic. Like we talked about in the above discussion of posture, when you are ready to speak, hold your arms and hand comfortably at your sides so that you are free to move. If you feel uncomfortable or are not sure when to gesture or what types of gestures to use, start with the most basic movements such as pointing to something on your visual aid or using descriptive gestures to illustrate concepts such as size or length.

The opposite of speakers who never gesture are those who gesture too frequently without purpose. Many times out of habit or nerves, a person will make a certain gesture repeatedly such as moving a hand in a circular motion or making a chopping motion with an arm. There is no meaning attached to this gesture, and due to its repetition, it can easily distract your audience. You might not be aware of using these types of repetitive motions, so a good way to get a handle on these is to either record yourself speaking or ask a friend, coworker, or instructor to give you feedback on how often you use certain movements. When you are speaking, concentrate on only using gestures that have meaning; use a gesture to illustrate a concept in your presentation and try to use emphatic gestures only once per main point so that the gestures will actually provide emphasis.

Another distracting type of gesture is an **adaptor** which is a form of self-soothing. When your body is stressed, which often happens during speaking situations as we discussed in the previous chapter, adaptors are a way for the body to restore equilibrium and calm itself. The problem with using adaptors is that the repetitive movements can be distracting to the audience and can also indicate to the audience that you are nervous or uncomfortable. To help yourself not use adaptors, there are two basic strategies you can employ. If your adaptors include fidgeting with something, such as a twirling a pen or twisting your hair, remove those things from your speaking situation. Don't hold any extra objects in your hand or pull your hair back. If your adaptive gestures involve touching, rubbing, or tapping, you can replace the distracting gesture with a smaller, less distracting movement that still provides a calming effect. For example, if you tend to rub your arms or hug yourself, try standing with just your thumb and pointer finger touching. The sensation of these fingers pushing together can be just as calming as tapping and is not at all noticeable to your audience.[11]

Here are a few tips for using gestures to your advantage:

- Imagine you have drawn a box around your torso from your shoulders to your waist. Make the majority of gestures within this square as gestures outside of this box are seen as less in control.
- Gesture with your palms facing upwards as this is more open and welcoming.
- Stand with your arms relaxed at your sides so you are free to gesture.
- Practice using gestures in your presentation. While this might feel artificial at first, the more you practice, the more natural they will start to feel.

Facial Expressions

A fundamental way we communicate our mood and feelings is with our facial expressions. One of the interesting things about facial expressions, as compared to other aspects of communication, is that many expressions are universally understood regardless of culture and language. Charles Darwin was the first to write about this idea, and while there have been later studies that show slight variations among cultures, expressions such as a smile universally communicate happiness whereas raised eyebrows communicate surprise.[12]

When presenting, there are two key things to remember in terms of your facial expressions. The first is that your facial expression should match the content of your presentation. If you are talking about something sad or tragic like a recent natural disaster, it would be inappropriate to smile broadly. On the other hand, if you are talking about how great and exciting a new product is while frowning, there is going to be a disconnect between your message and the emotion you are conveying. The second thing to consider is that you generally want to have a pleasant and welcoming expression unless you are talking about something negative. Smiling is not only the universal way to communicate happiness, but it also influences audience perceptions of your approachability, attractiveness, and credibility. People routinely evaluate smiling faces as more attractive, and more attractive speakers are seen as more credible and authoritative than less attractive individuals. Additionally, smiling people are viewed as more trustworthy,[13] so it is always helpful to begin and end your presentation with a smile.

Appearance

You may have heard the expressions "you cannot judge a book by its cover" or "it is what is on the inside, not the outside, that counts." While both of these sayings hold many elements of truth, the reality is that your audience is making judgments about you and your message based on not just your words but also on how you look. Even if audiences should not judge you based on what you are wearing or what you look like, it is very possible that they will. You should consider your audience and what impression you would like to make when planning what to wear. Think back to the example of the guest speaker at the beginning of this section. Now imagine that instead of a slightly wrinkled shirt, the speaker is wearing a ripped pair of jeans and a faded sweatshirt. You might be surprised to learn that this is your speaker and not an employee at the workshop venue or an underdressed workshop attendee. Obviously, there is no connection between what the presenter is wearing and his or her qualifications or the quality of the presentation. People, however, make assumptions about someone based on their appearance. Studies have repeatedly shown that professional dress can increase audience perceptions of a speaker's credibility, expertise, and professionalism.[14,15]

Two studies conducted on student assessments of graduate teaching assistants' credibility and authority found that the more professional an instructor's attire, the higher their ratings on course evaluations.[16]

So what should you wear for a presentation? The answer is that it depends on who your audience is and on the speaking occasion. A general guideline is that you should always be dressed as least as nicely and formally as your audience, and dressing slightly more formally can enhance your confidence and make a positive impression. If you are making a formal sales presentation at work, professional clothing such as a shirt and tie or dress pants and a blouse would be appropriate. You also need to consider your company or the company you are presenting to. If there is a more casual atmosphere, business casual may be more appropriate. Regardless of what level of clothing you wear, it is always important for your clothing to be ironed, clean, and tailored. Also, be sure that your hair is not covering your face so that the audience can easily see your eyes and facial expressions.

Verbal Delivery

This category of delivery components includes things that can be heard and are related to the voice but are still considered nonverbal. They are not the actual words that are said but the way they are said. Verbal delivery is especially important to master as it is a factor in all presentations including those where the audience cannot see you, such as podcasts, phone interviews, and some webinars. Like physical delivery, verbal delivery is something that you can work on and practice to develop your skills. In the following section we will discuss the different elements of verbal delivery and techniques for using your voice more effectively.

Rate

When you listen to someone speak, they may sound like a very fast talker making it difficult to follow and understand them, or you may notice that they seem to be talking so slowly that you find yourself getting impatient as you are waiting to hear the entire message. A speaker's rate is how quickly he or she speaks and is typically measured in words spoken per minute. In the United States, the average person speaks between 110 and 150 words per minute. A 2010 study conducted by researchers at University of Michigan analyzed the speaking rates of telemarketers and found that speakers who spoke at a more moderate rate were more persuasive than those with a faster or slower rate. Speakers with a faster rate were seen as trying to trick the listeners in some way, and those with a slower rate were perceived as being either less intelligent or condescending to the listener.[17] When people get nervous, they tend to speak more quickly, so you need to slow yourself down if this is your tendency.

Speed vs. Density of Different Languages

Have you ever wondered why some languages sound like they are being spoken far more quickly than others? You might attribute this to the words being unfamiliar to your ear, but there actually is a difference in the speed languages are spoken that is not due to variations in accent or speaking style but instead is due to the information density of the language. Information density is measured by how much information is contained in an average syllable. In more information dense languages, fewer syllables are needed to convey information. Spanish, which is spoken at a faster rate than English, has a much lower information density; therefore, speakers need more syllables to convey the same amount of information as compared to other languages such as English or German. One of the most information dense languages is Mandarin, whereas the least information dense language is Japanese. Japanese is spoken at a much faster rate than most other languages while Mandarin is spoken at a much slower rate.[18,19]

Volume

When speaking to a group or making a formal presentation, it is important that you are speaking loudly enough that everyone can hear you but not so loudly that it makes your audience feel as if you are shouting at them. The key to speaking loudly enough for your audience to hear when you are speaking to a larger audience or in a larger space is to project your voice. The human vocal cords work when air flows over them, so in order to speak loudly, you need to have enough air, which requires you to breathe deeply. When you are nervous, you might find yourself breathing more shallowly, so it is important to take deep breaths not only to calm yourself but also so your audience can hear you. In very large rooms you may need to use a microphone to amplify your voice.

Pronunciation and Enunciation

Pronunciation is the way a word sounds when it is spoken. In any language, words have a pronunciation that is considered correct, and errors can be embarrassing to the speaker or hurt the quality of the presentation. There are two primary reasons for mispronouncing a word. The first is because the word is unfamiliar to you, or you know the word but do not know how to pronounce it correctly. In this situation, your mispronunciation signifies to the audience a lack of knowledge and credibility. For example, I once had a student give a presentation about unique baby naming trends, and one of the names she talked about was Seamus, which had become very popular among celebrities. This was interesting information, but the problem was that she pronounced the name "see-mus," the way is looks, but the Irish name is actually pronounced "shay-mus." This minor error indicated to the audience that she had been reading up on this topic but did not really know the names. If you are preparing for a presentation and come across a word you are not familiar with or are unsure if you are pronouncing it correctly, you should always look it up or ask someone who knows.

Commonly Mispronounced Words in American Language

Word	Common Mispronunciation
Across	Acrost
Artic	Ark-tic
Espresso	Expresso
Nuclear	Nu-cu-lar
Escape	Excape
Jewelry	Jewel-er-y
Library	Li-barry

The second reason for mispronouncing words is due to having an accent or speaking in a nonnative language. It can be difficult to articulate certain sounds and words because there are some sounds that do not exist in some languages. For example, the "th" sound that is so common in English is not found in German and many Slavic languages which is why many native German speakers will substitute the "ze" sound for it. In Chinese, short vowel sounds do not exist, so it can be difficult for native Chinese speakers to articulate the words "pick" and "peek" differently. Because we learn to form and articulate sounds at a very young age, it can become almost impossible to learn how to pronounce new vowel and consonant sounds, and our accents are very much a part of ourselves. Even within the United States, there are a variety of regional accents, and someone from the southern part of the country will sound very different than someone raised, for example, in Boston.

While it may be difficult to pronounce certain words if you are not speaking in your native language or you have an accent, enunciation is something that anyone can work on as **enunciation** is saying words clearly. If you speak too quickly or mumble, it can be hard for your audience to distinguish the individual words you are saying. Part of enunciating effectively is speaking at a rate that is slow enough for you to clearly state each syllabus and sound. You also need to be sure you are opening your mouth enough so that your tongue and lips can make the necessary movements to create clear sounds. If you have an accent, enunciating your words is a great way to help your audience understand what you are saying. Even if some of the letters' sounds are slightly different, if they are clearly articulated, audiences will be more likely to comprehend the words.

Pitch and Tone

When thinking about your **pitch** and **tone,** think about the way your voice sounds to the audience. Pitch is where your voice falls on the musical scale. While some voices are naturally higher pitched and some are naturally lower pitched, we can all vary our pitch when speaking, just like we do when we are singing. As we speak, we naturally will raise and lower our pitch based on what we are saying. When asking a question for example, the voice will naturally rise at the end whereas if you are making a point or ending a sentence, your pitch tends to lower.

In general, your voice will be within a certain range such as high or low with females having higher vocal registers than males. One thing to consider is that higher voices are sometimes perceived as being less credible than lower voices, as higher pitched voices can sound younger and less powerful.[20,21] If you have a high pitched voice, this does not mean that you need to work to change it, but instead, focus your energies on making sure that your voice is full and that you are projecting your voice.

While pitch refers to how high or low the voice is, tone refers to the emotion or mood of the voice. The goal when speaking is for your tone to convey your personal enthusiasm, excitement, interest, or authority on your topic. The opposite of an enthusiastic tone is a bored tone that has little variation—often referred to as monotone. Perhaps one of the most notable examples of a monotone speaker can be found in the 1980s hit movie *Ferris Bueller's Day Off*. Whenever Ferris' economics teacher, played by Ben Stein, is on screen, he famously drones on with his monotone flat voice that easily puts his students to sleep. Audiences take their cues from the speaker, so a speaker who sounds bored and dull indicates to the audience that the presentation is boring and dull. On the flip side, if your tone is enthusiastic, audiences will pick up on that enthusiasm. Studies of audiences have found that speakers who use a confident and expressive tone are rated more credible and authoritative by audiences, regardless of the content of the message.[22,23]

Because your tone has such an impact on audience perceptions, it is important to avoid speaking patterns that detract from your credibility and authority. In the early 1990s, linguists and speech pathologists identified a common speech pattern among primarily young females in which they end their phrases and sentences with a rising intonation, which they dubbed **upspeak** or **uptalk.** This vocal pattern also referred to as talking like a Valley Girl, is perceived negatively as it sounds like the speaker is always asking a question and is unable to make a definitive statement. Not only can upspeak be annoying to the audience, but it also can make the speaker seem less intelligent and capable.[24] While this pattern was first unique to young females, more recent studies have found that young men are also starting to speak with this rising intonation.

Another more recent vocal pattern that has emerged as a trend and has actually been labeled as a speech disorder by speech pathologists is **vocal fry.** Made infamous by celebrities such as the Kardashian sisters and actress Zoey Deschanel, vocal fry is the vibratory sound made when a person speaks in a lower register than normal. The voice often sounds creaky or raspy and can actually damage the vocal cords because of the strain it places on them. One theory for why some women started using this technique is that it does lower the voice, and as we learned previously, lower voices may make a person sound more credible. In general, vocal fry is perceived negatively except for when females are speaking to other females of the same age. Because of the potential damage to the voice and the likelihood that others will perceive users as more immature or less serious, it should be avoided.

Vocal Fillers

Have you ever heard a speaker use a lot of filler words such as "like" or "um"? If you have, you most likely found that the longer you listened, the more focused you became on the filler words rather than what the speaker was saying. **Vocal fillers,** or more formally **vocal nonfluencies,** are words that are inserted into natural speech that have no meaning. Filler words act as a pause so the speaker can gather his or her thoughts without interrupting the flow of speech. Used occasionally, phrases and words such as "um," "you know," or "like" are fine, but using vocal fillers can become habitual, and when used in excess, they become annoying to the listener and can make the speaker seem less intelligent.[25]

Eliminating vocal fillers from your speech can be difficult as they are used subconsciously, and many do not realize the frequency with which they are using them. The first step is to become aware of how often you include vocal fillers in your speech. The easiest way to do this is to record yourself and listen, or have a friend or acquaintance listen and record how often you use vocal fillers. Once you are aware of the problem, here are some strategies for reducing your usage of filler words during a presentation:

> **Using vocal fillers can become habitual and when used in excess they become annoying to the listener.**

- Break your information into main points and subpoints;
- Know your material.
- Practice pausing when you are thinking instead of throwing in a filler word.
- Plan for and practice your transitions so you are not struggling with what to say.
- Have a friend give you a signal each time you use a vocal filler while you are speaking.

Pauses

In the previous section we learned that vocal fillers are used in place of a pause in speaking. Pauses are important in speaking because they give us time to breathe, indicate that we have reached the end of a sentence or idea, and give the audience time to process what they have heard. Used effectively, a well timed paused can create emphasis and help with the pacing of your speech. Used ineffectively, however, or used because the speaker has forgotten what to say or cannot gather his or her thoughts, long and frequent pauses can disrupt the flow of speech and signify to the audience that the speaker is unprepared or is struggling to present.

Overall Delivery

After reading through the prior sections, it is evident that speech delivery is comprised of multiple components. When these elements are combined, you create an overall impression on the audience. While more intangible and harder to define, the next two elements of presentation delivery, rapport and charisma, are what separates an average speaker from a great speaker.

Rapport

Rapport is the connection that a speaker has with an audience and implies some type of interaction. Even if the audience never speaks, an audience that laughs, sighs, and has an obvious interest in what the speaker is saying is one that is interacting with the speaker. When you have rapport with your audience, they are listening to what you are saying, and they want you to succeed. If you are trying to persuade them of something, you are more likely to be successful. Part of rapport building is based on the information you share, but your delivery style can also influence your connection with the audience. Maintaining eye contact, having an open posture, and smiling at your audience are all ways to bring them into what you are saying. Because rapport is a two-way relationship, you can gauge your level of rapport by noting how the audience is responding to you. If you are smiling and upbeat and your audience members are nodding off, you have not yet managed to establish rapport.

Charisma and Energy

If you think about some of the people we have talked about in the chapter as examples of great speakers, one thing they have in common is that they are charismatic. **Charisma** is an energy and magnetism that draws people in. A charismatic speaker is one who not only engages the audience but makes people want to listen. There is not a specific checklist for being charismatic as it is an overall trait, but there are things you can do to increase your charisma. The most important thing you can bring to any speaking situation is energy. If your audience can sense you are alert and excited to be there, and you are speaking with interest and passion, they are more likely to be engaged in your presentation. Your nonverbals such as posture, tone, and facial expressions are all key ways to express your energy. Some people are naturally more low energy or high energy, so depending on your personal energy level, you may have to work to sound and act more animated while speaking.

An interesting study out of UCLA found that speakers who were rated as being more charismatic tended to vary the pitch of their voice more going from their lowest to highest registers more frequently.[26] Another important component of charisma is appearing comfortable in the speaking situation. Nothing kills your charisma faster than appearing nervous or ill at ease in your speaking situation. Combining confident, open posture and meaningful eye contact with your audience with some of the public speaking anxiety management strategies is a way to convey your comfort in front of a group.

Chapter Summary

In this chapter, we examined techniques for delivering a presentation with confidence. Specifically, we explored the physical and verbal components of delivery as well as the overall impression your delivery can make on an audience. While the information you present is critical, it is equally important that you present in a way that demonstrates your confidence and capabilities.

References

[1] Newton-Small, J. 2016. "Hillary Clinton's Acceptance Speech Delivery Gets Panned on Twitter." *TIME,* July 29, 2016. http://time.com/4430082/dnc-hillary-clinton-speech-2/.

[2] Carson, C. 2009. "King, Obama, and the Great American Dialogue." *American Heritage* 59(1): 26–30. http://search.ebscohost.com/login.aspx?direct=true&db=aph&AN=37021863&site=ehost-live.

[3] Manam, A. A., S. Shamsudin, M. Puteh, and S. Said. 2016. "Effective Public Speaking Skills: A Case Study of Obama's Engaging Public Speaking Strategies." *Science International* 28(2): 1411–1416. http://search.ebscohost.com/login.aspx?direct=true&db=aph&AN=116773415&site=ehost-live.

[4] Mehrabian, A. 1972. *Silent Messages: Implicit Communication of Emotions and Attitudes.* Covington, KY: Wadsworth Publishing.

[5] Beebe, S. A. 1976. "Effects of Eye Contact, Posture, and Vocal Inflection upon Credibility and Comprehension." *ERIC.* http://eric.ed.gov/?id=ED 144121.

[6] Ozuru, Y., and W. Hirst. 2006. "Surface Features of Utterances, Credibility Judgments, and Memory." *Memory and Cognition* 34(7): 1512–1526. doi: 10.3758/BF03195915.

[7] Levine, T. R., K. J. K. Asada, and H. S. Park. 2006. "The Lying Chicken and the Gaze Avoidant Egg: Eye Contact, Deception, and Causal Order." *Southern Communication Journal* 71(4): 401–411. http://10.0.4.56/10417940 601000576.

8. Cuddy, A. 2015. "Strike a Power Pose—But Do It In Private." *TIME* 186(24): 80. http://search.ebscohost.com/login.aspx?direct=true&db=aph&AN=111352151&site=ehost-live.

9. Goldin-Meadow, S., and M. W. Alibali. 2013. "Gesture's Role in Speaking, Learning, and Creating Language." *Annual Review of Psychology* 64(1): 257–283. http://10.0.4.122/annurev-psyc-113011-143802.

10. Rudner, M. 2015. "Working Memory for Meaningless Manual Gestures." *Canadian Journal of Experimental Psychology* 69(1): 72–79. http://10.0.4.13/cep0000033.

11. Neff, M., N. Toothman, R. Bowmani, J. E. Fox Tree, and M. Walker. 2011. "Don't Scratch! Self-adaptors Reflect Emotional Stability." *Intelligent Virtual Agents*, 398–411. Heidelberg: Springer-Verlag.

12. Jack, R. E., W. Sun, I. Delis, O. G. B. Garrod, and P. G. Schyns. 2016. "Four not Six: Revealing Culturally Common Facial Expressions of Emotions. *Journal of Experimental Psychology: General* 146(6): 708–730. http://10.0.4.13/xge0000162.

13. Schmidt, K., R. Levenstein, and Z. Ambadar. 2012. "Intensity of Smiling and Attractiveness as Facial Signals of Trustworthiness in Women." *Perceptual and Motor Skills* 114(3): 964–978. doi: 10.2466/07.09.21.PMS.114.3.964-978.

14. Sebastian, R. J., and D. Bristow. 2008. "Formal or Informal? The Impact of Style of Dress and Forms of Address on Business Students' Perceptions of Professors." *Journal of Education for Business* 83(4): 196–201. http://search.ebscohost.com/login.aspx?direct=true&db=aph&AN=32013605&site=ehost-live.

15. Furnham, A., P. S. Chan, and E. Wilson. 2013. "What to Wear? The Influence of Attire on the Perceived Professionalism of Dentists and Lawyers." *Journal of Applied Social Psychology* 43(9): 1838–1850. http://10.0.4.87/jasp.12136.

16. Carr. D. L., T. L. Davies, and A. M. Lavin. 2010. "The Impact of Instructor Attire on College Student Satisfaction." *College Student Journal* 44(1): 101–111. http://search.ebscohost.com/login.aspx?direct=true&db=aph&AN=48646432&site=ehost-live.

17. Melnick, M. 2011. "Want to Be Heard? Try Changing the Way You Talk." *TIME*, May 20, 2011. http://Healthland.time.com/2011/05/20/want-to-be-heard-try-changing-the-way-you-talk/.

18. Pellegrino, F., C. Coupé, and E. Marsico. 2011. "A Cross-Language Perspective on Speech Information Rate." *Language* 87(3): 539–558. doi: 10.1353/lan.2011.0057.

[19] Kluger, J. 2011. "Why Some Languages Sound So Much Faster than Others." *TIME*, September 8, 2011. http://content.time.com/time/health/article/0,8599,2091477,00.html.

[20] Aguinis, H., and C. A. Henle. 2001. "Effects of Nonverbal Behavior on Perceptions of a Female Employee's Power Bases." *Journal of Social Psychology* 141(4): 537–549. http://search.ebscohost.com/login.aspx?direct=true&db=aph&AN=6002448&site=ehost-live.

[21] Gunn, J. 2010. "On Speech and Public Release." *Rhetoric and Public Affairs* 13(2): 1–41. http://search.ebscohost.com/logoin.aspx?direct=true&db=aph&AN=51231733&site=ehost-live.

[22] Alleyne, S. 2001. "In a Manner of Speaking." *Black Enterprise* 32(11): 73. http://search.proquest.com/docview/217900228?accountid=13360.

[23] Goman, C. K. 2008. "Watch Your Language." *T+D* 62(8): 94–95. http://search.ebscohost.com/login.aspx?direct=true&db=aph&AN=33650388&site=ehost-live.

[24] Baldoni, J. 2015. "Will 'Upspeak' Hurt Your Career?" *Forbes,* July 30, 2015. http://www.forbes.com/sites/johnbaldoni/2015/07/30/will-upspeak-hurt-your-career/#4dd7c4cc4edc.

[25] Pytko, J. L., and L. O. Reese. 2013. "The Effect of Using 'Um' and 'Uh' on the Perceived Intelligence of a Speaker." *Journal for the Behavioral Sciences– College of Saint Elizabeth:* 1–21. http://search.ebscohost.com/login.aspx?direct=true&db=aph&AN=95380385&site=ehost-live.

[26] Hotz, R. L. 2014. "How to Train Your Voice to Be More Charismatic." *Wall Street Journal:* 1. http://search.ebscohost.com/login.aspx?direct=true&db=aph&AN=99749558&site=ehost-live.

Chapter 4

Assessing the Speaking Situation

Objectives

After this chapter you will be able to:

- Explain the importance of assessing a public speaking situation.
- Distinguish between demographic, psychographic, and situational audience analysis.
- Utilize strategies for assessing a speaking situation.
- Identify ways to adapt your message in different speaking situations.

In 2016, Maria Elena Salinas, a prominent news anchor and journalist for Univision, the largest American Spanish Language television station, received her honorary doctorate from California State University's Fullerton School of Communication and was asked to speak at the graduation ceremony. During her speech she congratulated the student body and also spoke a few lines in Spanish, a move that seemed to be well received by the audience as nearly 40 percent of the University's student body speaks Spanish and many of the student's parents speak only Spanish. Given the nearness to the 2016 presidential election, Salinas made a few remarks about the candidates. After the university wide ceremony, Salinas was also asked to speak at a smaller reception for just the students graduating from the Fullerton School. She delivered a similar message in which she spoke Spanish, commended the Hispanic and Latino graduates in the group, and made a few disparaging remarks about the then Presidential Candidate, Donald Trump. This time, the audience was not as receptive, and several members started booing her. Some attendees even went on Twitter to criticize her talk saying that her political opinions and failure to recognize non-Hispanic and Latino attendees were offensive.

Let's Talk
- What mistakes did Salinas make when she was analyzing her audience?
- How could Salinas have adapted her message to avoid offending audience members?

Introduction

In any speaking situation, you will go in with a variety of goals. You might want to persuade your audience to make a lifestyle change, or your goal might be to let people know about a new volunteer opportunity within your organization. Regardless of the situation, one goal you will always have is to present your information and share your story in a way that resonates and connects with your audience.

In order to reach this goal, it is important that you are an audience-centric vs. speaker-centric presenter. A speaker-centric presenter is focused on what his or her message is and what he or she wants to convey to the audience. An audience-centric presenter is also concerned with his or her message, but is also concerned with how the audience will receive that message. An audience-centric speaker adapts the message in order to give the presentation its best chance to be successful. Being audience-centric does not mean that you pander to the audience or only tell them what they want to hear; instead, it means that if you are saying something, you consider how the message may be received and choose a way to deliver the message that your audience will hear and understand.

If you want to be an audience-centric speaker, there are four basic questions you need to ask yourself before going into a speaking situation:

- Who is my audience?
- What is my audience like?
- Where am I presenting?
- Why am I presenting?

By answering these questions, you can get a better handle on the speaking situation and adapt your message and your presentation plan accordingly.

Who Is My Audience?

One commonality among any type of presentation is that there is an audience. It may seem obvious who your audience is, but the reality is that you might not know, and failure to determine who is going to be listening to you speak can have negative ramifications. Let's say, for example, that you work for your city's public health department, and you are asked to come to a local high school to talk about food preparation. As you are preparing for your presentation, your supervisor asks who you are speaking to, and you realize that you are not sure. Are you speaking to cafeteria works, teachers and staff, students, or some combination of the group? Without knowing the answer to this basic question, it will be difficult to prepare a presentation that fits the needs of the audience.

Whenever you are going into a speaking situation, you always should determine who will be there. Sometimes the answer is obvious. If you are giving a presentation in a class, you know that your instructor and classmates will be the audience. If you call a meeting at work, you know who you have invited to attend. In other situations though, if you are not sure, you should always ask the person who has asked you to come and present. In the above example, a quick phone call or email can easily answer the question of who the audience will be.

Another important question to answer is how large your audience will be. By nature, presentational speaking involves a smaller audience than traditional public speaking. At work you may give a presentation to a small team of 4–5 coworkers, or you may present to a larger group, like your entire department of 35–40. In school you will often present to your classmates, so your audience size will be determined by your class size. You want to have a good idea of your audience because your presentation style and strategy will often differ based on size. Communication consultant Jim Anderson breaks audiences into four types. The first type is a group of less than 10 which he calls a conversational group. The next group contains 10–40 members is what he calls presentation size. The next groups, 40–100 and more than 100 members, are performance and show size.

When presenting to a smaller audience, a general rule is that your presentation can and should be more conversational. Given the smaller size of your audience, it is easier to be interactive and responsible. With a larger audience, you might still want to have a conversational delivery style, but your connection with each member will be difference and you will be less likely to have active engagement with the audience. Even if there is time for questions and answers, you will only be able to respond to a small portion of your audience.

Sometimes you may not be sure of how large your audience will be. Imagine, for example, that you are the president of your school's chapter of Big Brothers Big Sisters, and your group decides to have a call out for students interested in volunteering. Your group may advertise and promote your call out, but as you are getting ready for your presentation about the club, you really have no idea how many people will show up. The number could range anywhere from 1–100. In situations like these, you will want to have a plan for what you will do in either situation.

If only a few people show up, for example, you may want to adapt your presentation to being more conversational; instead of standing at a podium or using a microphone, you should sit or stand near the attendees. You could also ask the attendees to sit in the front. If a larger number than you anticipated arrives, you

> **When presenting to a smaller audience, a general rule is that your presentation can and should be more conversational.**

will want to consider where people will sit and make sure that your voice is loud enough to be heard. If you are using visual aids or have handouts, make sure everyone can see them. You also might investigate what prior attendance at call outs has been or how many people have shown up to other call outs.

What Is My Audience Like?

This next question goes beyond simply identifying who the audience is and asks you to consider what the people who comprise your audience are like. Going back to the previous example of giving a food safety presentation, imagine that you called the school principal who informed you that you would be talking to a group of students. This helps you to focus your presentation as you now know you are not speaking to a group of professionals working in the food preparation field. However, there is still a lot you do not know about this group, which is where audience analysis comes in.

Audience analysis is the process of learning more about your audience in order to appropriately adapt your message so that your presentation is understood, is useful to your audience, and is well received. Two fields that rely heavily on audience analysis are marketing and advertising. When designing a new product or determining how to best advertise a product or service, marketers invest a lot of time and energy in finding out what makes an audience tick. Take, for example, McDonald's. With a nearly $10 million advertising budget, the company can create ads meant to reach a variety of audiences include men, women, parents, and children. By researching each of these audience segments and creating a more detailed audience profile, McDonald's is able to create ads with messages and images that are the most likely to resonate with that audience.[1]

Within an audience analysis, there are two primary areas in which you should be interested: demographics and psychographics. By obtaining more information about your audience, you can develop a general audience profile that can help you plan for your message.

Demographics

Demographics are statistics about a population that include basic facts about a person such as age, sex, and geographical location. A great example of demographic research is the U.S. Census. Every 10 years, the United States Government surveys the entire population of the U.S. in order to determine who is living in the U.S. and basic facts about the people. The goal is for each adult living in the U.S. to fill out the survey in order to build a picture of what the population looks like. Some of the categories included on the census include sex, age, race, household income, primary language spoken, occupation, education level, address, group affiliation, and marital status. The U.S. Government and many of its agencies use this information to determine the makeup of the cities, counties, and states in the country. Additionally, this information provides vital information about what communities may need in terms of assistance and government programs. Similarly, an assessment of your audience demographics can give you an idea of what types of information your audience may need, want, or be able to relate to.

While there are endless categories of demographics, there are a few categories and terms that sometimes confuse people as they are unsure of what the terms mean, so we will define some of these categories. The first two categories that sometimes confuse people are sex and gender. Sex is the biological and physical characteristics that are male or female. Gender is often confused with sex, but gender is the societal beliefs as the attitudes, feelings, and behaviors that are associated with a biological sex. Traditionally, people have thought of masculine and feminine as being the two categories of gender, but more recently there has been a recognition that these two categories are limited, and there is a wide spectrum of gender identifications including transgendered, cis gender, and gender fluid. While a person's sex and gender may be aligned, for some people, their gender identity does not match their biological sex, and we cannot make assumptions about people based on their sex alone.

Two more categories that people sometimes confuse are race and ethnicity. Race is related to the physical characteristics a person has such as skin color and bone structure. Race is not based on country or origin or language spoken, so people across the globe are the same race, regardless of where they live. On the U.S. Census, the six categories of race are White, Black, Asian, American Indian and Alaskan Native, and Hawaiian or Pacific Islander. Additionally, people can identify as mixed race or biracial. This demographic does not provide much useful information as a person's race tells us very little. Ethnicity, on the other hand, is based on culture, and an ethnic group can be defined by shared values, customs, and beliefs. Terms like Hispanic, Latino, English, and American all refer to ethnicities. People are often members of multiple ethnic groups as an American might also identify as being Hispanic.

When you are going to give a presentation, you most likely will not need to conduct as thorough analysis as the Census Bureau, but you should ask yourself which categories will be most useful to you in planning your presentation. Think about our health department presentation. What are some basic facts you would want to know about your audience of students? Your list might include age, year in school, sex, and prior work experience. Knowing these things can help you determine what information might be most relevant and useful to the group. It can also inform what approach you take as you present, as well as what types of examples and references you can use that this audience could easily relate to. Because you are speaking to students vs. adults, you know you will want to use examples and references that this younger audience can relate to. When choosing restaurants to use as examples, you would want to choose locations that the students are likely to frequent and can relate to. Some demographics would not be as useful to you as they are not relevant such as religion, socioeconomic status, and home address; these are not related to the topic of food safety. The demographics you will want to gather will depend on your topic and the purpose of your presentation.

While there is a lot of utility in doing a demographic analysis, the information you collect is limited, and as a speaker, you need to be aware of these limitations. The largest limitation is that a demographic analysis has to rely on generalizations and presuppositions of what someone in a particular demographic is like. It is easy to make assumptions that a certain sex, age group, or group within a socioeconomic status thinks or acts a certain way or that all members of a group think and behave in the same way. These types of assumptions are called **stereotypes,** and if a speaker relies too heavily on stereotypes, he or she runs the risk at best not adapting the message correctly and at worst offending the audience.

This is what happened when the Texas A&M football team hosted a clinic for women to help teach them the basics of football. The clinic, Chalk Talk, included a presentation by two assistant football coaches. Attendees were quickly offended by the pair's presentation that began with a comment about the only reason for women being there was to learn enough about the game so they could talk to their husbands and boyfriends. Other jokes and comments in the presentation fell flat including rewriting lines of the school's fight song to say, "Maroon and white are the colors that we love. We are putting down our dish towels and taking off our gloves." In crafting their story, the coaches made a lot of

> If a speaker relies too heavily on stereotypes, he or she runs the risk of not adapting the message correctly and at worst offending the audience.

assumptions about their female audience including the belief that women have no interest in football and that they spend their time cleaning and taking care of the house when not watching the game with their partners. Several attendees complained to school administrators which resulted in the coaches being disciplined and the head football coach issuing an apology.[3]

Given the limitations of a demographic analysis, you might be wondering why even bother? Even though you have to be careful not to over generalize, you can glean useful information from a basic demographic analysis. If you know, for example, that the majority of your audience lives in a rural area, you know that the people in the audience have a certain frame of reference and have experienced life different than someone who lives in a large city such as Chicago. When it comes to presentations that you may give while a student, the majors of students in your audience is often an important demographic, as this one piece of information can provide insight into a person's interests or at least on some of the background knowledge this person has. For some topics this may not be relevant and other demographic might be. Imagine you are a sexual health educator at your university. The material you would include for an audience of all males would inevitably be different for a female audience.

Certain demographic variables can also key us more into the psychology of a person which are things we often look for in a psychographic analysis. Demographics such as religion, political party, and sometimes group affiliation can provide insight into the beliefs and attitudes of a person in regards to certain topics. For example, if a person is a member of PETA (People for the Ethical Treatment of Animals), one assumes that the person is a strong advocate for animal rights and will be interested in animals and animal related issues and, going a step further, would have positive attitudes towards subjects such as vegetarianism and limitations on hunting.

Knowing Your Audience's Age Range

One advantage of knowing an audience's age range is that it can provide information about what sorts of shared experiences, cultural references, and historical events your audience might be able to relate to. If, for example, a speaker references a now obsolete technology such as a VCR, he or she cannot assume that a group of college students will be familiar with what a VCR or VHS tape is. One tool that can help you to consider the lived experiences of an audience, especially an audience younger than yourself, is the annual Mindset List released by Belloit College each year. This list provides a list of facts about the typical incoming freshman class or 18 year olds. The list for the graduating class of 2020, for example, includes the facts that West Nile virus has always been a problem in the U.S., and Sponge Bob Square Pants has always been on TV. You can see each year's list starting back in 1998 at www.beloit.edu/mindset.

Psychographics

Because a demographic analysis is limited, a more thorough audience analysis will also include psychographics. **Psychographics** are variables related to an individual's interests, attitudes, and opinions. Psychographics go beyond demographics as they are not just labels we can put on a person but involve the way that a person thinks, believes, and behaves. The type of information you will want to gather will depend on your topic. If you are giving a presentation to your audience about harmful effects of eating too much sugar it would be helpful to know what your audience currently knows about sugar, their current beliefs about what sugar, does to the body, and opinions about sugar. If audience members already believe that sugar is unhealthy, you will not need to spend a lot of time convincing them that there is a problem with sugar, so you can get into specific effects. If your audience, however, believes that sugar is healthy and natural, you will have to spend more time at the beginning of your presentation presenting evidence to the contrary.

While there are a variety of factors you could consider in a psychographic analysis, there are some general categories of items that will frequently be useful to you as you think about how to craft your presentation.

Knowledge

You should try to determine your audience's general level of knowledge about your topic. Knowing this can help you to make sure you explain your information at level appropriate for your audience. If your audience has a low a level of knowledge, you will need to be sure that you are explaining the basic concepts, providing enough background, and defining unfamiliar terms. It is especially important that you are aware of jargon and terminology that is specific to your topic. Many times because it is so familiar to us, we forget that the special language we use is not universally understood. For example, Drew, a student at the state university, was asked to come and talk to a group of seniors at his high school about what his transition to college was like. Throughout the presentation he told the students about different programs, organizations, buildings, and majors on campus. Instead of referring to these by name, though, he used the acronyms he was familiar with such as referring to the Student Recreation and Sports Center as the SCRC and the very important freshman orientation program as NSBC instead of New Student Bootcamp, which effectively left his audience utterly confused and no more informed than before the presentation.

> You should try to determine your audience's general level of knowledge about your topic.

On the other side of the spectrum, if your audience has a high level of knowledge, you need to be sure that you are not boring or insulting your audience by covering information they already know. You also need to be sure that you are presenting information that is new, relevant, and interesting to this audience. People are most interested in stories that have new elements, an interesting plot twist, and relatability. Take, for example, Sophia who is a speech pathology major and is studying to work with children who have speech delays. The topic of her presentation is common articulation problems found in young children. If she were to present this topic to a class full of students not in her major, she would have to first explain what an articulation disorder is and then provide examples of each of the disorders.

In case you are wondering, an articulation disorder is when a child incorrectly pronounces a sound such as making a "w" sound instead of an "r" sound in the word "rabbit," pronouncing it "wabbit." If she was to give the same presentation to a group of her fellow majors, a basic explanation of what the disorders are would not be very interesting and useful, and instead, she would need to present a more in depth analysis of the causes and treatments of the disorders.

Interests

Another psychographic variable you might want to know is what your audience is interested in. Knowing your audience's interests can help you determine what to talk about or what types of examples to include. If, for example, you are presenting to a group with a lot of people with careers in STEM fields, you should consider using examples from science, technology, and engineering. Knowing your audience's interests can also help you link your topic to something your audience cares about.

Values and Attitudes

Values are the beliefs that a person has about what is good or bad, right or wrong, and important or unimportant. **Values** are generally deeply held beliefs that influence the ways we think about things and the way we live our lives. **Attitudes** are more specific than values and are a person's assessment of a specific thing or idea. Attitudes are often based on one's values. Going back to our sugar example, if your audience places a high value on personal health, it is likely that this will influence the attitudes they have about sugar. As you plan your presentation, you can tap into the value and illustrate to your audience how eliminating sugar from the diet can increase one's health.

Your audience's values and attitudes will often dictate what type of audience you are speaking to. Audiences whose values closely match those you are presenting will be a favorable or receptive audience whereas audiences whose values and attitudes are much different from yours will be a more hostile audience. Each of these types of audiences is unique, and there different things you should consider when approaching them.

We will start with the type of audience you would most likely want to speak to, a **favorable audience.** A favorable audience is one that already generally supports and agrees with your ideas. For example, an HR manager might call a meeting to present the new employee bonus program to the staff. Employees tend to be favorable towards getting compensated and awarded for the work they do, so they will be predisposed to like your content. When speaking to a mostly favorable audience, you need to be sure that you are providing them with new and relevant information. If all of your classmates currently have positive attitudes about volunteering, a general speech about the benefits of volunteering would be less useful to this audience than a speech providing specific examples of ways to volunteer on campus.

You may wonder if there is even a need to speak to a favorable audience if they already support what you are saying. The answer is yes, because it is an opportunity to increase their knowledge about the topic. Just because someone, for example, values financial security does not mean he or she knows everything about that topic.

One potential pitfall to speaking to a primarily favorable audience is assuming that they will be easy to present to and as a result, you do not prepare like you should. Even if your audience supports your basic idea, if you do a poor job of presenting that idea, your audience can turn against you. Poor speech delivery, lack of preparation, and subpar content can easily be detected by an audience.

> Poor speech delivery, lack of preparation, and subpar content can easily be detected by an audience.

A **neutral audience** is one that is neither favorable nor unfavorable to your ideas. This is an audience who is often unfamiliar with your topic. One of the benefits of speaking to a neutral audience is that you are speaking to what is a blank slate. Without deeply held beliefs, attitudes, and knowledge, it is easier to create a new belief or attitude in this group. One potential challenge of a neutral audience, though, is that it may not have the enthusiasm of a favorable or even hostile audience. When presenting, you need to engage this audience and also highlight the relevance and importance of your information.

Imagine, for example, you are giving a presentation to your classmates about investment options for retirement. Given the younger age of your audience, this might not be a topic they have thought a lot about and might not know why they should care. It is your job as the speaker to explain to them why they should listen and care about your information. Neutral audiences can also have little knowledge about your topic, so you must be sure to provide enough background information for your audience to fully understand your message.

The third type of audience you might address is a **hostile audience.** A hostile audience actively disagrees with what you are saying. Often an audience will be hostile when you are telling them information or news that will have a negative impact on them. For example, a school board member may have to speak to local residents about the need to lay off teachers to save money. At work, you may have to tell a team you lead that your group will be moving forward on a project that the team does not support. Many of us would prefer not to address an audience that is predisposed to disagree with us. The good news, though, is that people actually perform better when speaking to a hostile crowd.[2] Knowing you are headed into a difficult speaking situation can be a great motivator for doing your best.

As we think about how to best address a hostile audience, consider the following two situations.

Audience Homogeneity

As you are assessing and considering your audience, you should determine if your audience is **homogeneous** or **heterogeneous.** A homogeneous audience is one where the audience members are very similar on the key demographic and psychological variables you have determined to be relevant and important for your presentation whereas a heterogeneous audience is one where there is a lot of difference in these variables. Presenting to a homogeneous audience can be an easier task as you can more easily find a topic that the entire group will be interested in. It is also easier to know what level of explanation to include when the entire group has the same knowledge.

Presenting to a heterogeneous group can be much more challenging. With a diverse crowd, it can be difficult to know how to craft a story that will reach everyone. How you present will depend on where the differences in your audience lie. If your audience has a wide range of knowledge on the topic, you need to make sure that those with the lowest level of knowledge have enough basic information to follow your presentation. Acknowledging in your presentation that you are going to present some basic facts for those in the audience with less knowledge is a great way to let audience members with higher levels of knowledge know why you are including information they already know. It is also important to avoid using jargon when presenting to audiences with varying levels of knowledge.

When your audience is comprised of people who are a variety of ages or from a variety of places, it can be more challenging to know how to adapt your message. One of the most important things is to clearly establish the overarching purpose of your presentation. From there, as you begin to consider what examples and supporting evidence you will include, try to include a variety so that you can reach the different audience segments. For example, imagine you were giving a presentation to incoming freshman about how to survive academically the first year. If all of your examples came from just one major such as English, those in STEAM majors might not find your presentation as engaging or useful. During a business presentation, consider what areas of a company the attendees are from such as marketing, accounting, or project management and be sure to address the informational needs of each of these areas.

Where Am I Presenting?

In addition to analyzing your audience, you also need to spend some time considering where and when you will be presenting. If you prepare a great slide presentation for your sales update at work only to learn when you get to the meeting that no computer or projector is available, you are going to find yourself in a bind. A little bit of research and inquiry prior to a presentation can help you better plan what you are going to say and how you are going to say it. One of the reasons it is important to consider the environment in which you are presenting is because of potential distractions or noise that interfere with your presentation. If you recall the communication model from Chapter 1, you will remember that noise is something that interferes with the transmission of the message from the speaker to the receiver. Noise can be external or internal, and when you are presenting, noises are the barriers that prevent your audience from fully processing the message. As a speaker, you will want to either eliminate the noise or adapt a message in a way that can overcome the noise.

When thinking about where you are going to be presenting, here are a list of things you will want to consider:

- The size of the room,
- Availability of technology,
- Size of your audience,
- Ability to block out distractions, and
- Time allotted.

One reason it is important to know about the size and setup of your speaking location is so you can be sure that your voice can be heard by everyone in the room. In a very large room, you may need to use a microphone to help amplify your voice.

If some of your audience will be seated very far from you, you will have to consider this as you plan your visual aids and consider their ability to be easily seen from a distance. You may also want to ask or investigate what your speaking space will look like. Are you going to be up on a stage and addressing people in an auditorium, or will you just be in a room with tables and chairs?

Another important thing to consider is whether or not you will be speaking from a podium. Some people prefer a podium because there is comfort in being able to stand behind something while speaking, and it also provides a place for your notes. If you are only used to speaking from behind a podium, you may feel quite awkward if you have to just stand in front of the group. Some people prefer not to speak from a podium as they like to be able to walk around, but if the microphone is affixed to the podium, you might not have a choice.

If you do find yourself in a situation where you are using a podium, here a few tips for using the podium most effectively:

- Avoid clutching the sides or top of the podium.
- Stand one of two steps back from the podium so you do not lean on it or use it as a crutch.
- If you are using the podium microphone, make sure it is at the right height.
- Don't forget to gesture.
- Be sure your gestures can be seen above the podium.

You must never assume that technology will be available to you or that if it is available, that it will work. We have become so reliant on technology that sometimes we are at a loss for what to do if it is not available to us. A fellow instructor was once scheduled to teach a course at an off-campus site. She knew the classroom was equipped with a computer and projector, so she planned her lecture and slides accordingly. Given that she was teaching public speaking, she also created a playlist on YouTube of videos to illustrate different concepts of speech delivery. She was quite surprised to learn her first day of teaching that internet available in her off-site classroom was the business providing the classroom space to block nonessential websites which included YouTube; consequently, she could not show any of her examples.

Because you can never be sure that your technology will work, you always want to have a backup plan. If you are prepping for a big presentation at work where people from multiple organizations are attending, something like a power outage or a server going down is not going to be reason enough to reschedule the meeting, so you need to be able to go through your presentation without the help of technology. A great backup plan if you are using some type of slide presentation is to print out your slides, and if technology fails, you can always pass out your slides to your audience. If you are unable to show a video clip, be sure you can provide a good summary to your audience.

Another important factor to consider is the time of day when you are presenting. After doing some research of organizations and the human internal clock, Andrew Bradbury, the author of *Successful Presentation Skills,* concluded that the best possible time to give a presentation is on a Tuesday morning at 10:30. The reasoning behind this is it is late enough in the day that people have gotten over their initial sleepiness, and it is early enough that people are not worn out by the day. Tuesday is not Monday, a day when many people are still getting back into the swing of things, and it is early enough that the weekend is still far away.[4] Now obviously, we cannot limit our presentations to only Tuesday mornings, but we can consider specific adaptations we might want to make if we are giving a presentation at a time that might seem less than optimal.

Some times of day that might be more challenging than others to get and maintain your audience's attention are very early in the morning, right before or after lunch, and at the end of the day. In the early morning, your audience might still be tired and may have trouble getting enthusiastic about your presentation. If you know you will be presenting at an early hour, it is important that you yourself do not come across as tired and unenergetic.

Adding in components to your presentation that will allow your audience to participate and interact is a way to wake them up and keep their attention. If you are presenting right before lunch, there is a high chance that your audience members will be hungry and thinking more about food than you, and right after lunch, audience members might be full and drowsy. Again, you will want to engage your audience, and depending on the situation, bringing snacks or setting up your presentation as a lunch meeting is a great way to reduce the noise created by hunger.

Another time that can be challenging is a presentation that is scheduled for the end of the work day or in the evening. In these situations, people are often eager to leave and get home. Being engaging and providing useful and relevant information is very important. Additionally, you should try to be as succinct as possible so that your presentation does not run over time.

The amount of time you are given to present is also a key thing you need to consider when getting ready for a presentation. We have all probably been in the situation where each person in a group is given about 5 minutes to present on a topic, and there is one person who keeps talking for at least 20 minutes. Taking more than your allotted time is not only annoying to your audience, but it is also implying that your time is more important than theirs. On the flip side, if you have been invited to a local group to present about a topic for 30 minutes and you only talk for 10 minutes, you are letting the group down. When you know about how long you have to present, you can start to consider how much information you can and should include on a given topic.

Another thing to consider is that you may run into a situation where you do not have as much time to present as you thought. Imagine a Friday afternoon staff meeting and the person presenting before you has gone over time, meaning that instead of 15 minutes to present an update on the budget, you only have 10.

Why Am I Presenting?

The final question you need to answer is why you are presenting? What is the goal of your presentation, or what is the situation that has called for this presentation? This question is not just asking you to identify your main purpose or thesis statement but more broadly to think about this from your audience's perspective. Answering these basic questions can help you focus on the story that you want and need to share. Consider a college instructor's lectures; while each lecture has a specific topic the instructor is covering, the purpose of the instructor's presentation is to increase the class' knowledge about that topic. Students will come to class with an expectation that the material covered will be useful and relevant to them in either helping them be successful in the class or in their future careers. An instructor who showed up and spent the entire class period discussing his trip to the Amazon last summer might be interesting, but it would not be meeting the needs or expectations of the class. If you are asked to come and speak or you invite people to hear you speak, it is important that you and your audience have a shared idea of what the purpose of your presentation is.

Another consideration in why you are presenting is whether your audience is their voluntarily or because their attendance is required. A **captive audience** is one that is required to be there and does not have the option to not hear your presentation. A **voluntary audience** comes because they are interested in your topic and they want information, or they are there to support or oppose a cause you are advocating. One advantage of speaking to a voluntary audience is that you do not need to spend a lot of time establishing relevance of your topic to them, and they are often enthusiastic and engaged with your message.

One challenge of a voluntary audience, though, is that they have clear expectations of what they will hear and learn from your presentation. While it is great to a have a voluntary audience that supports you when you are in a persuasive situation—think political rally or political convention, it can be very challenging to have a voluntary audience that is opposed to your ideas.

When you know you will be presenting to a captive audience, you can assume that for one reason or another not everyone in the room would have chosen to come and listen to you speak had he or she been given the option. Your classmates are a great example of a captive audience. Many of them come to class not just to hear the presentations but instead because attendance in class is required or they need to learn the material to do well in the class. The challenge when speaking to a captive audience is to immediately grab their attention and explain to them why the information in your presentation will be relevant, interesting, or beneficial to them in some way. A required audience may be less enthusiastic about being there, so you will want to be enthusiastic yourself and find ways to engage your audience with your presentation.

Another thing to consider when presenting to a captive audience is that they do not have the choice as to whether or not to listen to. When you are thinking about addressing a controversial or potentially emotional topic with a captive audience, you need to be very careful as they have not come to listen to you on their own volition. Kelsey, for example, gave a presentation to her class about ways to fight sex trafficking in the U.S. As part of her presentation, she wanted to discuss some of the terrible physical, emotional, and sexual abuse that many sex trafficking victims endure. She knew that this content might be difficult for many of her audience members to hear. Because of this, she decided to limit the amount of graphic details she used in her account, and during her introduction she warned her audience that some of her content may be disturbing.

Conducting Your Assessment

Now that you know the different things you want to learn about your audience, you might be wondering how you can get this information. The method or methods you use will depend on several factors including how much time you have, your resources, and your connections to your audience. In the following section we will look at some of the formal and informal methods you can use.

Interviews

For very large presentations, you might consider conducting interviews with some of the audience members. Formal interviews allow you to identify several demographic and psychographic factors about these audience members. While you most likely would not want to interview all of your audience members, especially if it is a large audience, you also do not want to interview only one person and make the false assumption that this person represents everyone who will be listening to your presentation.

Surveys and Polling

Another great way to gather information about your audience is to send members a survey or poll to fill out. One advantage of surveys over interviews is that it is easier to administer a survey to a large group of people, and the information collection process is much less labor intensive. While you can conduct very comprehensive surveys, you can also create relatively short surveys that will provide you with the key information you need. Imagine you have been asked to give a presentation at work about creating a more environmentally friendly office. As you are planning your presentation, you might distribute a brief survey to ask the staff about their knowledge and awareness of different environmentally friendly strategies.

> **Demographic Tools**
>
> In addition to surveying and compiling information, the U.S. Census Bureau also has publicly available tools you can use to find out the demographic makeup of a city, town, county, zip code, or state. By visiting https://factfinder.census.gov you can type in the area you are interested in knowing more about, and within seconds you have reports on everything from the average age of the population to the average income.
>
> If you are more interested in the psychographics of your audience, Claritas, a firm specializing in market research and audience segmentation, offers free tools at their website, www.mybestsegments.com. Their zip code finder tool allows you to look at the different types of people who live in a given area. In this tool, people are classified into groups based on demographics such as age and income. It also includes additional factors such as interests, like the television shows they are likely to watch, and values.

Observation

You can learn a lot about people and groups of people by taking some time to observe them. In many work situations, you may present many times on different topics to the same groups of people. You may also sit in on other presentations with these groups and by paying attention to the reactions the audience has, their question and comments, and the material they present, you can begin to put together a good understanding of who these groups are and how to best communicate with them.

Informal Conversation

While a formal interview is a great way to gather information, we do not always have the resources for this, and it is not always the most appropriate technique. Having conversations with people in the group you are presenting to, with the person who requested you present, or other people who are familiar with the group you are presenting to is a less resource-intensive way to gather information. If, for example, you are giving a presentation for a new potential client, you might ask people in your network if they know about the client's company.

Internet Research

With the increased amount of information about people and organizations available online, audience analysis has become much easier to do in some cases. Going back to the previous example of a sales pitch for a potential new client, a quick internet search can easily give you some information about the company in terms of their company missions, values, and past clients. If you are asked to give a presentation to a group in the community that you are not familiar with, reading the organization's website or perusing their social media can let you know more about the organization and what the members are like.

So Now What?

You can spend all of the time in the world analyzing your audience and creating a detailed profile of your average audience member, but if you do not use that information to adapt your presentation, your assessment will be futile. Remember, the reason for adapting your message is not to simply say only things that your audience wants to hear. Instead, the purpose is to get information that can help you create and present your message in a way that will help you reach your goal of informing, educating, entertaining, or persuading your audience.

It is also important to note that although this chapter has focused on how to use your assessment to plan your story, this is not the only time you should be assessing the situation and making adaptations. You should also be assessing the situation and the audience's response while you are speaking. One of the primary benefits of an extemporaneous delivery style vs. a memorized or manuscript style is your ability to adjust and adapt your message to best meet your audience needs. If we go back to the communication model again, you will remember that as someone is sending a message, the receiver is providing feedback even if the receiver is not speaking. If your audience looks confused, this is a good indicator that you need to provide more explanation or clarifying information. If several audience members look bored, are on their phones checking messages, or are yawning, this means that you have not grabbed their attention, and you may need to increase your own energy or provide information that will be more interesting to your audience.

Summary

In this chapter we have talked about the importance of assessing your speaking situation so you can adequately prepare for your presentation. The first step in this process is determining who your audience will be. After determining who your audience will be, you need to identify key traits about your audience. These traits fall into two general categories: demographics and psychographics. You can then use this audience profile to determine how you are going to adapt your message so it is received well and understood by your audience.

Case Study Conclusion

When Salinas was giving her presentation, she was speaking to parts of her audience but failed to consider the entire audience. In doing so, she upset and alienated many of the people listening to her speak. As this chapter illustrated, speaking to a diverse audience can be difficult, but it can be done.

References

[1] Svrluga, S. 2016. "'Get Off the Stage!' Crowd Yells at Commencement Speaker after She Uses Spanish, Mentions Trump." *The Washington Post*, May 24, 2016. https://www.washingtonpost.com/news/grade-point/wp/2016/05/24/commencement-speaker-gets-booed-after-speaking-briefly-in-spanish-and-criticizing-trump/?noredirect=on&utm_term=.0138f5cee708.

[2] "McHistory: Timeline of Major McDonald's Marketing Moves." 2016. *AdAge*, April 25, 2016. http://adage.com/article/news/mcdonald-s-timeline/303717/.

[3] Rajan, G. 2016. "Two Coaches Suspended after Texas A&M's 'Chalk Talk' for Women." *Houston Chronicle*, July 29, 2016. https://www.chron.com/sports/aggies/article/Two-coaches-suspended-after-Texas-A-M-s-chalk-8635826.php.

[4] Bradbury, A. 2006. *Successful Presentation Skills* (3rd ed.). Bodmin, Cornwall: MPG Books Ltd.

Chapter 5

Information Literacy

Objectives

After this chapter you will be able to:

- Select the most appropriate investigative methods for retrieving and accessing information for your speech.
- Evaluate information critically.
- Recognize that information has economic and legal issues and use information ethically.
- Select appropriate supporting material and communicate it in your speech.
- Present supporting materials in effective ways for your given audience.

Chapter 5   Information Literacy

On December 4th, 2016, Edgar M. Welch, a 28-year-old father of two, drove from his home in Salisbury, N.C., to Washington D.C., with an assault weapon to Comet Ping Pong, a pizza restaurant. Mr. Welch was hoping to stop a ring of child sex traffickers who were using the restaurant as a front for illegal activity. After arriving at the restaurant, Mr. Welch shot off the lock on the back door entered the kitchen and began searching for the basement where he believed children were being held captive. He continued to fire his semi-automatic weapon inside the building.[1,2] Fortunately, no one in the restaurant was hurt. After police arrived, it was revealed that Mr. Welch had read a series of news articles on Twitter, Facebook, and the web linking the pizza restaurant with a child sex trafficking ring lead by Hillary Clinton.[3,4] These stories, however, were falsified. They were fake news reports that were circulated through the internet to distract attention from more substantial issues regarding the election. We have recently seen more and more of these fake news stories, but this one had terrible consequences both for the pizza establishment and for Mr. Welch. He was ultimately sentenced to four years in prison and three years probation, and he must pay $5,744 in restitution to Comet Ping Pong Pizza. The owner of the pizza company, James Alefantis, said he is relieved this situation is over, but his reputation has been tarnished by the whole ordeal.

While this example of a fake news report is an extreme case with a horrible outcome, the internet and social media make the viral spread of misinformation like this easy and contagious. (Image above: By Elizabeth Murphy from Alexandria VA, United States (Comet–NW DC) [CC BY 2.0 (https://creativecommons.org/licenses/by/2.0)], via Wikimedia Commons)

Let's Talk

1. How can you tell a fake news story from a real one?
2. Are there things you can easily identify that differentiate real news from fake news?
3. Should you investigate all news stories to verify their veracity? Why or why not?

Introduction

The concept of information literacy is helpful when we consider issues like fake news. According to the American Library Association, information literacy is the ability to locate, evaluate, and effectively use information to support your ideas.[5] This chapter will guide you and provide some tips for improving your own information literacy so that you can enhance the ideas in your presentations. We will also point out how to locate images and other supporting material that can help illustrate your ideas. In addition to locating material, the chapter will provide guidelines on the best practices for using support to enhance your argument and illustrations in your presentations.

Locating Supporting Material

Part of being information literate is knowing when you need to use information to support your ideas. The need for information or support may shift from situation to situation depending on your audience. More reluctant or hostile audiences are going to require more support to get your ideas across. Spending a good deal of time analyzing your goals in relation to your audience will give you good insight into the types and amount of support you will need. Once you have decided that you need support, where might you find it? The following section will focus on helping you locate good and reliable information to support the ideas in your presentations.

If you are like other students, the first place you might seek information is Google and Wikipedia. Google and Wikipedia are great places to start, but they aren't sufficient for finding all of the information you will need for your presentation. The following section provides ideas and resources that are available at almost any university library or online. These resources should aid you in collecting valuable supporting evidence.

Online Resources

Google Scholar

Google Scholar is a specialized Google search. It is a search engine that allows you to search a multitude of places for scholarly articles. It cuts across disciplines so it provides a wealth of information on almost any subject. These include articles, theses, books, court opinions, information from academic publishers, professional societies, online repositories, and universities.[6] If you link Google Scholar to your own university library through settings and library links, you should have access to many full-text versions of the articles that you find in your searches. If your university library provides access to the full-text article, after providing your credentials, you too should be able to access the full-text version from the comfort of your own home. If you have trouble with this feature, speak with a librarian. They should be able to help customize your settings.

Organizational Websites

Organizational websites are terrific places to look for information. They often publish information about themselves but also link to other information on their industry or related material that could prove useful in your search for information. Consider the American Society for the Prevention of Cruelty to Animals as an example. This website has a wealth of information and statistics on the humane treatment of animals. They also have current headlines and the latest information on regulations and legislation on this issue. If you were planning a presentation on animal rights, this organization's website could be crucial to your research.

Crowd Sourcing Platforms

Crowd sourcing platforms like Reddit are a type of social news aggregation but also provide the opportunity for members to rate content and discuss it with each other. Another similar type of platform includes StackExchange. These platforms assemble groups of people who are interested in a particular topic. They have forums on all types of topics such as math, movies, parenting, science fiction—the list is really endless. People pose questions, others answer, the answers are voted on by other users, and the best ones rise to the top.

Ranking of the answers provided to questions and discussion threads is what is important with this type of resource. The "crowd" controls what is popular thereby providing some quality control of the content or answers. However, the control or oversight will only be as good as the members are knowledgeable on a particular topic. This is something to consider when using this type of source for gathering your data.

Blogs

Blogs can be an interesting source of information for supporting material. Blogs are usually written on a variety of topics by an individual, a group of individuals, or even an organization with some sort of expertise in an area. They are usually specific to a defined topic and provide the latest developments or reviews on something relevant to the topic. Some extremely popular tech blogs include *Mashable, GigaOM,* and *Gizmodo.* Some popular science blogs include *Overcoming Bias, Bad Science,* and *RealClimate.* You can find blogs on virtually any topic from decorating to gun control. However, authors of blogs may vary in expertise or reputation in their field. The popularity of a blog is some indication to how useful the information is, but the credibility of the author or authors is also a factor for you to consider. Some blogs are run by traditional media outlets, so they enjoy the prestige that goes along with the traditional media outlet's name. The *New York Times* has several blogs, for example. You will have to consider all of these factors and decide if the information in the blog will be credible with your particular audience.

Twitter and Other Social Media

Twitter and other social media provide good material for supporting evidence, as well. By searching hashtags you can locate any topic and see what the experts are saying about it. You can follow a leading expert and mine their tweets for important information. Although it probably won't provide a lot of supporting material, it can provide insights and "digital access" to an expert. In a way, it provides you access to an expert that would otherwise be difficult to obtain. Be sure that the person you are following is a legitimate expert. Anyone can create a website and Twitter account so make sure that you are citing someone your audience will respect.

Online Newspapers and Magazines

Online newspapers and magazines provide excellent information as well. You can usually go straight to a source and download a limited amount of initial information for free. Most of the more popular newspapers and magazines are also indexed at your library and provide you with unlimited access. Newspapers and magazine are timely, and the material you find in the latest issues will be current. Traditional newspapers and magazines also go through an editorial process that is arduous. The articles are usually fact checked, and it provides an added layer of protection against collecting false or inaccurate information. That is a real benefit to this type of source.

News Aggregators

News aggregators are software or web applications that pull all of the news together from syndicated sources into one place so it is easy to find. Google News and Apple News apps are examples of this type of resource. They pull syndicated stories and headlines from all over the world and show the latest headlines. They are good for catching up on current news and stories. If you are looking for timely information on a topic that is currently making news, this is where you would want to go.

Some news aggregators are specialized. For example, *PoliticsToday* and *Memorandum* are two that are specific to politics. If you subscribe to an aggregator, you likely will have little control over the information in your feed because it has been tailored for your reading preferences. If you aren't currently subscribing, you can control the content and target the topic you are interested in learning more about. In order to make sure you are seeing a variety of content, and not specialized content you will have to look at your settings to make sure you are getting a broad look at what is out there. This is one limitation with this type of source.

Databases

General databases at your library provide great access to a variety of different types of material that could be important to your presentation. These databases search a wide variety of subjects and are good places to begin general searches. The following table lists some of the most popular with a description of what they index.

Popular Databases

- **Nexis Uni:** Provides full-text access to U.S. and international newspaper articles, information on 80 million companies, information on federal and state court cases, laws, regulations, European Union law, patents, tax law, and law review articles.
- **Academic Search Complete:** Provides a large collection of full-text journals. It includes peer-reviewed full-text for STEM research as well as for the social sciences and humanities.
- **Academic Search Premier:** General academic index that indexes more than 8,200 magazines and scholarly journals from every academic discipline and provides some full-text access.
- **Newswires:** Provides near real-time access to top world-wide news from Associated Press, United Press International, PR Newswire, Xinhua, CNN Wire, and Business Wire.

(Descriptions taken from EBSCO and Purdue libraries.)

Scholarly Peer-Reviewed Articles

Scholarly articles that are published in peer-reviewed journals go through a special editorial process before they are published. The author, usually an expert in the field, submits the article for publication to the journal. The journal editor then sends the paper out to other experts in the area and asks them to review the article. These outside reviewers then read the article and decide if it will be published in the journal or not. A paper that is chosen to be published will probably go through edits by the reviewers before it is published. This process is the most stringent, and peer reviewed articles are believed to be the most prestigious. Every subject area (e.g., sociology, nutrition, theoretical physics, drug and alcohol abuse) has peer-reviewed journals and they can be very specialized. They can also be hard to read for someone who isn't an expert in the field. However, they are very credible sources of information due to the rigorous review process. You can find peer-reviewed articles in Google Scholar and in general and specialized databases in your library.

Books

Good old books can also provide information for supporting material. Books enjoy one marker that can help distinguish quality, and that is the press that printed the book. Different presses have different status among readers, and you can usually tell how important a book is by who printed or published it. It is one method of determining how credible the material might be.

> By the time a book gets to the library or on the bookshelf, it may already be out of date.

One limitation with books, however, is currency. Books take a while to publish, and the author does not have the ability to write something and get it out to their readers immediately. By the time a book gets to the library or on the bookshelf, it may already be out of date. For historical topics, this may not be an issue. For topics that require constant updates, this can be problematic.

Librarians

Librarians are also a great source of information. Don't be afraid to seek out a librarian for assistance especially if you are looking for something that is a little bit obscure. Many libraries often have online sessions where you can speak to a librarian without even having to go to the library. Students rarely take advantage of these services, but we encourage you to. Nobody knows the library like a librarian, and it is his or her job to help. You will find better material more quickly if you utilize their services.

Interviews

If you have access to someone with subject expertise or someone with special experience that makes them credible on a particular topic, you may want to interview them and include their opinion or testimony in your presentation. As mentioned earlier in the chapter, you can often access some experts over social media. Don't be afraid to reach out and ask for a quote or answer to a particular question. Experts are often surprised to be contacted by students and welcome the opportunity to speak with them.

Being on a college campus provides ample access to all kinds of experts who are conducting cutting edge research. Their busy schedules don't always allow them to sit down and talk through 30 minutes of questions, but they may be able to answer a quick question over email.

There are a few things to keep in mind if you do get access to an important interview. First, arrive to the interview prepared and ready to go. Second, be respectful of the interviewee's time constraints and keep the questions to a minimum. Finally, make sure that you quote the expert accurately. It is important that you summarize the key ideas and read them back to the interviewee to ensure that you have captured his or her ideas correctly. Interviews can have an impact on your ability to persuade your audience, so if you think they might add to your argument, use them to add support.

Evaluating Your Supporting Material

Once you have determined that you need supporting material to enhance your ideas and have located sources to retrieve supporting material, you have to evaluate the credibility of that material or the source. Exactly how valid or credible is the support you want to use? The standard questions—when, what, where, and why—apply when evaluating your material. In order to evaluate supporting material, it is important to consider the authority of the source.

Authority and Supporting Material

Authority, as it relates to information, is associated with perceived expertise and credibility of the person or organization that created that information or material. Authority is a complex concept. Just who has the legitimate power to be an authority on any particular issue? Well, that depends on who is consuming the material. That is why it is extremely important that you conduct adequate audience analysis in order to determine exactly which experts or sources will resonate or be accepted by a particular audience.

Authority can be accrued on an individual level (e.g., single author) or at the institutional level (e.g., news agency). Regardless of the level of authority, it occurs within a particular context, and different communities respond to different authority in different ways. Consider, for example, the way political conservatives and liberals in the U.S. respond to the authority of information presented by MSNBC and Fox News. Conservatives are extremely skeptical of information presented by MSNBC, and liberals are skeptical of anything on Fox News. You have to know your audience and who they believe has authority.

In order to evaluate the particular authority of any document that you may use in your presentation, we typically consider expertise, societal position, and special experience of the source of that information. Let's take a closer look at each of these and explore ways they can be used to evaluate the sources you consult for supporting material.

Subject Expertise

Subject expertise usually refers to the scholarship of information.[7] It is the information created in the pursuit of knowledge in a particular area or endeavor such as chemistry or art history. Subject expertise is usually defined by an agreed upon set of criteria that industry or discipline experts create to bestow mastery of an area. It usually includes a formal educational degree (e.g., PhD, MD, JD, or MFA) along with special experience in the subject area that leads someone to be considered an expert and have subject expertise.[8] For example, a student who receives a Masters of Fine Arts in art history is beginning to establish their expertise but probably won't be an expert until they establish significant years of additional work experience and/or research in their specific area of specialization.

When examining the subject expertise of a resource, you might ask the following questions: Just what is the particular expertise of the author of a particular document? Does the author have formal education that makes them an expert in the area? In other words, do they have an advanced degree in the area, or have they been conducting research in the area? If so, the author is probably considered an expert and has the education and experience to be an authority on a given subject.

Consider the level of expertise in the following two examples. A neurosurgeon will have more expertise on issues related to the brain than a pediatrician, for example. Two individuals with advanced degrees in particle physics may both have some expertise, but the one who has also worked conducting research at the Fermi National Accelerator Lab will likely have more expertise because of the prestige of the lab experience.

In addition to people, organizations may also have expertise. Many of the documents you use to support your claims in your speech may be from organizations. Again, ask yourself what special expertise a particular organization has and what special knowledge it might have to produce this information. For example, few of us would doubt the expertise of NASA in regards to information on the space programs or the history of the space program in the U.S. Medical associations such as the American Dental Association or the World Health Organization also have expertise in their own domains. These are just a few examples of organizations that would have subject expertise.

When you gather your information for your presentation, it is important that you recognize subject expertise as an important factor. Choose resources and information created by individuals and organizations with appropriate credentials. As mentioned earlier, it is also important to consider the context in which you will present your information and your audience. What sources will they most readily recognize and validate? A room of undergraduate accounting majors will have a very different view of expertise regarding accounting regulations than a room full of Certified Public Accountants. So, when choosing resources to support ideas in your presentation, consider expertise and the criteria for expertise that your audience may also require.

Societal Position

Sometimes expertise is associated with a position or role someone plays rather than a set of degrees or certifications someone has earned. For example, politicians usually earn expertise related to issues in their jurisdiction based on their experience in office, and members of the clergy are often considered expert on a variety of issues beyond their specific training. Take, for instance, Pope Francis. He has been an outspoken advocate against poverty around the world. While he does not hold advanced degrees in finance or business, he does garner credibility because of his leadership role in the Catholic Church.

The important thing to remember with using sources based on their societal position is that they may not actually have the expertise you need, and, even if they do, they may be perceived as biased on certain topics. Consider a politician like Hillary Clinton who is an expert on foreign policy. Through her role as Secretary of State, she has gained a wealth of information about global relations and tensions. However, her stance of specific topics (e.g., Russia, Taiwan, Israel) may be skewed because of her political affiliation (as would a Republican's perspective).

Special Experience

In special cases, people develop expertise in an area, and it isn't related to a formal degree or directly related to their profession. For example, Ed Yong is a British science writer for the *Atlantic*, who also writes a popular blog called *Not Exactly Rocket Science* hosted by National Geographic. He has developed an expertise in microbes and parasites that impact the behavior of all animals. He has even written a book on the topic and delivered a wildly popular TED talk on the subject. Although he has researched the area for a long time and has a wealth of knowledge in the area, he is not an expert in the same way that the actual biologists who made the discoveries that he writes about are. Yong examines the original research that comes from these scientists' labs, synthesizes it, and then presents it in a way that can engage larger audiences. While he is an expert, his authority is different than the authority generated by the actual scientists in their labs.

> Sometimes people have expertise because they have had a special experience.

Sometimes, people have expertise because they have had a special experience. Perhaps they were part of a military deployment or maybe they were at Progressive Field when the Chicago Cubs baseball team won the World Series in 2016. These experiences make them uniquely qualified to talk about those particular experiences or topics related to those experiences.

It is important to keep in mind that their accounts are anecdotal in nature, and that can be a limitation. However, anecdotal accounts are sometimes extremely entertaining and can arouse strong emotion from an audience and help tell a great story. Ultimately, it depends on the goals that you have for your presentation. However, this is something that is important to be aware of as you evaluate your material.

Other Considerations for Choosing Quality Sources

Once you have determined the appropriate level of authority for the supporting material included in your presentation, there are some additional things to consider. The following sections present criteria to consider when selecting supporting material.

Consult Reliable Sources

The places that you look for information should be credible and respected. Known entities with established reputations are usually more embraced by audiences than websites that no one has ever heard of. Also, certain sources are known to be biased in particular ways. As we mentioned earlier in this chapter, Fox and MSNBC are perceived as being politically biased. Keep all of this in mind as you consider using a particular source. Your instructors may have criteria that they want you to use when consulting sources so make sure that you check with them concerning any specific guidelines.

Consider Primary and Secondary Sources

One thing to keep in mind is the difference between **primary** and **secondary** sources. **Primary sources** are the originating sources of the information. When the *New York Times* publishes an article on the benefits of exercise for brain health, it usually bases the article on the peer-reviewed research published in a medical journal. The peer-reviewed piece in a medical journal is the primary source, and the secondary source is the article in the *New York Times*. The original or primary sources are always more reliable. Secondary sources reinterpret the information in primary sources, so there are always chances for information to be unintentionally misinterpreted.

Secondary sources are not inherently flawed, however. Many times the information is presented quite accurately. In some cases, this is the only mechanism for sharing information to wider audiences. Few of us have the educational requirements to ferret through medical journals. This would often require detailed background in the specific medical area being discussed as well as a sufficient background in experimental methods and statistics to fully appreciate the information. Science journalists take the information and present it in a way that mass audiences can understand. This is extremely important because findings from important studies may never make their way to the public if it were not for these secondary sources.

However, information in primary sources can be misinterpreted and presented inaccurately. Sometimes, the material is just hard to communicate, and the secondary source gets it wrong. The secondary source can also use and manipulate the data to make its own point. So, it is important that you consider whether your source is primary or secondary and if you should consult the primary source to check for accuracy. Some audiences will be fine with secondary sources and some will not. It is important that you take that into consideration.

Verify Your Material from More Than One Source

Once you have found information that you think you may want to use, it is important that you verify that information or check to see that it has been reported in a similar way by more than one legitimate source. Consider the following situation that occurred in December of 2016 about a dying child and a Santa Claus actor.

Eric Schmitt-Matzen, a professional Santa Claus actor, claimed that he had received a call from a

> You need to check that your information has been reported in a similar way by more than one legitimate source.

local Knoxville, Tennessee, hospital that a child was dying and wanted a visit from Santa Claus. He claims that he rushed to the hospital to bring the child a present, and the child died while he held him in his arms. The story was originally reported to the Knoxville *Sentinel News*. The *Sentinel News* did not initially verify the story with other sources and printed the story as part of a regular column. The feel-good story went viral spreading quickly across the internet and more traditional news outlets. When the Knoxville *Sentinel News* followed up and decided to verify their sources, no hospital in town could verify such an event happened or even identify a patient who could fit the profile in the story. The *Sentinel News* retracted the story and so did many other media outlets across the U.S. The *Sentinel News* should have verified the facts of this story before they printed it, but they claim they received the information from a regular and trusted source. Regardless, they should have followed up and verified the source.[9]

If the second news outlet had conducted due diligence to investigate whether or not these events took place, they could have prevented the questionable story from going viral across several other resources. Eric Schmitt-Matzen maintains that the events did, in fact, happen, but he refuses to provide more detail to protect the child and family who were involved.

The lesson we can learn from this event is that it is important to verify facts, stories, and statistics. Facts from one source are rarely sufficient to make a claim. It is important that you seek information from more than one source to verify that your information is indeed correct.

Include a Global Perspective

It is important to get a global perspective on many topics. Sometimes, it isn't sufficient to check for bias just nationally—only among U.S. outlets. We live in a global world, so it becomes important to consult the perspective of others who live outside of the U.S. If you were, for example, to give a presentation about the Syrian refugee crisis, a U.S. perspective would be limited, and information from the places closer to and more directly impacted by the crisis would be both valuable and informative.

Therefore, consult newspapers and other sources published in other countries to make sure you have considered your topic from more than just one angle. Some of the databases recommended earlier in this chapter search outlets that are based outside of the U.S. Look for diversity in perspective; it can be important to remaining unbiased.

Ensure the Currency of Your Information

Currency means that your information is new, up-to-date, or current. We live in the information age, and things change rapidly. Information is everywhere, and it can be spread in a viral fashion. It is important for you to have the most up-to-date information as possible. If you cite information on a health issue, for example, that is two years old, it may already be out of date. If your audience has more up to date material than you do, they will question your credibility.

Be Skeptical of Information

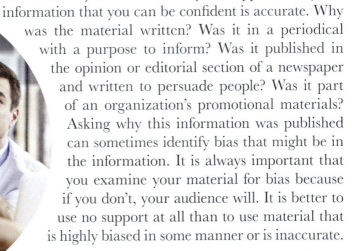

If something sounds suspicious, it probably is. Be skeptical about the sources you examine for your support. Only use information that you can be confident is accurate. Why was the material written? Was it in a periodical with a purpose to inform? Was it published in the opinion or editorial section of a newspaper and written to persuade people? Was it part of an organization's promotional materials? Asking why this information was published can sometimes identify bias that might be in the information. It is always important that you examine your material for bias because if you don't, your audience will. It is better to use no support at all than to use material that is highly biased in some manner or is inaccurate.

Types of Supporting Material

Now that you have considered the credibility of sources that you may want to consult for your supporting material, let's examine the specific supporting material itself. In the following section we review several types of supporting material, suggest good places to find that type of supporting evidence, and make recommendations on how to use that supporting material effectively.

Statistics

Numbers and statistics can have a strong impact in a presentation because we believe, accurately or not, that they are less subject to interpretative bias than other types of supporting material. If used responsibly and if the speaker understands the statistics they are using, they can be incredibly powerful. Statistics can easily make a point in ways that words alone could never make. Consider the claim that the movie *Titanic* was incredibly popular. However, saying that according to the Internet Movie Database, the movie, *Titanic,* has grossed over 2 billion dollars world wide as of August 2015 has a stronger effect than simply saying it was popular. The second statement is much more descriptive and has more impact.

When we talk about statistics, it is important that you differentiate between two types: descriptive and inferential. **Descriptive statistics** describe a sample or particular group. They summarize important characteristics of a particular group or phenomena. The example above about the movie *Titanic* is a descriptive statistic. Descriptive statistics may also report specific demographics of a group in terms of gender, ethnicity, or any number of socio-economic data. In addition, descriptive statistics can report percentages, or central tendencies (e.g., mean, median, mode).

Inferential statistics, in contrast, often seek to determine differences between groups or identify relationships between variables and are used when you want to move beyond mere descriptions. Whenever people speak about a statistically significant difference, they are talking about inferential statistics that are based on probability theory. For instance, a study might find that women are significantly more likely to suffer from a certain health issue than men. Another study might find that people who consume certain foods are significantly more likely to suffer from certain health issues. Both of these examples show that inferential statistics go beyond simply describing a single variable or group by making meaningful comparisons or highlighting certain relationships.

Where to Find Statistics

There are many places to find statistics. Many figures and statistics will be mentioned in the articles and reading you do to prepare for your presentation. However, sometimes you will need a particular figure to prove your point and will need something very specific. Here are some good places to start when looking for statistics.

First, you may consider using a reference source or database. Any library will provide access to a wide range of databases that provide information on statistics. Some of these will be specific to an industry or segment like *Agricultural Statistics (USDA)* or *CountryWatch*, which provides demographic, political, economic, business, and cultural information on specific countries. There are also more general databases like the *Data-Planet Statistical Datasets* that provide information from more than 70 source organizations and 90 billion data points. You can find information all the way from education to travel to commerce. *Statistical Abstract of the United States* also provides a wealth of statistical data from both governmental and nongovernmental sources and is produced by the Census Bureau. Visit your library home page for the list of databases that are available to you. They are usually indexed by topic and provide a wealth of information.

The second strategy for locating information would be to find agencies or organizations that may collect that information and publish it. These may include governmental organizations, NGOs, Academic Institutions, or even commercial firms. One great place to begin is with organizations that collect a wide range of data and publish it regularly like the Pew Research Center and Gallup.

Another place you may find data and statistics is in research articles. Many of the articles you find in periodicals and scholarly papers will provide a wealth of data and statistics that will provide good supporting material.

The following table presents some webpages that are good places to start when looking for statistical information on a variety of topics.

> **Webpages to Reference for Statistical Information**
>
> - **U.S. Bureau of Labor Statistics:** Has links to sites both nationally and internationally and by specific country. https://www.bls.gov/bls/other.htm
> - **FedStats:** Provides information on a range of official information produced by the federal government. https://fedstats.sites.usa.gov/about/
> - **World Health Organization Data Page:** Provides data on all kinds of worldwide health issues. http://www.who.int/gho/en/
> - **Pew Research Center:** Nonpartisan organization "fact tank" that provides poll, demographic, and content analytic data. http://www.pewresearch.org/
> - **Central Intelligence Agency:** Provides data on 267 world entities. https://www.cia.gov/library/publications/the-world-factbook/

Using Statistics Effectively

There is a very famous book called *How to Lie with Statistics* by Darrell Huff. The point Huff tries to make is that you can manipulate numbers in a variety of ways that bias them in your favor.[10] However, he correctly argues that this isn't ethical, and it is important to make sure that the statistics you do use represent your claim accurately. Here are some tips to keep in mind when you use statistics as supporting evidence.

Why and How Was the Data Collected?

Anytime someone collects data, there is a reason. The person has an agenda and is trying to answer a particular question. This can bias the data. When you use information such as statistics, it is important that you think about who collected the data and why they collected that data. Some good questions to ask:[11]

- What issue prompted the poll/survey?
- What policy or event may rely on the outcome of the poll/survey?
- Who or what organization may benefit from the data that is collected in the poll/survey?

Asking these questions may help you decide if the data may reflect a bias. You won't find any information that is completely free from bias but examining it by asking these questions may help you see any potential problems, if they exist.

It is also important to let the audience know how the data was collected. Was it a survey project collected over the phone or via online surveys? How many people did they survey? What were the demographics of the survey? Was the survey representative and who collected the data? All of this information can impact exactly what this data means. Knowing this information can alert you to problems with certain statistics and may impact how you choose to use the information. If the poll reflects a small sample collected in a non-scientific way, it may not be very reflective of the larger population it purports to represent.

Has the Data Been Interpreted Correctly?

Correlation vs. Causation

One of the mistakes we often see in presentations is confusing correlational data with data use to make causal claims. In order to make causal claims—a claim that one variable causes another—three things have to be present. First, the causal variable has to precede the variable it impacts. Second, all extraneous factors that could also be impacting the variables have to be ruled out. Finally, the two variables in question must move together in a systematic way, or in other words, the variables are **correlated.** In order to meet these three criteria for a causal claim, an experimental design must be used in the study. Experimental designs allow researchers to control for extraneous factors, control for order, and test whether variables are related or correlated. No other research design can meet all of these criteria. Unless the study used an experimental design, the authors cannot make causal claims.[12]

Correlational studies merely argue that two variables are related or move together. They only meet one of the criteria for causation. As one variable goes up, the other variable goes up, or as one goes up, the other goes down or as one goes up the other goes down or vice versa. Say you find a study that claims that after surveying a group of people on optimism and after looking at their medical data, researchers discovered that participants with high optimism scores also had healthier hearts. You examine the article and learn that the researchers merely used survey data and medical chart data and found that people who were more optimistic had healthier hearts. Because the study did not use an experimental design, the researchers can't prove that that optimism caused the participants to have healthier hearts. Maybe something about healthy hearts causes people to be more optimistic. Without an experimental design we couldn't tell which variable caused the other or if either one caused the other—maybe it was some other variable all together. The only thing we know for certain is that when optimism is higher so is heart health.

Many health-related studies that are reported in popular press pieces cite correlational data. Read the article carefully to see what kind of data was collected to see if causal claims can be made. The original research article will often explicitly describe the experimental design in the method section if it was indeed experimental. If you aren't certain that they have causal data, then you cannot make a causal claim. Causal claims are more powerful than correlational claims and can mislead your audience. Consequently, be careful and examine claims carefully.

Report the Margin of Error

When polls are conducted, they also have a margin of error. This is basically a confidence interval in which we expect the larger population to fall. If I say that 55 percent of students report dissatisfaction with dining services with a margin of error of 7 percent, what I am really saying is that I am 95 percent confident that the dissatisfaction with dining services lies somewhere between 42 percent and 62 percent in the larger population. Why would this matter? Say the university dining services said that the number went down to 52 percent dissatisfaction, so they make an argument that they had actually improved things. Well, a 3 percent improvement isn't outside of the margin of error, so the change could have been due to sampling error. Margins of error matter, and they help audiences interpret the data, so make sure that you report them as well as percentages.[13]

Report the Correct Central Tendency

Say that you visit the campus placement office, and they report that the average salary for recent graduates in your major is over $208,000. That number seems extremely high to you. You are friends with several people who graduated recently, and none of their salaries are that high. What the placement office is reporting is an average—an arithmetic mean. What they may not know about the arithmetic mean is very sensitive to outliers. Maybe your program or major happened to have a diver who won a gold medal at the Olympics and is very well compensated for all his TV appearances, book deals, and speaking engagements. So while most of the graduates in your major make around $42,000 per year, he makes 1.2 million. This skews the data toward the high end. It makes it seem that recent alumni, on average, earn more money than they really do. Consider the following annual salaries reported from recent alumni in your major:

Recent Graduate Alumni and Their Annual Salary

- **Student 1:** $25,000
- **Student 2:** $32,000
- **Student 3:** $32,000
- **Student 4:** $47,000
- **Student 5:** $57,000
- **Student 6:** $63,000
- **Student 7:** $1,200,000

If we examine these using three measurements of central tendency (mean, median and mode), we get very different numbers. The **mean** or average is $208,000. The **mode** or most common number or salary is $32,000, and the **median** or number in the middle is $47,000. These measures provide extremely different views of this data. The average skews the salaries, and students' expectations for what they may receive after graduation would be unrealistic. In this case, the mode and median provide more realistic representations of reality. However, the mode may be too low. The median provides a truer picture of the typical student salary after graduation in regards to this data. It is important that you examine your data to ensure that the statistic you are reporting accurately reflects the point you are trying to make. Doing otherwise is misleading at best and unethical at worst.

Contextualize Your Statistics

Statistics can have a big impact, but sometimes those numbers are hard for an audience to visualize or interpret. Make it easier for them. When possible, contextualize your statistics. In other words, relate the numbers to something the audience is already familiar with or something that they can visualize. For example, simply saying that as of 2011, there were 500,000,000 active Facebook users is a little overwhelming for an audience. How do we visualize a number that big? How can you help your audience contextualize or visualize that large data point a little easier? Well, you could tell them that means 1 out of every 13 people on Earth is a Facebook user. That has more impact and brings that 500 million into focus for your audience. Whenever possible, relate your statistics to something the audience can process more easily.

Inferential vs. Descriptive Data

There are real differences between inferential and descriptive data, so make sure you know what type of data you have. If the article where you found your data talks about statistical differences, you probably have inferential data and can make claims about changes, trends, etc. If not, you may only have descriptive data, so you need to be careful about moving beyond statements that merely describe your sample and data.

Simplify Your Statistics

Round off your statistics so that an audience doesn't get distracted by the details. It is much easier for an audience to process 1 million than 1,035,325. So, unless it is extremely important for you to be specific, simplify numbers by rounding.

Another method for simplifying statistics and data in general is using visual aids. Whenever possible, use simple graphs to show trends or percentages. This way your audience hears the data, but they can see it too.

Use Statistics Strategically

Statistics can become boring for audience members who aren't highly motivated to process your information. Therefore, make sure that you use statistics strategically. In other words, don't bombard your audience with statistics. It is a quick way to lose your audience. Pick and choose places where statistics will have the greatest impact and use them there.

Opinion Statements

Another type of evidence you may want to use is opinion statements. The opinion of an expert or someone who has had a particular experience can go a long way toward supporting your ideas. Using the experience or claims of an expert or someone who has more experience than you can actually enhance your credibility on a topic. It is one thing for you to say that identity theft is increasing. But quoting or paraphrasing the same statement from Andrew Weissmann, the Chief of the Fraud Division of the U.S. Department of Justice, carries much more impact.

Types of Opinion

The first type of opinion we will cover is **Expert Opinion.** Expert Opinion is exactly what it sounds like. It is the opinion or claim of a professional in the field. This person has the occupational position or educational credentials to be considered an expert in a particular area. You can find expert opinion in scholarly and peer-reviewed articles. Experts are also quoted in newspapers and other popular press pieces. You can even reach out to an expert to see if they will allow you to conduct an interview to gain insight to their ideas and opinions as well. As mentioned earlier, you can also use social media to capture the opinion of an expert. Business and industry leaders as well as research scientists tweet and post to Facebook pages, and this can be used for testimony as well.

The second type of opinion is **Lay Opinion.** Lay opinion is the testimony of someone who has had direct experience with a particular area. For example, your friend Mary may not be an expert on the Indy 500, but she has gone to the race for the last ten years. This experience would provide her with the insight to give advice on the best way to enjoy the race. Your friends and family are good sources for lay opinions.

Tips for Using Opinion Effectively

Provide Context for the Opinion

Unless the person is extremely famous, you will want to let your audience know how their background and experience gives them authority. You may answer some of the following questions to establish their credibility. What is their education level? What is their occupation? What kind of work experience have they had? How many years have they been in the industry? Have they made any important discoveries, written any major books or articles, or appeared on television? Relating this type of information to your audience will make the authority's words have more impact.

Make Sure the Person Is an Expert

Don't confuse expertise with celebrity. While Jennifer Aniston, the actress, may endorse skin care products, that doesn't make her an expert on skin care. A dermatologist or plastic surgeon is an expert. Aniston would not be. Be careful of confusing the two.

Quoting vs. Paraphrasing

Should you directly quote the opinion or paraphrase the opinion? Both have their strengths. Paraphrasing allows you to keep a conversational style and doesn't require that you memorize or read the quote from your notes. However, it isn't always ideal to paraphrase. Here are some practical tips for deciding what to do when incorporating opinion.

Use paraphrasing when the idea you need to communicate is more important than the quote itself. Use paraphrasing when the quote is too long or too complicated to recite verbatim.

Use a direct quotation when the exact language the person used is important. Sometimes a person speaks in a unique manner and that becomes important to capture. They may have a quirky vocabulary, or the quote may reflect a historical time period. You should also use an exact quote when paraphrasing may change the meaning. These guidelines should help you when weaving opinions into your supporting evidence.

Examples

Examples or short narratives are another type of evidence that you can use to support claims you make in your presentation. They can bring your ideas to life for an audience. They extend your ideas by providing an illustration or a specific instance for a general case. Examples can be brief or extended and real or hypothetical in nature.

Brief Examples

Brief examples can be a word or two or a sentence or two. They provide an instance of the concept or idea you are trying to convey. Maybe you are presenting information on the world's largest rollercoasters, and you want to provide a few specific examples. Maybe you want to provide a couple of different examples of vegetables that provide vitamin C: yellow bell peppers, kale, and kiwifruit.

Extended Examples

Extended examples are useful when you need something more substantial to support your ideas. An extended example or mini-narrative can have a lot of impact on an audience and can bring abstract ideas to life. They are a powerful way to pull an audience in, and they can keep an audience engaged.

Occasionally, examples come from real experiences, actual cases or from historical documents. You can find them in newspapers and in magazines. Sometimes, however, no matter how hard you try, you simply cannot find real examples, and you have to ask your audience to imagine a scenario or provide a hypothetical example for them. You may not have any actual scenario or extended example to explain how a specific nano-medicine may change our lives, but you could ask your audience to project how this technology may work in the future by creating a hypothetical situation.

Tips for Using Examples Effectively

Examples can be powerful tools so use them to clarify, reinforce, and make your ideas come alive for your audience. Try to use real examples whenever possible. Hypothetical examples will never have the impact of a real example. If you are using an extended example or narrative, make sure that you include a beginning, middle, and end to your story. Give your characters names and use adequate details so that your audience identifies with the action and actors in the story. Chapter 7 provides more detail on using narratives in presentations, so be sure and consult this information when using an extended example.

Images

Images can add even more support to your ideas. The old cliché, "a picture is worth a thousand words," is definitely true. We recommend that you use images to support your ideas when you can. There are several different types of images that you may consider using. A few examples include pictures, graphs or charts, diagrams, infographics, maps, and even flow charts. While we talk at length about how to use visual aids in Chapter 9, it is important that we consider images briefly as a form of supporting material here.

Places for Finding Images or Graphics

Google Images is a great place to locate images of all kinds. Simply search for images instead of performing a general Google search. Getty Images also has wonderful images in all kinds of categories. One problem with images is that they are usually copyrighted quite heavily, and you will need to pay to obtain permission to use them. There are, however, some images that operate in the public domain. The following table points you toward some sources that provide some images in the public domain, and Creative Commons licenses content that will not require you to purchase the image. Although many of these sites can be used for free and are in the public domain, check each picture and read the restrictions for each image you want to use. Many are free to use, but you still need to cite the source in specific ways (see the tip below for the ethical use of images). When in doubt about a particular image, find a different one.

Images in Public Domain

- **Creative Commons:** Searches a variety of sites for images that you can "share, use and remix" Make sure you check the appropriate box at the top. http://search.creativecommons.org/
- **College Art Association:** Provides links to many depositories of images. http://www.collegeart.org/ip/ip_image
- **U.S. Government Photos and Images:** https://search.usa.gov/search/images?affiliate=usagov&query=

Tips for Using Images Effectively

Make Sure the Content and Tone Are Appropriate

Sometimes the graphic nature of an image is just what you need to convey a particular idea. Think about the Yulin Dog Meat Festival. Imagine that you are delivering a persuasive speech asking people to protest this cultural event. While you could talk about this festival all day, nothing could do your description justice like the photos that have been taken at the event. However, these images are terribly graphic in nature and probably too intense for many audiences. The same is true for gruesome pictures of war images. Really think about how much emotion is appropriate to arouse in your audience. Upsetting an audience or causing emotional distress is rarely appropriate. Excess emotion may be troubling for an audience, but it also has implications for you as a speaker. Sometimes, arousing too much emotion can backfire and your appeal will not have the intended consequence.

Ensure Ethical Use of Images

Since images are the work of others and potentially have monetary value, they aren't all available for use in your presentation. Examine the rights of images you find carefully. Important questions to ask: Can they be used for free? Can they be manipulated? How do I give appropriate credit? After determining that you have the right to use an image, make sure that you provide appropriate credit. The following section provides guidelines for appropriate citations during presentations that may be helpful when citing images as well.

> Upsetting an audience or causing emotional distress is rarely appropriate.

First Lady Eleanor Roosevelt votes in the 1936 presidential election. National Archives (NARA). This photo was used from the public domain. https://www.flickr.com/photos/127744844@N06/28295079594

As you can see in the slides above and below, all of the details concerning where this image was found and who published it are printed at the bottom of the slide. In addition, the speaker should also mention where the photo was found during the presentation.

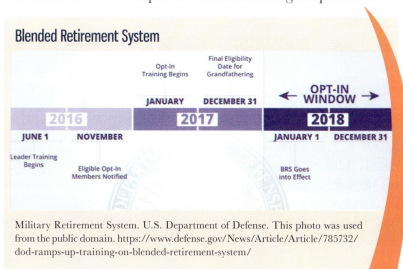

Military Retirement System. U.S. Department of Defense. This photo was used from the public domain. https://www.defense.gov/News/Article/Article/785732/dod-ramps-up-training-on-blended-retirement-system/

Using Supporting Material Ethically

As discussed in Chapter 1, plagiarism can present a problem for individuals. In this section, we highlight the fact that information has value, so it is important to recognize the intellectual property of others and give credit to other's ideas if you borrow them. Although sometimes we hear that some cultures view plagiarism and individual contributions differently, current research is calling that into question. It seems that most, if not all, cultures respect the independent and unique work of others. In a comparison study of children between the ages of five and six in the U.S., China, and Mexico, researchers found that children rated people more favorably when their drawings were unique and creative vs. mere repetitions of others' drawings. The authors argue that this finding indicates that even small children have well-developed ideas about unique contributions and original work.[12]

Providing Appropriate Citation

Given that information others create has value and belongs ultimately to them raises issues of ethical use. We can use the ideas of others if we provide appropriate credit. Sometimes, that may seem awkward to do orally, and it becomes difficult to decide just how to give credit to other's ideas during a presentation. While it is important to give others credit, there is a bonus for you as well.

Citing others can also improve your own credibility or authority. This section will walk you through some strategies for giving others credit during your presentation.

Oral Citations During the Presentation

Speeches do not have bibliographies or work cited pages, so you must use oral citations to give appropriate credit. You will always want to simplify an oral citation. Your audience doesn't appreciate you reading a full citation. There is just too much information for them to process. Speakers are often confounded about just how to simplify a citation and present bibliographic information eloquently during a presentation. There are no foolproof rules for accomplishing this. Because authority is contextual, it will be important for you to determine just what part of your citation will have the most impact for your particular audience. Will the support have credibility due to the organization that it is affiliated with (e.g., *New York Post,* scholarly journal), or does the support have impact due to the author of the material? It may come from someone that your audience highly respects and that imbues it with authority (e.g., Neil deGrasse Tyson or Warren Buffet). Ultimately, you will need to decide which part of your citation carries the most impact and present that information to your audience. Your instructor may also have some guidelines as well, so make sure you seek this information.

One portion of the citation that is usually important is the date it was published. The audience often wants to know that the information you are presenting is current. If you are persuading your audience about dietary guidelines that are from 2006, the information won't have much impact. Nutrition and medical research changes rapidly, and it is important for your audience to know that you have up-to-date information. You usually don't have to cite the month and year unless your circumstance is really unique.

Here are some examples and suggestions for citing support during your presentation.

- Spending on pet care has grown 60 percent from 1996 to 2012 according to a 2017 article appearing in the *New York Times*.
- Cassia Denton, personal-training and group-exercises director for Balance Gym in Washington, was recently interviewed in January 2017 and said, "You should look for something that energizes you in a fitness routine."
- According to their website, the National Rifle Association was founded in 1871.
- In Gary Taubes' 2017 *New York Times* best seller, *The Case Against Sugar*, he claims that sugar is a "dietary trigger."
- "Apollo in 1969. Shuttle in 1981. Nothing in 2011. Our space program would look awesome to anyone living backwards thru time," says, noted astrophysicist, Neil deGrasse Tyson.
- In a recent study published in the journal *Current Biology*, they reported data that provides evidence for episodic memory in dogs.

Boolean Operations That May Help You Search More Effectively

- **AND:** Strings two words together and makes sure search engine only returns information that contains both words. It will actually decrease the number of results returned. Google assumes there is an "AND" whenever you type more than one work in the search box. Other search engines and databases do not make this assumption, and you must type them in.
- **OR:** Use "OR" when you want to gather words of similar meanings and expand your search. **Example:** friend OR colleague OR peer
- **NOT:** Excludes terms and helps you narrow a search when you are overwhelmed by material.
- **Exact Match "…":** In Google, put quotations around a phrase, and it will only return exact matches for that phrase.
- **Hashtag Search:** Put "#" in front of word.

Chapter Summary

In this chapter we highlight the importance of information literacy and provide information on the role of supporting evidence to support ideas in your presentation.

The authority of a particular source has implications for you as the speaker. We also describe specific kinds of supporting evidence and the best practices for using that evidence. Citing sources in your presentation is important. There are various methods that you can use when citing sources in your own speeches.

Case Study Conclusion

Fake news isn't something new. It has just been in the news more recently because it played such a pivotal role in the 2016 presidential election. Fake news has also increased in popularity across social media by people trying to make money by driving ad revenue to their illegitimate news sites. Consequently, we are seeing it now more than ever. Just remember, if a piece of supporting material sounds too good to be true or makes you question the veracity of its claims, you should probably dig deeper. The tips and recommendations made in this chapter should help you avoid fake news and help ensure you use the best information possible. You can also visit factcheck.org and Snopes.com. These websites are designed to answer questions about bad journalism and fake news and may provide you with confidence that you haven't been dubbed into believing something that is untrue.

Edgar Welch, the misinformed shooter mentioned at the beginning of this chapter, in above should have recognized the bizarre nature of his story and asked himself a series of questions about the events. First, if this child trafficking ring was so well known, why hadn't someone in authority stopped it? Secondly, was the story verified across multiple media outlets? He should have searched in both conservative and liberal news sites. When something sounds as bizarre as this story, it should cause you to investigate.

References

[1] Robb, A. 2017. "Anatomy of a Fake News Story." *Rolling Stone*. https://www.rollingstone.com/politics/news/pizzagate-anatomy-of-a-fake-news-scandal-w511904.

[2] Haag, M., and M. Salam. 2017. "Gunman in 'Pizzagate' Shooting is Sentenced to 4 Years in Prison." *New York Times*, June 22, 2017. https://www.nytimes.com/2017/06/22/us/pizzagate-attack-sentence.html.

[3] Goldman, A. 2016. "The Comet Ping-Pong Gunman Answers our Reporter's Questions." *New York Times*, December 7, 2016. http://www.nytimes.com/2016/12/07/us/edgar-welch-comet-pizza-fake-news.html?_r=0.

[4] Fisher, M., J. W. Cox, and P. Hermann. 2016. "Pizzagate: From Rumor, to Hashtag, to Gunfire in D.C." *Washington Post*, December 6, 2016. https://www.washingtonpost.com/local/pizzagate-from-rumor-to-hashtag-to-gunfire-in-dc/2016/12/06/4c7def50-bbd4-11e6-94ac-3d324840106c_story.html?utm_term=.6a3eb4ddb042.

[5] "Information Literacy." *American Library Association*. Accessed April 18, 2018. http://www.ala.org/Template.cfm?Section=Home&template=/ContentManagement/ContentDisplay.cfm&ContentID=33553.

[6] "Information Literacy Competency Standards for Higher Education." *American Library Association*. Accessed January 4, 2017. http://www.ala.org/Template.cfm?Section=Home&template=/ContentManagement/ContentDisplay.cfm&ContentID=33553.

[7] Venable, S. 2016. "Story of Santa with Dying Child Can't Be Verified." *News Sentinel*, December 14, 2016. http://www.wfaa.com/life/holidays/story-of-santa-claus-with-dying-child-cant-be-verified/370047564.

[8] Venable, S.

[9] "Information Literacy Competency Standards for Higher Education." *American Library Association*. Accessed January 4, 2017. http://www.ala.org/Template.cfm?Section=Home&template=/ContentManagement/ContentDisplay.cfm&ContentID=33553.

[10] Huff, D. 1993. *How to Lie with Statistics*. New York, NY: W.W. Norton & Company, Inc.

[11] "Statistics." The Writing Center at UNC Chapel Hill. Accessed March 3, 2018. http://writingcenter.unc.edu/handouts/statistics/.

[12] Yang, F., A. Shaw, E. Garduno, and K. R. Olson. 2014. "No One Likes a Copycat: A Cross-Cultural Investigation of Children's Responses to Plagiarism." *Journal of Experimental Child Psychology* 121: 111–119.

[13] "Polling Fundamentals—Total Survey Error." 2018. *Roper Center for Public Opinion Research.* https://ropercenter.cornell.edu/support/polling-fundamentals-total-survey-error/.

Chapter **6**

Presentation Preparation

Objectives

After this chapter you will be able to:

- Prepare your presentation in an organized manner.
- Craft a presentation narrative.
- Understand the importance of organizing your ideas.
- Articulate different ways to organize presentation material.
- Create an introduction, organize main points and corresponding supporting points, use transitions, and prepare a conclusion.

There is often a presentation given as part of commencement ceremonies. This speech tends to have an inspirational tone and asks graduates to consider their future as they mark the end of this chapter of their educational journey.

This was the norm at the University of Maryland-University College (UMUC), who invited Richard T. Jones, an actor, to deliver a commencement address in 2011. Unfortunately, Jones scrapped his original remarks and improvised his presentation.

He started the speech by saying, "Wow! I had this great speech ready for you guys and then you put me behind a bunch of doctors. You put an actor ... behind a bunch of doctors ... and then they said everything I wanted to say so I figure I'll keep talking until I say something. I had such great analogies. I had such great quotes ... And every one was used already. I'm glad I looked up a word called "improv" because that is what is going to happen here."[1]

Because Jones was unprepared to deliver his presentation, he jumped from topic to topic without any discernable organizational format/goal. The Huffington Post, who also reported this story, described Jones' commencement address as "embarrassing" and left readers with this piece of advice: "If you're keen on delivering a great speech, a wise strategy would be to actually write one."[2]

Let's Talk
1. Why is it important for speakers to prepare for their presentation?
2. Why is it important for speakers to keep their ideas organized?
3. Do you think the audience was able to follow Jones' ideas as they were presented?
4. What could have helped make Jones' message clearer to his audience?
5. Did Jones craft a narrative during the commencement presentation?

Presentation Preparation

How do you prepare for your presentation? This is an important question because as any experienced speaker will tell you, preparation is one of the keys to a successful presentation. There is a lot to consider when preparing a presentation, like a topic choice that is appropriate for the speaking situation, your goal, your audience, the organization of main points and supporting ideas, your an organizational structure, and the use of the basic presentation template (introduction, body, and conclusion). This chapter will help you prepare for your presentation by detailing these components as you begin to craft a narrative/presentation.

Your presentation will ultimately be a narrative that you will create. Even if you are giving a presentation on new data you have collected or giving a training at work, you will still be creating a narrative for your audience to take in. You will choose a topic and share a story that has a beginning (introduction), middle (body), and end (conclusion). The narrative that you craft is important as it will help you organize your information into a coherent story and will allow your audience to follow along and remember key points more easily.

Topic Selection

The speaking situation often dictates the general topic of your presentation and then you, as the speaker, will narrow down the specific topic. Consider a director of human resources at an organization who is tasked with running new employee orientation. There are specific topics that the director must cover in order to get the new employees acclimated to the organization, such as the culture, vision, mission, and structure, as well benefits, payroll, and opportunities. In a sales pitch, you will need to talk about your product and service to potential clients and customers. Other times, you may have more freedom to select a topic that you deem important.

Before narrowing your topic from general to specific, you must also make sure that you choose an appropriate topic for the situation, your goal, and the audience. These factors will help you determine the specific topic of your presentation.

Speaking Guidelines

When you know that you will be giving a presentation, the first thing you need to do is determine some of the specific parameters of your presentation. Thing that you need to consider include the purpose/goal of the presentation (informative, persuasive, ceremonial), time limits, and your ability to use visual aids. This information should help you to start the process of choosing a topic and should be used in conjunction with brainstorming and creating an association web.

Once you understand the basics of your upcoming presentation, you can start the process of narrowing your topic. There are a plethora of presentation topics to choose from. If you are having trouble narrowing down your ideas, then consider brainstorming or creating an association web. Brainstorming is the term used to describe the act of generating a list of possible topics to talk about[3] whereas an association web is a brainstormed list of topics that is formed around a central idea, like "college life." The web format helps you to visualize how potential topics are connected to and stem from each other (see a sample below). These processes will allow you to consider a variety of possible presentation topics, some of which you may not have initially thought of when you were first given your speech assignment.

When thinking about possible topics, there are a couple of guidelines that you will want to follow: (1) they are appropriate to the classroom setting, (2) they can fit within the assignment time limits, and (3) they are novel.

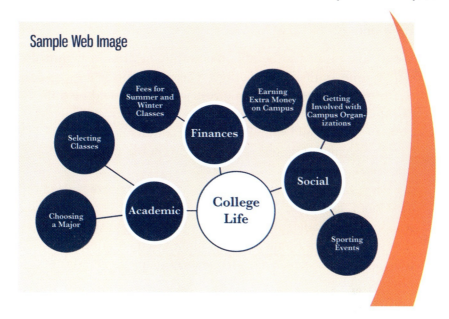

Appropriate

Choose a topic that is appropriate for the setting. You need to consider how your audience will respond to your topic, especially if you are speaking on something controversial. For example, if you are going to speak about something that may alienate a large portion of your audience (e.g., the 2016 Presidential election), you need to be aware of this and determine if the time and place you are doing this is appropriate. You will learn more about your peers and their attitudes, values, and beliefs after completing an audience analysis.

An appropriate topic is also one that is ethical. By this we mean that you do not want to incriminate yourself or encourage anything illegal. Also, you do not want to say anything that could potentially lead to negative consequences for your audience.

For example, you would not want to give a presentation about how using Adderall has helped you study during college if you are not prescribed the medication. This type of topic could lead to physical harm (e.g., a bad reaction to the medication) or invite legal problems (e.g., possession of a controlled substance). These are important considerations to think through as you choose a topic.

Time Limits

Your topic must also be able to be fully addressed within the stated time limits. On average, classroom presentations last 5–7 minutes. Given these time restrictions, it would be difficult to inform the audience about federal gun control regulations. However, you could simplify the topic and focus on the right to carry concealed weapons on college campuses, which is a policy that Texas adopted in 2016.

Time limits are important in all contexts, even outside of the classroom. For instance, if you are asked to speak at a training session about leadership for 30 minutes, then you want to make sure you speak for roughly half an hour. Going over or under this time limit can be perceived as disrespectful and may indicate you are not prepared.

Novelty

You will also want to make sure that your selected topic is novel. By novel, we mean that the topic is new and original. We all know that we need to brush our teeth twice a day or should turn off electronics when not in use. Your audience probably does not need to be informed about or persuaded to adopt these behaviors. However, with a little effort you can choose topics that are creative and new to your audience. For example, you could persuade people to never wear shoes in their homes (because they track in germs, bacteria, and viruses), to not eat deli lunchmeat (because of the risk of listeria and high levels of nitrates), or to adopt "meatless Mondays" (for health and environmental reasons).

Determine your Goal

In order to give a good presentation, you need to determine what the goal of the presentation is. You need to answer the question, what is the purpose of telling your story? Typically, the goal of a presentation falls into three broad categories: (1) informative, (2) persuasive, or (3) ceremonial.

> An **informative goal** is one that seeks to provide new details, data, or information to an audience about a given topic. It is important to gauge the audience's understanding of

the topic when preparing an informative presentation so that you can focus on new information that will keep the audience engaged. Informative presentations will be further discussed in Chapter 8.

- A **persuasive goal** attempts to influence or change an audience's stance on topics of fact, value, or policy or to adopt/change behaviors. Persuasive presentations will be detailed in Chapters 10 and 11.
- A **ceremonial goal** is one that is delivered during special occasions and includes toasts, eulogies, and speeches of introduction or acceptance. These types of presentations will be covered in Chapter 13.

These categories are broad and do not have to be mutually exclusive. For example, President Trump gave a ceremonial speech at his inauguration in 2017. During this presentation he also informed the public of his goals for the next four years and attempted to persuade his audience to mend political party divides. With that said, the dominant goal was to deliver a ceremonial address; however, you can see aspects of informative and persuasive speaking as well.

Considering the Audience

The audience is an important aspect in the presentation preparation process. Speakers must be aware of the knowledge, opinions, and values that the audience holds in order to choose a topic of interest as well as select appropriate information to include. For example, if you were speaking to a group of high school seniors about your college experience, your presentation would include different information than if you were talking to a group of parents about your college experience. When talking to high school seniors, you may decide to include more practical aspects for high school students, like how to choose a major, register for classes, become involved on campus, and find the best places to eat on campus. In contrast, when talking to their parents about your experience, you may want to talk about the financial needs of students, costs associated with registering for winter or summer courses, and detail how you have grown/what you have learned during your time on campus. Chapter 4 covers audience adaptation in more detail.

Communication Choices

While your topic (and corresponding assignment, goal, and audience) determines some of your communication choices so do aspects of your culture. National culture plays a key role in determining the type of communication style that is preferred by a given audience and should be adopted by the speaker. However, in the technologically connected world we live in, audiences are made up of people who represent a variety of national cultures and speakers have to be aware of this fact as you prepare presentations.

Geert Hofstede,[4,5] along with others, developed **six dimensions of national culture,** which include (1) power distance index, (2) individualism vs. collectivism, (3) masculinity vs. femininity, (4) uncertainty avoidance index, (5) long-term orientation vs. short-term normative orientation, and (6) indulgence vs. restraint. These dimensions vary from country to country and are often compared to one another to provide context related to similarities and differences.

Hofstede's Dimensions of National Culture

- The **power distance index** refers to how power is distributed and accepted in a given culture.
- **Individualism vs. collectivism** determines how members of a society view their role in a given community. Are members of a culture expected to care for themselves or the larger community?
- **Masculinity vs. femininity** refers to a culture's preference for masculine (e.g., toughness) or feminist (e.g., tenderness) characteristics.
- The **uncertainty avoidance index** measures the level of ambiguity a culture is comfortable with.
- The **long-term orientation vs. short-term normative orientation** discusses the prioritization of maintaining tradition or adapting to modernization.
- **Indulgence vs. restraint** refers to the norms in place regarding self-gratification.

Communication Choices Continued

Take a minute to reflect on why these differences matter in a communication context. For example, if speaking to people who are not comfortable with ambiguity, your presentation must be more explicit. In contrast, if you come from a culture that appreciates ambiguity and implicit messages, then you may feel uncomfortable delivering direct, persuasive messages that tell the audience what to think or believe. As a communicator, you need to be aware of how dimensions of culture impact your communication behavior as well as your audience's preferences.

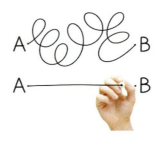

Moreover, these dimensions come together to determine preferred **communication styles.**[6] For example, some people prefer linear communication while others appreciate circular forms. Linear is more direct. Picture a straight line where the speaker moves from one point to another in a very clear manner. In contrast, the circular communication style relies on aesthetics features and narratives to build context and help an audience understand a point. When thinking of the circular communication style, picture a spiral.

In both these styles, the audience gets to the same point (from A to B) but does so in different manners. However, these styles do not need to be mutually exclusive. There could be certain passages that are more circular than others.

Communication Styles
- Linear vs. circular
- Direct vs. indirect
- Detached vs. attached
- Intellectual engagement vs. relational engagement
- Concrete vs. Abstract

Source: Communication Styles

Organize Your Main Points

Now that you know your goal and topic, you must organize your thoughts and materials so that your message is communicated to your audience.

Outlines

In most speaking situations, you will prepare a **framework** and a **speaking outline** rather than a **manuscript outline.** You may be tempted to write out what you are going to say word for word, but there are few situations where a manuscript is a good idea. In most presentations, you want to be conversational and adaptable. A manuscript does not allow for flexibility. This type of outline encourages speakers to try to memorize every word of their narrative or tempts them to read from the page. These two styles of delivery, manuscript and memorized, are problematic because they limit interaction with the audience and appear inauthentic. A memorized presentation can cause a speaker to lose his or her spot in a presentation and may appear robotic in nature. A manuscript form of delivery limits eye contact and tends to encourage students to take on a monotone type of voice without normal vocal inflections and variations.

A framework is the first step in your presentation preparation process. Here, you will write out your main points and supporting ideas. Drawing on a building metaphor, this step serves as a detailed blueprint that indicates where each room (main points) will be situated in a house (presentation) and where the load-bearing walls (supporting ideas and supporting evidence) are located.

The next step is to transition your detailed framework to a speaking outline. Continuing the building metaphor, the speaking outline is a simplified depiction of the blueprint you created that guides you through the house. It should include key words that serve as reminders of where you are going in your presentation. This type of outline helps speakers deliver their presentations in an extemporaneous manner or a conversational tone that is practiced but not memorized (see Chapter 3 for more information on delivery styles). This is the type of delivery that is encouraged in presentational speaking classes since it appears more genuine and natural.

Parts of the Narrative (Introduction, Body, and Conclusion)

The simplest way to think about preparing a presentation can be summarized by the phrase, "tell the audience what you are going to tell them (introduction), tell the audience (body), and then tell the audience what you told them (conclusion)."

> **Basic Presentation Sections**
> - Introduction
> - Body
> - Conclusion

This format may seem repetitive, but presentations need repetition since, unlike books, your audience can't go back to pick up a point that was missed. We will go through each of the three basic presentation sections in the remainder of the chapter.

Body

While this may seem counterintuitive, the best way to approach your presentation is to start with the body of the presentation rather than the introduction. This way, you will know what you are planning to say before you start to think about the best ways to introduce the topic to your audience.

To begin, you must determine what the **main points** are that you want to include in your narrative. Once you know your topic and the goal of your presentation, you are ready to start thinking about the primary idea that you want to share with your audience. These ideas are the main points that ultimately support your goal and are major landmarks in your narrative.

There are some guidelines that you will want to follow as you develop your main points. First, you will want to limit yourself to two to four main ideas. Some speech structures (see below) will determine how many main ideas you have. For example, a presentation that uses a cause-effect structure will have two main ideas while a presentation that is organized using a topic structure may have up to four main ideas.

With that said, three seems to be the magic number in terms of providing enough information to your audience while not overloading them with too much detail. In fact, there is a **"Rule of Three."**[7] This rule claims that people tend to remember only three things from a presentation. If this is the case, then consider what you want those items to be, and these should form your main points. On a side note, you can also see the "Rule of Three" come out in the basic sections of the presentation (introduction, body, and conclusion). Again, this is helpful for speakers to remember where they are in their presentations. If you have more than three main points, you may need to assess them to see if you can reorganize or categorize your thoughts. You may also be including supporting points, which cannot stand on their own since they are used to support main ideas.

Second, you will want your main points to be balanced, meaning that they will take roughly the same amount of time to present or include the same amount of material. For example, if you were to give a presentation that informs your audience about how the flu vaccines work, you would want to talk about how the World Health Organization determines which viruses to target each year, how the vaccine prevents the flu, and how to determine the vaccine's efficacy. These would be your three main points that would serve as the backbone of your presentation, ultimately telling the story of vaccines. You would then further add to your narrative by adding supporting ideas and supporting evidence (see Chapter 6).

As the name suggests, **supporting points** are the pieces of information that support your main points by providing details and context to your main idea. Under the main point of how vaccines work, you could include information about the immune system, antibodies, and immunity. This information is subordinate to the main idea and as such should be noted that way in your key word outline to help keep you on track. This process is called **ranking** as it allows you to prioritize your main ideas and scaffold them with supporting points and supporting evidence. Below is a sample key word outline that includes main points and supporting points.

- **(Main Point)** How the targeted vaccines are selected
  - **(Supporting Point)** Strands of flu viruses
  - **(Supporting Point)** Predicting upcoming strands
- **(Main Point)** How the vaccine works
  - **(Supporting Point)** The immune system
  - **(Supporting Point)** Antibodies
- **(Main Point)** Determinants of efficacy
  - **(Supporting Point)** Matching flu strains
  - **(Supporting Point)** Age of patient
  - **(Supporting Point)** Health of the patient

This is one way to organize your presentation; however, this presentation can be presented in a variety of ways. The next section covers multiple ways to organize a presentation.

Thesis Statements

Once you have determined your main points, you will want to develop a thesis statement. Your thesis statement is one sentence that summarizes the topic and main ideas of your presentations. In the above example of about the flu vaccine, your thesis might be something like, "In order to understand how the flu vaccine works, you need to know how the strain is targeted, the science of vaccines, and what influences the vaccine's effectiveness." This statement clearly states what you presentation is about and what information will be included in the presentation.

A strong and clear thesis statement is beneficial to both you and your audience. For you, a thesis statements helps you focus on what you want to say and how you want to organize your information. As you are preparing your presentation, information that does not fit into your thesis statement is information that you do not need to include. Your thesis statement also helps prepare the audience for what they are going to hear. By laying out your main points at the beginning, the audience is better able to follow along as you are speaking.

Organizational Structures

Organizational structures are templates that can be used to organize your main points. Depending on your topic, certain organization structures will work better than others.

> **Common Organizational Structures**
> - Chronological/temporal (informative)
> - Spatial/geographical (informative)
> - Topical (informative)
> - Comparative advantage (informative/persuasive)
> - Cause-effect (persuasive)
> - Problem-solution (persuasive)
> - Monroe's Motivated Sequence (persuasive)
> - Refutational (persuasive)

One organizational structure is to talk about it chronologically or temporally. In this method, you would think about the major events that took place in the story and follow the sequence. A trademark of the chronological organizational structure is the use of signposts, like "first, second, third" or "first, next, then, and last."

- **Sample Chronological Organizational Structure**
    - (**Main Point**) First, the targeted flu strain is selected.
    - (**Main Point**) Second, scientists develop the vaccine for that strain.
    - (**Main Point**) Third, the vaccine is administered.

The spatial/geographical pattern organizes information by place or region. In continuing with the flu vaccine example, a presentation could be structured by the areas of the body that the vaccine impacts

- **Sample Spatial/Geographical Organizational Structure**
    - (**Main Point**) Location of vaccine administration.
    - (**Main Point**) Vaccine's interaction with the immune system.
    - (**Main Point**) Vaccine's interaction with the circulatory system.

Topical organization is the most common and easiest pattern. It is a catch-all that allows the most flexibility in sharing the narrative you created. It can include two or three main ideas that are somewhat different from one another (e.g., not based on time or location).

- **Sample Topical Organizational Pattern**
    - (**Main Point**) History of the flu vaccine
    - (**Main Point**) Development of each year's vaccine
    - (**Main Point**) Efficacy of the flu vaccine

The previous organizational structures are often used for informative presentations. The remaining organizational structures (comparative advantage, cause-effect, problem-solving, and Monroe's Motivated Sequence) are more often reserved for persuasive speaking.[8] These structures will be discussed in more detail in the chapter on organizing persuasive presentations, but they are also presented here so you are familiar with them. Imagine now that instead of just informing your audience about how the flu vaccine works, you are trying to persuade your audience to get a flu shot.

The comparative advantage organizational structure is one structure you can use. This structure is used to compare or contrast two items (person, place, thing, or idea). In a persuasive format, these items can be solutions, one of which you will advance in your presentation as being the better option.

- **Sample Comparative Advantage Organizational Structure**
    - (**Main Point**) Comparison: There are some options to avoid contracting the flu including getting a flu shot and taking personal precautions such as not sharing personal items and washing your hands frequently.
    - (**Main Point**) Contrast: The flu shot has been shown to be more effective in preventing the flu than taking personal precautions.

The goal of the cause-effect organizational structure is to show a direct relationship between a problem and an outcome—or the (1) cause of an (2) effect. This is difficult to accomplish since you will have to show causation, which is a difficult relationship to establish, especially given the time restrictions of in-class presentations.

- **Sample Cause-Effect Organizational Structure**
  - (**Main Point**) Cause: Many college-age students do not receive their MMR booster before moving to campus.
  - (**Main Point**) Effect: The lack of protection from mumps has caused localized outbreaks on college campuses.

As the name suggests, the problem-solution organizational structure first details a problem (need) and then provides a solution that could solve the presented problem.

- **Sample Problem-Solution Organizational Structure**
  - (**Main Point**) Problem: The flu can lead to serious medical outcomes including death.
  - (**Main Point**) Solution: People should get their flu vaccine each year.

Monroe's Motivated Sequence is an organizational structure with five steps: (1) attention, (2) need, (3) satisfaction, (4) visualization, and (5) call to action.[9] The persuasive chapter will go into this technique in much more detail.

Include Transitions

Transitions are an important part of any presentation. They are tools that let your audience know that you are moving from one section or idea to another. You will need to signal that you are concluding your introduction and starting to talk about your first main point, or moving from your first main point to your second. Remember, being explicit is key here since your audience won't be able to go back and see what they missed, so lay it out for them even if it seems a bit repetitive.

Types of Transitions

- **Linking transitions:** These link ideas and concepts together for the audience. They signal to your audience where you have been and where you are going.
  - Example: As you've heard, nitrogen is very important to high corn yields, but the timing of the application is also very important.
- **Sign posts:** They help you audience focus on what is important in the presentation and where you are.
  - Example: The critical step in setting up your firewall …
  - First, second, third, finally
  - In conclusion,
  - The most important point
  - To begin
- **Internal summaries and internal previews:** when your material is very complex, you may need to summarize or preview within the body or our presentation.
  - To reiterate, you need 3 documents when you meet with your tax attorney.

Guidelines

The first guideline is to make your transitions clear. Again, audience members can't go back if they get lost in your presentation, so take the time to tell your audience when you are wrapping up one point or section and moving on to the next.

Second, make sure your transitions review what you just said and preview what you are going to talk about. Think of the transition as a bridge that connects one idea/section to the next.

Finally, feel free to physically show the move from one idea/section to the next. This is a good place to take a few steps (physical delivery) to reinforce that you are moving forward in your presentation.

Examples

- **Introduction to body:** Now that you know the topic of my presentation, I want to describe how the World Health Organization determines what flu strain to target.

- **One main point to the next:** Now that you understand what the flu vaccine is intended to fight, we will look at how the actual vaccine works.
- **Body to conclusion:** As you have heard, the efficacy of the flu vaccine depends on a variety of factors, so in conclusion …

Prepare an Introduction

Introductions are one of the most important parts of your narrative since they serve as the first impression of you as a speaker and set the expectation for what you will be talking about. This is the section where you tell the audience what you are going to tell them. There are four parts of the introduction: (1) attention-grabber, (2) practicality, (3) goal, and (4) main ideas.

- **Use an attention-grabber:** How are you going to draw your audience in to the story you are telling?
- **Establish the practicality:** Why should they care about the topic?
- **State your goal:** What is your goal (tell your audience)?
- **Preview your main ideas:** What are your three main points (tell your audience)?

Attention-Grabbers

Attention-grabbers refer to the ways to draw your audience in to your presentation/narrative. There are three ways to accomplish this task: (1) craft a small story, (2) share a startling fact, or (3) find a relevant quotation.

> **Ways to Start Your Presentation**
> - Small stories
> - Startling facts
> - Quotations
> - Rhetorical question
> - Technology (image, video, and/or audio clip)
> - Humor

Small Stories

Small stories are the short stories that speakers use to pull the audience into the presentation. They include personal experiences, hypothetical examples, and real-world examples.

Personal experiences are stories that the speaker uses to tell the audience about their experience with the topic at hand. For example, a presentation about flu vaccines could begin with a personal anecdote about getting the flu.

Example: "In 2015, I never got around to getting my flu shot, but I figured that since most of the people I knew had, I would be okay. I could not have been more wrong. I woke up with a cough and assumed I had a cold. As the day went on, I felt worse and worse. I spiked a fever, was achy all over, and could not even think about eating anything. I continued to feel worse and worse until I was so weak that my mom decided to take me to the ER where I was treated with IV fluids and medication."

Hypothetical examples use fictitious characters and events to make a point about the topic. A way to start a presentation on flu vaccines might be the following:

Example: "Imagine being sicker than you ever have been in your entire life. You are achy, chilled, and coughing so hard you feel like you might crack a rib. This is what you may experience if you contract the flu."

Finally, a real-world example uses a true story to introduce the topic. They often stem from the news or current events. This is the way we begin most of our chapters because it shows how the concepts we discuss in the book are applicable to real-world settings.

Example: Adam York was one of the last people in his family to get the flu in December 2017. While his children had been ill but recovered, York continued to get worse. As his condition deteriorated, his wife took him to the ER where he was admitted due to his poor lung condition. Despite treatment, his condition worsened, and he was admitted to the ICU and placed in a medically induced coma as a last attempt to allow his body to heal.

Startling Facts

Startling facts can be used to surprise the audience and pique their interest in the topic. These facts can have a great impact on your presentation. Besides demonstrating the importance or pervasiveness of a topic, it can also add to your credibility by showing that you did research, especially if you incorporate an oral citation into your attention grabber (see Chapter 5 for information on oral citations).

Example: According to the Centers for Disease Control, more than 26,000 people die each year in the United States from the flu.

Quotation

Using a **quotation** to open up your narrative is an effective attention grabber as well. The quotation or the source of the quotation needs to have an obvious connection to the topic of your presentation since it is the audience's first impression of your presentation.

Example: When asked about the current flu vaccine, Dr. Pritish Tosh, an infectious disease specialist said, "We need more research so we can develop an influenza vaccine that works 100 percent of the time, for 100 percent of people."

Rhetorical Questions

Rhetorical questions are a common, and sometimes overused, device to begin a presentation. Speakers use a rhetorical question by asking a question that does not require a verbal response. Even though many speeches start with a rhetorical question, many are not used effectively. In order to be done well, you must practice asking your question, then briefly pause—giving your audience time to process your question. This pause gives them time to think about what their response would be and to situate themselves to the topic.

Example: Have you ever wondered how a shot can protect you against contracting a deadly virus?

Technology

Using **technology** can also serve as an effective attention getter. For instance, speakers can show an image (picture, map, or diagram) on the screen as they begin to speak; they can show a short video clip that corresponds directly to the topic at hand; they can play a snippet of music. All of these techniques work to grab the audience's attention if done well. Again, in order to use a technology-based attention-grabber, the speaker must practice with whatever device they selected. By practicing, you can become familiar with the technology in the presentation room as well as determine the amount of time that the attention-grabber should use. In terms of length, a video or audio snippet should last for less than 30 seconds for a 5–7 minute speech and no more than a minute for longer presentations. Moreover, the clips need to be cued to the starting point. Nothing is more distracting than seeing a speaker scroll to the right time marker or to watch a commercial first.

Example: Showing a map of the country indicating how high flu rates were during the 2017–2018 flu season.

Humor

Some speakers are able to use **humor** (telling a joke or sharing a funny story) to begin their speech. However, it can be tricky since everyone has a different sense of humor, so you have to be careful about using this kind of attention-grabber. In addition, some people are naturally better at using humor; they have what is called comedic timing, which can make a joke come alive.

If you plan to use humor as an attention-getter, then you must practice your delivery and test out the joke/story on friends or family to make sure it translates well. You also need to be aware of your topic. Some topics lend themselves well to starting with a funny attention grabber (informative presentation on *The Big Bang Theory*), while others do not (e.g., informative presentation on Zika).

Practicality

The second component of the introduction is to establish the **practicality** of the topic in the introduction. Explain why your audience should care about the topic you are presenting. Think about the applications.

Example: Each year we all have to make a decision about whether or not to get a flu shot. Understanding how the flu vaccine works can help you make a more informed decision.

State Your Goal

It is important to explicitly **state your goal** as well. This serves as a thesis statement that you use in your writing classes. This is where you let your audience know what they should learn/gain from listening to your narrative.

Example: To inform your audience about how the flu vaccine works.

Preview Your Main Points

Finally, you will want to preview your main ideas before transitioning from the introduction to the body of your presentation. Here, you will "tell the audience what you are going to tell them." List out your main ideas, so the audience knows the main points of your presentation.

Example: Today, I will explain how the targeted strain of the flu is selected, how the vaccine works, and what determines the efficacy of the vaccine.

Craft a Conclusion

A **conclusion** signifies the end of your presentation. This is the tell them what you told them part of the phrase from the beginning of the chapter. There are three components to a well-crafted conclusion: (1) restate your goal, (2) review your main ideas, and (3) create a circular or cyclical narrative.

- **Restate the goal:** What was the purpose of the presentation?
- **Review your main points:** What were your three main points?
- **Complete the circular or cyclical narrative:** How can you leave your audience thinking about your presentation?

Restate the Goal

As you conclude, you will want to **restate the goal** you had for this presentation. Here, you remind them of the purpose for your talk.

Example: Today, I discussed how the flu vaccine works.

Review Your Main Ideas

Next, you will **review your main points.** Again, you will list off your main points as you remind the audience of the main ideas you want them to take away from your presentation.

Example: Specifically, I explained how the WHO determines which flu strain to target and how vaccines work with the immune system. Finally, I discussed what factors determine the efficacy of the flu.

Complete the Circular or Cyclical Narrative

Finally, you will **complete the circular or cyclical narrative.** This device is used so that your presentation/narrative ends in the same place it begins.[10] In oral communication, this literary device is often called a circular device.

It is used so that a speaker can connect back to the introduction—specifically the attention-grabber. Think back to your introduction—how did you start? Then think about how you can bring your topic full circle. This is a powerful device to include in your presentation as it provides a sense of closure for your audience by referring back to the introduction.

For instance, if I used the statistic about deaths due to the flu to grab the attention of my audience, I might conclude by saying something like the following example:

Example: The flu can be a deadly disease as evidence by the large numbers of deaths caused by it each year. The flu vaccine is one way that medical professionals are trying to decrease that number.

Chapter Summary

In this chapter, we discussed the steps needed to prepare for your presentation. Specifically, we talked about how to choose a topic that is appropriate for the assignment, your goal, and your audience; how to organize main and supporting; how to select an organizational structure; and how to use the basic presentation template (introduction, body, and conclusion). While there is a lot to consider when preparing a presentation, the information provided in this chapter will help you answer the question, how do you prepare for a presentation?

Case Study Conclusion

In the opening case study, we discussed Richard T. Jones' embarrassing commencement address at UMUC. It serves as an example for why preparation is important when tasked with delivering a presentation. Jones would have benefited by choosing an appropriate topic, selecting an organizational pattern, and developing main and supporting. Unfortunately, he failed on all of these fronts. The presentation was such a mess because he ended up talking in circles, which confused the audience and ultimately obscured his message. Ultimately, Jones crafted a narrative during his presentation, but it was one of being underprepared and less credible than other commencement speakers, which was not his intended goal.

See the commencement address here:

❱ **The Urban Daily** *https://theurbandaily.com/1324645/actor-richard-t-jones-gives-embarrassing-commencement-speech-at-umuc-video/*

❱ **The Huffington Post** *http://www.huffingtonpost.com/2011/06/02/richard-jones-commencement-umuc-_n_870301.html*

References

1. The *Urban Daily* Staff. 2011. "Actor Richard T. Jones Gives Embarrassing Commencement Speech at IMUC." *The Urban Daily*, May 26, 2011. https://theurbandaily.cassiuslife.com/1324645/actor-richard-t-jones-gives-embarrassing-commencement-speech-at-umuc-video/.

2. "Actor Richard T. Jones Improvs Embarrassing UMUC Commencement Speech (VIDEO)." *HUFFPOST*, June 2, 2011. https://www.huffingtonpost.com/2011/06/02/richard-jones-commencement-umuc-_n_870301.html.

3. The Writing Studio. 2017. "The Definition of Brainstorming." Colorado State University. http://writing.colostate.edu/guides/teaching/gentopic/pop4a.cfm.

4. Hofstede, G., J. Hofstede, and M. Minkov. 2010. *Cultures and Organizations: Software of the Mind* (3rd ed.). New York: McGraw-Hill.

5. Hofstede, G. 2001. *Culture's Consequences: Comparing Values, Behaviors, Institutions, and Organizations Across Nations* (2nd ed.) Thousand Oaks, CA: Sage Publications.

6. "Communication Styles." (n.d.) University of the Pacific. http://www2.pacific.edu/sis/culture/pub/1.5.3_-_Communication_styles.htm.

7. "The Rule of Three." 2017. *Presentation Magazine*. https://www.presentationmagazine.com/presentation-skills-3-the-rule-of-three-7283.htm.

8. "Organizational Patterns: Patterns for Persuasive Speeches." n.d. University of Northern Iowa. http://www.uni.edu/chatham/cdrom/spcho_23.htm.

9. "Monroe's Motivated Sequence." 2017. *Changing Minds.Org* http://changingminds.org/techniques/general/overall/monroe_sequence.htm.

10. Hansen, E. 2017. "What Is a Circular Narrative Style?" *The Pen and the Pad*. https://penandthepad.com/circular-narrative-style-3143.html.

Chapter 7

Narratives and Storytelling

Objectives

After this chapter you will be able to:

- Explain why stories are an effective oral communication tool.
- Explain the neurological reactions to stories.
- Identify the key components of a story.
- Determine where stories can effectively be used in presentations.

Compassion International's mission is to bring children around the world out of poverty by providing developmental resources. These resources range from basic necessities such as food and clothing to educational programs designed to help children grow socially, economically, spiritually, and mentally. Currently, Compassion works with children in over 25 countries from three continents. The primary way that Compassion funds its work is through direct child sponsorship. Under this model, individuals across the world who feel compelled to help a child in need can sign up to sponsor a child by providing a monthly donation. This money is used by the local Compassion organizations to provide for the unique needs of that child. Sponsors are given basic information about their sponsored child including a picture and have the ability to exchange written letters with the child. One of the constant challenges Compassion faces is finding sponsors willing to make a monthly financial commitment to a sponsored child. One tactic Compassion uses is their website where visitors can learn about Compassion's programs and services and read some stories about different children that have been or are in the program. While the website offers a lot of information and attempts to bring their work to life through the stories posted, Compassion knew this was not enough and looked to find ways to share their work with a broader audience.

In 2008, Compassion launched the Compassion Blogger program. The idea of the program was to have small groups of popular bloggers with large followings travel to a country where Compassion was on the ground working. Throughout the trip, the bloggers would share stories with their readers about their visit and the people and communities Compassion was working with. The first blogger trip to Uganda was very successful as the unique and first-hand stories the bloggers shared compelled several of their readers to become sponsors. Since 2008, Compassion has continued to host blogger trips. As forms of social media have increased, so too are the ways that trip participants can share stories with friends and followers back home. In 2016, six bloggers traveled to Uganda. Throughout their trip they shared stories about the what they were seeing and experiencing. Not only did they write their stories, but many posted and shared videos of themselves in which they talked about what they had experienced that day and allowed their followers to see first-hand where these stories were taking place.[1]

Let's Talk
1. Why do you think the blogger trips are so successful at attracting sponsors to the Compassion program?
2. What can Compassion Bloggers share that lists of facts and statistics cannot?

Introduction

Humans, as a species, are addicted to stories. We love to hear them, and we often love to tell them. Think about in a given week how many articles you read online, television shows or movies you watch, podcasts you listen to, or stories you share with friends about something that recently happened to you. Some argue that it is this ability, the ability to understand and create stories, that makes humans unique from other species. While this method of communication is innate to the way we think and speak, it does not mean that there is not a skill or art to creating and telling stories. This chapter will give you some of the information and tools you need to be a great storyteller.

Now you may be thinking, I thought this book was about giving presentations; why am I worried about telling a story? Storytelling may seem more informal to you, like something that people interested in entertaining others may do, but the truth is that stories are and should be an important element of your presentations. Whether your sole purpose in presenting is to share a story or use a story as a type of supporting evidence, there are specific techniques that can make your story more memorable and effective.

In this chapter, you will read about the foundations of storytelling, a communication format that has existed since ancient times, as well as the scientific reasons that storytelling is such a powerful tool. You will then learn about the key elements that every story needs to have and reasons that some stories resonate with the audience more than others. Finally, you will learn about storytelling in different fields and contexts.

The Foundations of Storytelling

While no one can identify when the first story was told, we can assume that it was soon after human language developed. Early speakers were using stories to let others know about recent events such as a successful hunt. Very quickly, oral storytelling became one of the primary ways that people were able to remember and share history. Prior to the invention of the written word, oral stories were one of the only ways that a group could keep a record of that group's past. Even after the first written systems of language were developed, the number of people who were able to read words or had access to the tools needed to record words were few. In addition to recording history, stories were also an important teaching tool. Religions frequently used stories and parables to impart lessons and wisdom to followers who had no way to engage with religious texts.

Even after the modern printing press had been invented in the 1500s, the majority of the world's population remained illiterate. In 1820, only 12 percent of the world's population could read or write. Today, that number has drastically increased to 83 percent.[2] In the U.S., it was not until the early 1900s when major reforms in public education took place that literacy rates began to rapidly rise. Even with the explosion of literacy, written forms such as books and newspapers favored a narrative format, and people continue to learn about history and current events through stories rather than simple reporting of facts.

Beyond a means of information sharing and education, stories have also played a key role in providing entertainment. As early as the 5th century BC, the ancient Greeks were performing fictional plays.[3] Epic poems, early novels, radio serials, and silent films are all examples of how innovations and technology expanded the ways stories could entertain the public. Today, as we noted in the introduction, stories are so present in our lives and everyday interactions that we often forget that the things we are hearing or reading are in fact, stories.

> Stories are so present in our lives and everyday interactions that we often forget that the things we are hearing or reading are in fact, stories.

Narrative Paradigm

Although stories have seemingly existed since almost the beginning of oral communication, it has been more recently that scholars and researchers have considered the role of stories and narratives in the ways we experience and understand the world. In 1984, Walter Fisher introduced his narrative paradigm. He argued that humans are "essentially storytelling creatures" because he believed that humans are born with the innate ability to create stories. He further argued that each person makes decisions based not on logic, but on the stories that one knows and believes about the situation.[4] For example, a person deciding whether or not to buy a lottery ticket will not base his or her decision on the numerical odds of winning, but more likely will make a decision based on stories he or she has heard about other winners or the potential story of what it would be like as a multi-millionaire.

Another key component of Fisher's theory is that multiple stories exist in the world, and multiple stories can be created to explain an event. A story by definition is the way an individual puts together events that occurred over a given period of time. As people create and tell stories, their recollection and interpretation of events may be influenced by a multitude of factors. This means that the stories we encounter are not always accurate or reasonable.

Fisher argued that we evaluate stories based on two criteria: **coherence** and **fidelity**. Coherence refers to the story being structurally sound. In other words, do the events make sense and hang together? A story where elements are out of place or a character is depicted as being in the two places at the same time would fail the coherence test. The second element, fidelity, has more to do with each person's perception and evaluation of how the story fits into his or her understanding of the world. If the elements of a story do not ring true to a person's sense of how the world works, it will fail the fidelity test.

Narratives and Persuasion

One of the things that has long been understood about stories is that they are a great persuasive tool. After reading, being told, or watching a story, people are more likely to engage in a desired action such as donating money, participating in healthy behaviors, or supporting a position. One field that has used this phenomena to its advantage has been the nonprofit sector. Earlier you read about Compassion International and the creative way they found to increase potential donors' access to stories about its work. These stories were successfully used as a means of persuasion as these stories resulted in an increased number of people signing up to be sponsors.

Many nonprofits rely heavily on donations of money, items, and time. While these organization can and do talk about the needs of the population they are serving and the work they do, long lists of statistics and facts can have a limited impact. When those lists and facts are paired with stories of need or stories of the work the organization is doing, the audience is more likely to donate or engage in a desired activity for that organization. The stories these organizations tell help the audience attach a face, meaning, and emotion to the problem which makes it more likely that a persuasive appeal will succeed.

For example, the National Court Appointed Special Advocates (CASA) is an organization that trains and assigns advocates for children involved in the legal system due to abuse or neglect. The role of a CASA is to represent and be a voice for the best interests of the child in legal proceedings. One of the challenges CASA programs across the country have is having enough trained volunteers to serve as CASAs which means that hundreds of children in counties across the United States have no advocate representing their best interests during court proceedings. In trying to recruit volunteers, CASA has two primary challenges. One is lack of awareness of the program and what volunteers do. The second is motivating people to volunteer for a position that is time consuming and potentially emotionally taxing. CASA's recruitment strategies tend to focus less on the statistics about children in the legal system such as the number of children in the foster care system or a list of problems caused by abuse. Instead, CASA focuses on telling the stories of children who need CASAs and children who have been helped by CASAs. They also share the stories of CASA volunteers. These stories often shared online in the form of short videos or brief articles have been able to break through the clutter of requests, and volunteer numbers have risen. The question then becomes, why? Why are stories so powerful? The next section provides some answers to that question.

The Science of Storytelling

So far, this chapter has looked at some of the historical and philosophical foundations of storytelling, and it has provided examples of the power of storytelling as a persuasive tool. In order to better answer the question of why stories work the way they do, we will look at the science behind storytelling. Understanding the neurological implications of telling and hearing stories can help you consider how you can skillfully use stories to reach your communication goals. It has long been known that people enjoy stories and use stories to share information. More recently, communication scholars and neurobiologists have begun to study the cognitive, psychological reasons that stories are so powerful.

One thing these researchers have found is that humans process narrative information differently than other types of support. For example, studies have found that people can read narrative text twice as fast as expository text.[5] Other studies have found that people can more easily recall information presented in a narrative format vs. information presented as a list.[6]

Not only did scientists see that stories are easier for the brain to process, but they also seemed to play a role in the persuasive process. As researchers looked into why this was happening, they discovered the concept of transportation. Green and Brock found that sometimes when people read or listen to a story, they become so absorbed in the story that they are psychologically transported into the story.[7] Have you ever been watching a movie or reading a book and gotten so lost in the story that you became unaware of time passing and what was going on around you? This happens when the brain and the imagination are transported into the story, and the audience feels as if they are actually in the story observing what is occurring.

When transportation happens, the listener not only feels as if he or she is there in the scene, but also becomes emotionally involved in the story. When something bad happens to a character the listener cares about, she goes beyond just feeling bad for that character and feels some of the pain herself, an indication of an empathetic response. This empathetic response is one of the reasons that a narrative can be so powerful in encouraging listeners to do something for others. If a listener is transported while listening to a story from Compassion International about a child who is living in poverty, the listener experiences empathy for that child and is more likely to be willing to donate money to help that child or children like her.

One of the interesting things about transportation and the persuasive process is that persuasion does not need to be explicit to be effective. People interested in promoting healthier behaviors have long known this and found ways to include health-related storylines in entertainment programs. The field of entertainment education is dedicated to helping television and movie producers include storylines in programs that provide accurate health information with the goal of promoting healthier behaviors in the audience. For example, in the mid 90s, the long running day time soap opera *The Bold and The Beautiful,* included storylines focused on HIV infection and prevention. After the programs aired, the National STD and AIDS hotline reported a drastic increase in calls from people seeking out more information about the risks of HIV and ways to protect themselves.[8]

Being transported into a story also means it is more likely that listeners will adopt the world view presented in the story.[9] If, for example, a story about students in an underfunded public school system presents a consistently negative view of the school and system, the listener, who may not have experience with that school system, will be more likely to express negative views about the system. If the story, however, presents a more positive outlook, perhaps it focuses on the work of dedicated teachers or on students who have been able to beat the odds, the listener will express more positive views.

In addition to psychological and cognitive processes, some researchers wondered if there are any physical reasons that stories have such a profound impact on people's thinking and decision-making processes. In order to answer these questions, researchers began to scan people's brains to see what was happening when they were listening to a story. In the early 2000s, neurobiologist Paul Zak and his team of researchers began to wonder why people feel so personally connected to characters in stories and what if any changes occur in the brain while listening to a story. His team found that when a person is engaged in a story, the brain actually produces oxytocin.[10]

Oxytocin is a powerful hormone that generates feelings of love and affection and in turn promotes bonding between people. Oxytocin, sometimes referred to as the love hormone, is naturally produced by the brain in response to different forms of physical contact such as hugging and kissing. Oxytocin is not relegated to romantic relationships; it also plays a key role in developing the relationships between parents and children as well as friends. When oxytocin is released, people engage in more social activities and are more likely to engage in reciprocal behaviors with a person. The release of oxytocin also increases feelings of trust.[11]

What Zak and his team found was that this powerful hormone was released in the brain not as a result of actual human contact, but merely from listening to an engaging story. Just as it would in a real-life encounter, the released chemical increased feelings of connection to and bonding with the characters. This helps to explain why audiences sometimes have such powerful emotional responses to events in stories to the point where it feels almost as if the listeners themselves are having the same experience. As a result of the oxytocin viewers feel empathy for the character, and the viewer also has an increased desire to engage in social behavior with the character. Additionally, because ocytocin, increases feelings of trust, the listener is more likely to trust the storyteller and agree with him or her.

Although the viewer cannot actually interact with the characters, viewers can develop ideas and opinions that are sympathetic to that character. In turn, viewers may be more likely to support or engage in actions that would help people in a similar situation. For example, if a character in a story is the victim of domestic violence, an engaged listener or viewer is more likely to feel sympathetic to the situation of other domestic violence victims. In turn, when that person is asked to support the local domestic violence shelter with a donation or support legislation that would enforce harsher penalties for abusers, he or she is more likely to say yes.

Another powerful phenomena that explains why stories can have such powerful impacts is **neural coupling,** which is when the storyteller's and the listener's brains engage in synchronous activity.[12] In order to look at what occurs in the brain, researchers at MIT placed storytellers into MRI machines. They found that when someone is telling a story, depending on what elements are being described and what emotions are being conveyed, different parts of the brain light up indicating action in that area. Researchers went a step further and placed a listener into an MRI machine as well and looked at what areas of the brain were activated. They found that as the listener heard more and more of the story, the same areas of the brain as the teller began to light up. The more involved the listener reported being with the story, the more the brain activity of the teller and listener mirrored each other.

The researchers found that when neural coupling occurred, the listener was not just understanding the words being shared, but by having similar areas of the brain activated, the listener was experiencing similar emotions. Much like the release of oxytocin promotes feelings of empathy, neural coupling does too. When the listener's brain is in sync with the teller's brain, the listener is also more susceptible to suggestions and ideas. If, for example, the speaker is telling a story that promotes the importance of energy conservation, listeners whose brains were in sync are more likely to state pro-energy conservation beliefs as their own.

> In order to best take advantage of the power of stories, we must know how to construct and tell the best stories possible.

What science and research tells us is that stories matter. They are not only central to the ways we think about and understand the world, but telling and hearing stories lead to physical and chemical changes in the brain. In order to best take advantage of the power of stories, we must know how to construct and tell the best stories possible. In the next section we will look at the specific components that make up a story.

The Components of a Story

Stories represent a unique form of communication that differs from other communication techniques such as sharing a list of facts or issuing commands. In this section, we will look at the four key elements that comprise a story.

Plot

The narrative arc is something you probably learned about in your English class. At the most basic level, a story has a beginning, middle, and end. Stories take place over a given period of time, and the events within that time are connected. This requirement of stories is why the following sentences are not a story: Ryan sat in a chair. Ryan has red hair. Ryan wants to go to California. While these statements all talk about Ryan as a character, these facts do not connect with each over time. In contrast, the following sentences are a story. Ryan, whose hair is red, sat in a chair. Ryan thought about wanting to go to California. Ryan decided to buy a ticket. Now, this is not an interesting story or one that many of us would consider worthy to share in a presentation, but by definition, it is a story.

If we go beyond the basic structure of beginning, middle, and end, we can flesh out the parts of the plot a little more. One way to think about the plot of a story is to look at it as a narrative arc. Visually, the plot of a story looks like this:

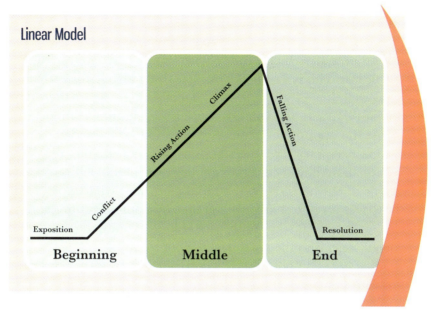

Pixar, the film company responsible for innovative and award-winning films such as *Toy Story, Wall-E,* and *Finding Nemo*, attributes it success not just to their innovative animation techniques but to their dedication to telling great stories. In a widely watched and shared TED Talk, animator Andrew Stanton, provides the following formula for creating a memorable and interesting story; "Once upon a time there was _____. Every day, _____. One day, _____. Because of that, _____. Because of that _____. Until finally, _____."

You can watch his talk at https://www.ted.com/talks/andrew_stanton_the_clues_to_a_great_story. This is similar to the idea of having a beginning middle, and end, but this helps expand our idea of what needs to be included in each of these sections.

First, once upon a time. Notice that this format starts out very much like a classic fairy tale. One of the reasons that these fairy tales are classics is because they are great stories that follow this format. The introduction is where you layout the foundation of the story and provide the background information your audience will need to understand and care about the story moving forward. The challenge in the exposition is providing enough information so that your audience understands the story but is not bored or overwhelmed. If you fail to layout the basics of the story that matter such as who, when and where, your audience will be lost. This is a common mistake when we tell stories that we know well. It is easy to forget that our audience was not there or is not familiar with the context, so we leave out important details.

At the opposite extreme is providing too many details that are not necessary for understanding the story. If you are telling a story about how a coworker got her current job, telling several details about her family, her childhood, and what type of car she drives is not essential. If you take too long to get to the next element, conflict, you run the risk of losing your audience before you even get into the good part of your story.

The next component is the **conflict,** which is the tension or problem in a story. This is the part of the story formula where one day something happened. Conflict can exist between two characters, a character and nature, a character and his or her circumstances, and even a character and himself. Conflict is the thing that makes a story interesting. Imagine, for example, that Brad, branch manager of a local bank, has been asked to come and speak to a class of business students about his career path. He tells them that he always knew he wanted to work in banking, went to college, got good grades, went to his first interview after graduation, got the job, and has had this job ever since. While you might be impressed by Brad's good fortune, or even slightly jealous of what seems like his incredibly good fortune, his story is not that compelling. Why? Because his story lacks conflict. There were not obstacles in his way, no challenges or situations he had to face or overcome to succeed. If Brad told his audience how he failed accounting during his freshman year and almost got kicked out of college, his story becomes more interesting as his failure introduces a struggle into the story.

Once the conflict has been introduced, the story continues to the **rising action.** This is the part of the formula where you fill in the blanks because of that _____ and because of that _____. One of the interesting things to note about this formula is the phrase "because of that." It may seem like a small thing, but the words "because of that" imply a linkage between actions. Storytelling can be quickly derailed when we share a lot of things that happened in a given time frame but fail to make a connection between those actions. As you think about how you want to tell your story and what details and events to include, ask yourself if the previous element leads logically to the next one. In Brad's story, the rising action would be his description of the things he had to do to keep himself in school and getting to a point where he was actually succeeding.

The next element in the plot line is the **climax** or **critical event**. If you look at the diagram, you see that this is the peak of your story. The climax occurs when the conflict has been building and reaches its strongest point. The critical event can be either positive or negative. Take, for example, Brad. After struggling to do better and working as he hard he could, the climax of the story could be his graduation day. In some stories, the climax might be when a character is at his or her lowest. For example, singer Demi Lovato has been very open in sharing her story of addiction to drugs and alcohol. The climax of her story is hitting what she describes as her rock bottom when she was waking up each morning and starting the day with a glass of vodka.

> The climax occurs when the conflict has been building and reaches its strongest point.

The final part of the story is the **falling action** and **resolution**. Another term for the resolution of a story is the French word **denouement,** which means tying the knot. This is a great way to think about the conclusion of a story. After getting to the peak of the story, the audience wants to know what happened. In the case of Brad, we know that he graduated, but we also want to know what happened as a result. Did he go on to get a good job? Did he find a completely different career? As a storyteller, you need to let your audience know how things ended or you will leave them with a sense of incompletion.

Characters

Every story you tell or hear has characters. Sometimes the characters in your story are familiar to your audience and you will not to have a spend a lot of time describing them. If the characters are not familiar, you as a storyteller need to determine what information you want and need to share about your characters.

In thinking about your characters, there are two main types of characters that most stories have. The first is the **protagonist,** sometimes referred to as the main character or hero. The protagonist is the character that needs to overcome the conflict. Another key character is the **villain.** The villain may not always be a person. If you look at the types of conflict that exist, only one of them is between two people, so the villain could be a force of nature such as a hurricane, or the villain could be an external force. In some situations, the main character can be both the protagonist and villain if the protagonist is facing an internal struggle. The villain is a powerful character because it is the villain that frequently brings the conflict and tension to a story.

In some stories, you may have additional supporting characters with varying amounts of importance to the story. It is important that your audience understands who a character is and why that character is there. Forgetting to introduce a secondary character and having him or her suddenly appear in the story is an easy way to confuse your audience and make it difficult for them to follow you.

When thinking about how to describe and portray the characters in a story, there are a few general tips to keep in mind. In general, the protagonist should be a sympathetic character that the audience is rooting for. A protagonist can certainly have flaws; a too perfect character can be hard to feel a lot of sympathy for, but if the protagonist is too flawed or unlikeable, they audience may not be rooting for him or her to succeed. Depending on the length of your story, your character will be more or less developed. One thing to remember is that if you want your audience to be engaged with the story, they need to be able to imagine themselves there. Providing a few key details about a character such as their age or occupation can help the audience more fully picture and relate to a character. Pixar's rules of great storytelling remind storytellers that audiences want to connect with a character who has opinions, who has emotions, and who faces challenges.

Setting

The setting is a where a story physically takes place. Depending on the content of the story, the setting may be more or less important. If you are recounting a conversation you had with a mentor, where that conversation took place is probably not very important unless the setting itself introduced some sort of tension or problem into the story. Other times though, the setting provides needed context for the story's events. If for example you are sharing a story about a natural disaster, the location is a critical element.

Point of View

All stories have a narrator. By telling a story, you assume this role. Depending on the story you are telling, you may be a first-person narrator, telling a story about something you experienced directly, or you may be a third person narrator telling a story about something that happened to someone or something else. As the narrator, it is important to recognize your point-of-view and the limitations this may place on you in terms of your reliability. If you are telling someone else's story, you are limited by what you have read or have been told and might not be able to convey a completely accurate account of the event.

Even if you are telling a first-hand account of something that happened to you or you observed, you are still presenting it from your perspective. We do not always have access to what other characters are thinking or their motivations, or we may not have been told all of the events that occurred. We are obligated to our audiences to acknowledge these limitations and be clear that we are sharing a story from a particular perspective.

Stories in Presentations

Now that you have seen how powerful stories can be in persuading others, captivating attention, and creating connections, as well as the components that make up a story, you may be wondering how and when to use stories in your presentations. Before we discuss the specific ways you can use stories, we must first identify three types of stories you can tell.

Fictional Stories

Fictional stories might be what first pop into your mind when you hear the term "story." Fictional stories are made up stories that often serve the purpose of entertaining an audience or teaching a lesson. This type of story is seen less often in professional presentations, but they are not completely absent. A fictional story can be a great tool for illustrating a key point to a group or team. For example, a manager may relay the classic fable, "The Ant and the Grasshopper," to help motivate a team to work hard to prepare for an upcoming busy season at work.

True Stories

True or non-fictional stories are accounts of events that have actually occurred. These will most likely be the most common type of story you use in your presentations. These can be stories of the things you directly experienced, stories that others have told you, or stories that you gather through research such as reading an article or watching a news report.

Hypothetical Stories

This is a specific type of fictional story in which you ask your audience to imagine a given scenario. These hypotheticals are often based in reality. For example, you ask your audience to imagine what it would feel like to come home hungry for dinner to an empty refrigerator and bare pantry. Hypothetical stories engage the audience by asking them to directly put themselves into a given situation and consider how they would feel or react.

Brief vs. Extended Narrative

Another categorization you need to be aware of that applies to all of the above types of stories is a **brief** vs. **extended** narrative. A brief narrative is a short story that is not fully developed and is often focused on a specific event and has limited detail regarding the characters, setting, and action. Brief stories are sometimes referred to as anecdotes. Even a short story can be powerful as long as all of the components of the narrative arc are there. In contrast, extended stories are often more complicated and spend more time developing the situation, characters, and setting.

Using Story Types

During a presentation, there are several different ways that you may use these types of stories. Here is a list of how stories can be used in a presentation:

- *The Presentation*—In some situations, the story itself is the presentation. Think about the earlier example of slightly boring Brad and his story of his career path. For this presentation, his personal story was the entire presentation. In different circumstances, you may be asked to share about a personal experience.
- *Attention Getter*—When you begin a presentation, the first thing you should do is say something to grab your audience's attention and pull them into your presentation. Because people are so drawn to narratives, a brief story that relates to your topic is an excellent way to do this.

- *Establishing Relevance*—Another important component of a presentation is informing your audience about why the topic is relevant to them. A story in which your audience can relate to the situation or characters is a powerful way to do this. Imagine that you have been tasked with speaking to a group of incoming freshman at the local college about the dangers of binge drinking. Starting your presentation with the story of a former freshman who went to a party during his first semester on campus and ended up in the hospital with severe alcohol poisoning after a night of over consumption is a quick and easy way to help your audience see why this is a topic that affects them.
- *Establishing Credibility*—When you are giving a presentation, there may be times when you have a personal experience that is relevant to the topic. Sharing your personal story is a way to demonstrate to your audience that you are qualified to address the topic. For example, Tony Dungy, former coach of the Indianapolis Colts, is a Super Bowl winner. There is no question that he is qualified to talk about football, but tragic events in his personal life also gave him the credibility to address the topic of suicide prevention. After losing his 18-year-old son to suicide, Dungy has worked to raise awareness of this issue.
- *Creating Rapport*—In Chapter 3 on delivery, you read about the importance of establishing a sense of rapport with your audience. Sharing a personal story can be a great way to create a connection with the audience. Your story may illustrate your similarity with the audience, or it may help them to see you as a person, and not just an expert or speaker. Sheryl Sandberg, the Chief Operating Office at Facebook and author of the bestselling book *Lean In*, has been incredibly successful in her business life. Part of her mission is to work for gender equality in the workplace, and she often speaks on the challenges women face in their careers as they try to climb the corporate ladder. Throughout her talks she includes numerous personal stories about work, her family, and her own challenges. Despite being wildly successful and holding a prestigious high-powered job, her storytelling allows that the average woman can still relate to her.

❱ *Supporting Evidence*—Another excellent way to incorporate stories into a presentation is to use them as evidence and examples. As you read earlier, the ways that the brain reacts to hearing a story can make stories a powerful persuasive tool, so stories can serve as compelling supporting evidence in a persuasive presentation. Stories can also be used in informative presentations to illustrate a concept or idea. A story can help your audience take more abstract information and see how it is applied. Imagine, for example, your task it to teach an audience about how to use different sales techniques such as door-in-the-face or foot-in-the-door. Including some stories about how these techniques have been successfully and unsuccessfully used is a great way to provide a concrete illustration to the audience.

Crafting Compelling Stories

One thing to consider as you intentionally tell stories and incorporate them into your presentations is that not all stories are created equally. Some stories are more effective, interesting, entertaining, and enjoyable than others. This is why some TV shows captivate large audiences and win Emmy awards while others are panned by critics and are canceled after just five episodes. Just because a story has all of the key elements does not mean that it is a good story. In the next section, we will look at some of the factors that influence the relative merit of a story.

As you read earlier, in his Narrative Paradigm, Fisher argued that people judge stories based on their fidelity and rationality. The **Story Model** created by Hastie and Pennington which is based on their work in the legal field, expands on these ideas and looks at the different components that influence how a listener or audience will evaluate a given story.[13] Hastie and Pennington were interested in how juries took all of the evidence presented in a trial and used it to make a decision regarding the case. They found that jurors put the pieces of evidence together in a story or stories to explain what happened. Jurors then make their decision based on which stories they deem to be the most rational. It is the role of the lawyers then to present evidence and explanations for the events that can be constructed into the most rational story.

Earlier we discussed Fisher's concept of rationality which is based on a story's coherence and fidelity. Hastie and Pennington describe what they term as certainty principles. When a juror is making a decision in a case, he or she picks the story that allows him or her to be most certain that the events in the story are what actually occurred. In the Story Model, certainty is based on coverage and coherence. Coverage refers to the amount of evidence that supports a given story. Their concept of coherence incorporates three elements: consistency, plausibility, and completeness. Consistency is similar to Fisher's concept of coherence. A consistent story does not contradict itself. Plausibility takes into account a person's knowledge and understanding of how the world works. A plausible story is one that the listener can see occurring based on his or her knowledge of how similar events may occur. Completeness refers to the story having all of the elements and structure of a story. If a defense lawyer cannot provide a reasonable ending for the story he or she is trying to present, the jury will be more likely to reject that story.

> A plausible story is one that the listener can see occurring based on his or her knowledge of how similar events may occur.

While based in the legal realm, the Story Model's concepts can be applied to multiple settings. If you are using a story as evidence to support your point, you should consider how the audience might evaluate the story. If your story seems too far-fetched, your audience may discount it and reject it as supporting evidence as it does not meet the plausibility test. It is also important that the elements of your story line up, and you avoid contradictions. When telling longer stories, it is easy to get timelines and events mixed up, and these small contradictions can lessen the impact of your story.

Conflict

Some may argue that conflict is the most critical element in a story. As we learned earlier, conflict is any tension that impedes the character's ability to achieve a desired outcome. In general, the more conflict or the greater the conflict, the more interesting and well received the story. A story about someone's recent bout with the flu, for example, may not be as interesting as a story about someone's recent hospitalization due to severe pneumonia. In terms of the stories, there are two key things to consider when it comes to conflict. First, when you are selecting what stories to share in your presentation, consider which ones have the more interesting or intense conflict. Second, consider how you will present the conflict. Using dramatic language and a dramatic tone can elevate a relatively minor conflict to a higher level.

Novelty

Another factor is the novelty or unexpected nature of the story elements. A story in which we can easily predict the outcome is not going to hold our attention in the same way that an unexpected tale will. This is one of the reasons that we love stories about ordinary people who do or experience what we call great things. It is unexpected to think that an impoverished single mother who struggled with depression would become one of the best-selling authors of our time as did J.K. Rowling, author of the *Harry Potter* series. When you are considering what stories to use as attention getters or support, select ones that have a novel element such as unexpected hero, a less common challenge, or a unique solution to a problem.

Suspense

Suspense is related in some ways to both conflict and novelty. Suspense is the audience's feeling of anticipation of wanting to know what happens next. Suspense is what keeps your audience listening. Suspense is created as you share the rising action and build to the critical event. In order to create suspense, there needs to be a question about what is going to happen. The easiest way to take away any sense of suspense is to tell the ending of the story at the beginning. This may seem obvious, but far too many people give away the ending as they set up the story.

> Suspense is the audience's feeling of anticipation of wanting to know what happens next. Suspense is what keeps your audience listening.

A great way to build suspense is to break up the parts of the story throughout your presentation. You may begin your story at the beginning of your presentation by introducing the key characters and conflict. As you move to the body of your speech, you can include elements of the rising action as pieces of evidence until you reach the critical event. Finally, when you are concluding your presentation, you can include the resolution as a way to tie together your entire presentation.

Details

Earlier we talked about not providing extraneous details that do not add to the story. This does not mean that details and description are bad. Instead, you need to determine what details will help your audience better connect to the story. One simple detail that is often overlooked is sharing the names of your characters with your audience. Imagine you are talking to a local community group about the need for more volunteers at the local food pantry. As part of your presentation, you share about one of the food pantry patrons. Referring to her simply as "her" or "the woman who came" depersonalizes her whereas calling her by her name such as "Mary" makes her seem real. Research on the psychology of names has shown that names are a powerful cognitive tool. When the listener can link a description of a person with a name, this actually assists in the creation of mental maps, which assists in the overall processing and recall of the story.[14]

Another thing to consider when adding details to a story is how those details will stimulate the audience's senses. When a listener is transported into a story, he or she feels as if she is there. Helping your audience to image how things look, smell, sound, and feel can strengthen feelings of transportation and immersion. Take, for example, Tia. She is sharing a story of a cold January day when she was locked out of her house. Her description of the cold can have a large influence on how her listeners evaluate her story. If she says that it was a pretty cold day in January, her audience is going to think about it being cold. If she provides some key details such as it was bitterly cold, the temperature was hovering around 0 degrees, the wind was howling, and within a few minutes, the tips of her fingers were starting to go numb, the audience has more information to help them picture the scene.

When sharing details, using fewer highly descriptive words or a strong verb is more powerful than putting together a stream of adjectives. Adding the word "bitterly" above, changes a cold day into something more serious and, in turn, makes the conflict of the story, being locked out in the cold, a more intense situation.

The Way It Is Told

You can have an amazing story with an incredible plot, intriguing characters, and a ton of action, but if you do not tell the story well, it may fall flat. Just like all types of presentational speaking, the information you have is only as good as the way it is told. Take a minute and think about the people you know who are great storytellers. What is it that makes them such great storytellers? Partly they may have really good material as they might have had a lot of interesting experiences. But often, it is their enthusiasm, expression, and sense of timing that transform a good story into a great one.

Here are some key things to think about in terms of how you deliver the stories you share.

- Match the emotion and tone of your voice to the emotion and tone of the story. If you use a monotone voice to tell your audience that a character was overcome with excitement, it is going to be hard for the audience to believe or imagine that enthusiasm.
- Don't be afraid to be expressive. This goes beyond your tone. Your facial expressions, gestures, and body movement can convey a lot of emotion and energy as well.
- Remember the power of a pause. A well-placed pause before a critical moment or a key detail can go a long way in creating suspense.
- Know your story. Great storytellers know their material. If you keep losing your place or forgetting key elements, it interrupts the flow of the story, and it calls your credibility into question.
- Look your audience in the eyes. Great storytellers speak directly to their audience. If you are looking down at your notes during most of your presentation, your audience is going to feel like you are reading to them instead of simply telling them a story.

Storytelling in Context

This chapter has explained the whys and hows of using stories in your presentations. In this section, we will look at how stories are used in specific contexts and fields. Particularly, we will look at some contexts where you would not naturally assume that storytelling was a commonly employed or useful tool.

Storytelling in Science

Remember earlier when we discussed Fisher and his ideas about the narrative paradigm. One of his primary contentions was that people use narratives rather than logic to make decisions. For those in the field of science where facts and data reign supreme, this contention can be difficult to accept. Data and facts are vital to learning about and understanding the world, but the challenge for those in scientific and technical fields comes from being able to share and explain their work and findings with those outside of their fields. Another challenge is getting audiences to have an emotional connection and response to the facts and data. This is where storytelling can play a helpful role in translating highly technical information to a lay audience.

Neil deGrasse Tyson has his PhD is astrophysics from Columbia and has gained a large following of fans through his books, television appearances, and weekly podcasts. His fan base is not just fellow astrophysicists but ordinary people who are interested in science and learning more about how the universe works. What makes him so popular is his ability to take incredibly complex ideas and translate them into stories he can share with his audience. These stories provide a lay audience with a context for understanding. Through his storytelling and conversations with his audience, he has been able to make a highly technical field more accessible to the average person.

When presenting about science and technical information you should include statistics and data. Your presentation can be even more effective if you use these alongside stories so your audience can better connect to and understand the information. A story can be used to illustrate the significance of a research finding. For example, in 2017, a team of scientists discovered that an elixir extracted from a common mushroom can effectively kill Varroa mites. The average person may not find this very interesting or significant unless they are told the story behind this discovery. It is believed that Varroa mites are one of the primary causes of the declining honeybee population. Honeybees are not only needed for honey production but more importantly for their key role in pollination which allows crops to grow. Varroa mites invade a colony and weaken bees by slowing sucking their blood. They are resistant to most pesticides. The newly discovered mushroom elixir is fatal to the mites yet does not harm the bees, so the elixir became a way to defeat the villian.[15] With this further explanation, the audience can now understand the relevance and importance of the research.

Stories can also be used to personify abstract concepts. Audiences may have a difficult time understanding or picturing how a chemical reaction takes place. If you are able to explain that reaction as a story in which the components of atoms are characters who are taking specific actions that lead to the final reaction, an audience has a better chance of making sense of the reaction.

Sara ElShafie, a doctoral student in integrative biology, recognized the importance of taking her highly technical work and finding a way that she could explain it to people outside her field, including her family. She said the hardest part for her was to get away from the multiple details that informed her work so that she could tell the overarching story of her research which focuses on how climate change impacts animals over time. Once she was able to step back and identify the key characters, events, and plots that informed the need for her research as well as her findings, she found that she got a much better response from general audiences when she talked about her work. Inspired by her successes, she has gone on to develop and teach workshops to fellow scientists on how to use the storytelling techniques of organizations such as Pixar to discuss their own work.[16]

Storytelling in Management

Managers have multiple responsibilities in terms of helping an organization succeed. In terms of leading an organization or team, some of the most important responsibilities include helping the group understand the mission and vision of the organization and motivating the team to reach its goals. One thing that highly successful managers and leaders do is use stories to inspire and motivate their teams and customers. Steve Jobs, founder of Apple, and considered by many to be a visionary leader, was adept at creating and telling stories that captivated and inspired not only his employees but also the public.[17] When a new Apple product was launched, the presentation did not just focus on the newest features of the iPhone or MacBook. Instead, Jobs would come on stage and cast his product as a hero that was working to overcome a villain such as a poor interface or lack of connectivity. In this way, he transformed Apple products from technical gadgets that could perform tasks to a force that assisted people in making the world a better place.

One way leaders and managers can use stories is to create an understanding of what the organization is and what the organization desires to be. Sometimes referred to as an origin story, this story not only lets the listener know more about the company, but if the story is engaging enough, it also creates buy-in from the listener. The Disney corporation is not only masterful at telling stories to captivate audiences, but its own origin story has been a shaping force for the company as a whole. When Walt Disney dreamed of creating Disney Land in the early 1950s, his desire was to create a place where people could enjoy spending time with their families, experience some Disney magic, and feel like they were honored guests. This story was told and continues to be told to all Disney employees as a way to help them understand that whatever their job is in the corporation, their actions should align with this goal. This story has played a key role in developing and sustaining the incredible customer service that Disney is known for.

Storytelling in Teaching

Teaching is another area where storytelling can play an essential role. Remember that prior to widespread literacy, stories were one of the primary means of teaching and sharing information. It is also important to note that teaching is not only the work of those who work within the school or university system. Many jobs include an element of teaching in the form of training or employee development. Research has consistently shown that presenting information as stories assists in the retention and recall of the information.[18] People are so familiar with the narrative structure of beginning, middle, and end that their brains are primed to take in information this way. Because a story has characters and events that relate and connect, it is also easier for the brain to make connections between key concepts.

Chapter Summary

This chapter began with a discussion of the role stories have played in human communication throughout time. It then looked at some of the research done on the impact stories have on the human brain. Next, the chapter described the key components that constitute a story as well as ways to incorporate stories into different types of presentations. The chapter also provided tips for telling the best story possible. Finally, the chapter examined the role storytelling can play in different contexts and fields.

Case Study Conclusion

After Compassion started its blogging tours, the number of children sponsored following each trip increased dramatically. For example, as a result of the story sharing from the 2016 trip to Uganda, 292 children were sponsored. Based on what you have read and learned from this chapter, why do you think the stories the bloggers shared from the different Compassion sites were so successful in gaining sponsors? It is highly likely that when viewers heard and saw the stories of what life was like for many children in Uganda they were transported into the story and developed strong feelings of empathy. When the viewers were then asked to become a sponsor, they were more likely to say yes.

References

[1] "The Definitive Guide to Compassion Blogger Trips." 2016. *Compassion* (blog), January 29, 2016. https://blog.compassion.com/the-definitive-guide-to-compassion-blogger-trips/.

[2] Roser, M., and E. Ortiz-Ospina. 2018. "Literacy." *OurWorldInData.org*. https://ourworldindata.org/literacy.

[3] "The Greeks–The Origins of Theatre–The First Plays" (Continued). *PBS*. Date Accessed: April 17, 2018 http://www.pbs.org/empires/thegreeks/background/24b_p1.html.

[4] Fisher, W. R. 1985. "The Narrative Paradigm." *Journal of Communication* 35(4): 74–89. http://onlinelibrary.wiley.com/doi/10.1111/j.1460-2466.1985.tb02974.x/abstract.

[5] Cervetti, G., M. Bravo, E. Hiebert, P. D. Pearson, and C. Jaynes. 2009. "Text Genre and Science Content: Ease of Reading, Comprehension, and Reader Preference." *Reading Psychology* 30(6): 487–511. https://doi.org/10.1080/02702710902733550.

[6] Fisher, W. R. 1985. "The Narrative Paradigm: In the Beginning." *Journal of Communication* 35(4): 74–89. http://onlinelibrary.wiley.com/doi/10.1111/j.1460-2466.1985.tb02974.x/abstract; Fisher, W. R. 2009. "Narration as a Human Communication Paradigm: The Case of Public Moral Argument." *Communication Monographs* 51(1): 1–22. https://doi.org/10.1080/03637758409390180.

[7] Green, M., and T. Brock. 2000. "The Role of Transportation in the Persuasiveness of Public Narratives." *Journal of Personality and Social Psychology* 79(5): 701–721. doi: 10.1037//0022-3514.79.5.701.

[8] Kennedy, M., A. O'Leary, V. Beck, K. Pollard, and P. Simpson. 2004. "Increases in Calls to the CDC National STD and AIDS Hotline Following AIDS-Related Episodes in a Soap Opera." *Journal of Communication* 54(2): 287–301. doi: 10.1111/j.1460-2466.2004.tb02629.x.

[9] Zak, P. J. 2015. "Why Inspiring Stories Make Us React: The Neuroscience of Narrative." *Cerebrum*, February 02, 2015. http://www.dana.org/Cerebrum/2015/Why_Inspiring_Stories_Make_Us_React__The_Neuroscience_of_Narrative/.

[10] Zak.

[11] Kosfeld, M., M. Heinrichs, P. J. Zak, U. Fischbacher, and E. Fehr. 2005. "Oxytocin Increases Trust in Humans." *Nature* 435: 673–676. doi: 10.1038/nature03701.

[12] Stephens, G., L. Silbert, and U. Hasson. 2010. "Speaker-Listener Neural Coupling Underlies Successful Communication." *PNAS* 107(32): 14425–14430. https://doi.org/10.1073/pnas.1008662107.

[13] Pennington, N., and R. Hastie. 1993. "Reasoning in Explanation-Based Decision Making." *Cognition* 49(1-2): 123–163. https://doi.org/10.1016/0010-0277(93)90038-W.

[14] Butler, J. 2017. "Mindcrafting: The Semantic Characteristics of Spontaneous Names Generated as an Aid to Cognitive Mapping and Navigation of Simulated Environments." *SAGE Journals* 48(5): 588–602. http://journals.sagepub.com/doi/10.1177/1046878117712750.

[15] GrrlScientist. 2017. "Can a Mushroom Save Honey Bees?" *Forbes*, June 5, 2017. https://www.forbes.com/sites/grrlscientist/2017/06/05/can-a-mushroom-save-honey-bees/#6d7346ca5322.

[16] Dong, T. 2017. "PhD Student Pioneers Storytelling Strategies for Science Communication." *Berkeley Arts and Design*, June 6, 2017. http://artsdesign.berkeley.edu/literature/news/phd-student-pioneers-storytelling-strategies-for-science-communication.

[17] Gallo, C. 2012. "7 Ways Tim Cook Gave a Steve Jobs-Like Presentation." *Forbes*, March 8, 2012. https://www.forbes.com/sites/carminegallo/2012/03/08/7-ways-tim-cook-gave-a-steve-jobs-like-presentation/#2b50b09d162e.

[18] Emde, K., C. Klimmt, and D. M. Schluetz. 2015. "Does Storytelling Help Adolescents to Process the News?" *Journalism Studies* 17(5): 608–627. https://doi.org/10.1080/1461670X.2015.1006900; Abrahamson, C. E. 1998. "Storytelling as a Pedagogical Tool in Higher Education." *Questia: Education* 118(3). https://www.questia.com/library/journal/1G1-20494609/storytelling-as-a-pedagogical-tool-in-higher-education.

Chapter 8

Informative Presentations

Objectives

After this chapter you will be able to:

- Understand the key features of a speech of awareness.
- Identify the necessary components in a speech of demonstration.
- Recognize and apply the important strategies for using elucidating explanations.
- Recognize and apply the strategies for using quasi-scientific explanations.
- Recognize and apply the strategies for using transformative explanations.

The Three-Minute Thesis Competition began at Queensland University during a massive drought. At the time, citizens in Australia were being encouraged to take three-minute showers to conserve water. People used egg timers to limit their time in the shower. This phenomenon spurred the Dean of the Graduate School at Queensland University, Alan Lawson, to come up with the idea for a three-minute thesis competition. The competition asks graduate students to present their research—typically a dissertation project—to an audience of non-specialists in a manner that is free from jargon or scientific language in three minutes or less.

This is quite a challenge. Dissertations or thesis projects contain about 80,000 words. It would take nine hours to present a dissertation of this length. This competition challenges students to condense their ideas to just three minutes. As you can see, this seems like an impossible task. However, graduate students around the world were up for this challenge and these competitions occur all over the world. I bet there are competitions on your own university campuses because over 200 universities in the U.S. alone host competitions. You should visit the website https://threeminutethesis.uq.edu.au/ and check out some of the winning presentations. Some of the specific skills these speakers use are going to be highlighted in this chapter.

What is key here is how to take the complex research that these students conduct and explain it to an audience that has no expertise in their specific research area. This is a skill that all of us will have to engage in at one point or another. And many times, you only get three minutes with your boss, or client, or investor. How can you inform them about what you do and why it is important in that length of time?

Let's Talk
1. What are the challenges a competition like 3MT might present for an audience?
2. What are the challenges inherent in communicating information to a non-expert audience?
3. How can you cut down information in a way that will still be meaningful to your audience.

Introduction

This chapter focuses on speeches that serve to inform an audience. Informative speeches can make an audience aware of a new idea, be instructional, or even explain information. You may want to make an audience aware of a new vaccine or new policy. You may even be asked to explain complex information to a particular audience. Maybe you need to explain to a group of farmers how a pesticide for example, will affect a particular pest population. All of these examples are informative in nature. In fact, most of the presentations you deliver will be informative in nature. We all like to be persuasive, but don't underestimate the importance of informative speaking. While we often think of informative speaking as easier than persuasive speaking, this isn't the case. A good informative presentation is as hard to craft as a persuasive presentation. There are many things to consider and decisions to make when planning an informative presentation, and many of them surround the audience. Here are some key issues that you should know about your audience before you begin presentation preparation:

- Are they knowledgeable about your topic?
- What expectations do they bring to the presentation?
- What ideas might they hold that may make it difficult for them to process your presentation?
- How motivated are they toward your topic?

Answers to all of these questions are important. They will help you arrange your materials in a particular way that will have the biggest impact on the audience. Your audience will either have no information, some information, old information, or, given the propensity of people to look things up on the web, even wrong information. It's highly likely your audience won't be homogenous; that is, you could have a portion of your audience members with no information and some members with a lot of information. It is up to you to be able to relate your presentation to all these audience members.

This chapter will focus on three types of informative speaking: awareness, demonstrations, and explanations. If you follow these guidelines we discuss throughout this chapter, you will have a better chance of being effective.

Speech of Awareness

An informative presentation of awareness does exactly what you think it does. It makes your audience aware of an event, person, place, thing, or even raises awareness of a problem that they didn't know about before you began your presentation. Perhaps you want to deliver a presentation on a person who was influential in a particular way. A speech on James Naismith, the inventor of basketball, is an example of a presentation of awareness and fits this bill. Another example is a presentation about cheap places to stay when attending a music festival. Both of these examples present new information and make the audience aware of some important or interesting information they were unaware of before.

Suppose you work at the student success office on campus. Part of your job is to make your colleagues aware of the programs offered around campus. You decide that stress is a major problem for your audience. You have heard everyone in class talking about how stressed out they are. So, you decide to make them aware of services on campus for addressing stress. You might outline your presentation along the following lines.

Thesis Sentence: There are three free programs on campus that can reduce stress in college students.

- (Main Point) First, our health mentor program provides one-on-one counseling to reduce stress.
- (Main Point) A second program you can take advantage of is Wellness on Demand.
- (Main Point) Finally, the Stress Smash Session allows you to physically work through your stress by breaking things.

This example presentation is organized topically by program type. The speaker would go into more detail providing enough information to allow the audience to determine if these programs were right for them and how to get enrolled in them.

Any organizational pattern appropriate for an informative speech can be used with a speech of awareness. These include chronological, spatial, topical or comparative advantage and were discussed in Chapter 6.

It is important when thinking about topics for a speech of awareness that you make sure to present something new to an audience. If they already know about your topic, you've just wasted their time, so make sure that you have adequately analyzed your audience and are actually presenting novel and useful information. What might be novel for one audience won't be for another. Really do the research so that you can make a valuable contribution to your audience. As an audience member, nothing is more frustrating than sitting through a presentation and learning nothing new.

Speech of Demonstration

Demonstration or Instructional presentations explain to an audience "how to do something." The U.S. is obsessed with this type of informative presentation. Ratings for the Food Network and HGTV are off the charts.[1] Much of this programing shows an audience how to make a casserole or update a stale bathroom. YouTube is also a big avenue for instructional videos. The authors of this text have learned to crochet from YouTube videos, and one of us has been able to avoid costly service repairs and even fixed our own washer and refrigerator by watching this type of video on the web. These are important presentations and if delivered well can help an audience achieve some important goal.

In a speech of demonstration, your goal is to move audience members from their current level of knowledge (e.g., knowing that their vacuum cleaner is broken) to some desired goal or outcome (e.g., being able to fix their vacuum cleaner).

There are two things that you have to accomplish before you just start explaining how to do something. First, you have to establish your credibility. If you are going to explain to your audience "how to" generate more followers on Twitter, you have to be willing to disclose how many followers you have and how many of your own tweets have gone viral. Why should the audience listen to you regarding this topic? Provide them a reason why. This isn't a time to be shy. You don't have to be boastful, but the audience should get a good sense of why they should consider you an expert and follow your advice. Explain your expertise and show how it directly relates to the material at hand.

Second, as the speaker, you must also convince the audience that the process is something that they can achieve and be successful at. If they believe it is too complex, they won't listen. As part of your strategy, you need to be encouraging as you lead your audience toward the end state. Cheer them on at each step and provide encouragement as the presenter.

Once you establish your credibility and set the right tone, you are ready to get down to the important stuff. Effective demonstration presentations move through four steps.[2] First, you must clearly explain to your audience the **end goal.** What is the goal or outcome you are hoping audience members will be able to accomplish? State that clearly so the audience knows exactly what they will be able to do or achieve as a result of your presentation. Maybe you won't be able to teach your audience to fix their vacuum cleaner, but you may be able to help them identify what the problem is so they are informed when they take it to the repair shop. The audience should have a very clear understanding of what success means at the end of the presentation.

Second, you must address any **prerequisites** audience members must achieve. What do audience members need to have or need to complete before they begin the task to ensure success? Are there tools or supplies that they need? Are there accounts that they need to set up? If so, make sure you are clear about what needs to happen before they begin.

Once all the prerequisites have been explained, you can begin to address the "how to" process or outline the **procedures.** The stated **procedures** comprise all the steps you move through as you head toward your goal. It is important that you use a chronological pattern here with plenty of transitions so that the audience knows what to do first, second, and so forth. If the presentation is delivered to a live audience, watch their reactions and be adaptable enough to slow down and reiterate specific steps if audience members appear confused or lost.

During the "how to" portion of your presentation, it is important that you use minimalist instruction. Minimalist instruction encourages an action-oriented approach[3] in demonstration speeches. That is, audience members attending instructional presentations are eager to act, to perform this new task. So don't unnecessarily delay getting to the information needed to make that happen. This means keep your instructions brief and to the point. This is particularly important in asynchronous presentations. Since they are watching online they may give up if the pace isn't appropriate.

The final step that must be addressed in a "how to" presentation is **things to avoid.** These are things that are undesirable and will impede the process. People attempting to learn new skills can spend 25 to 50 percent of their time making and recovering from errors.[4] The best way to remedy that is to prevent those mistakes from occurring in the first place, which reduces frustration on the part of the learner. Tell your audience where the landmines are to begin with, and they can avoid them.

Imagine that you are teaching your audience to make a melt in your mouth meatloaf. Say the recipe calls for two pounds of 80 percent ground beef. If the quality of this ingredient impacts your recipe, make sure you let the audience know that up front. If they have the wrong type of beef, explain what will happen, perhaps the meatloaf will be too tough, etc. Be explicit about these things with your audience so they don't start off on the wrong track or end up with results that aren't ideal.

> **Effective Speech of Demonstration Should**
> - Explain the expertise/credibility of the speaker.
> - Encourage the audience during the process.
> - Describe the end goal.
> - Describe any prerequisites.
> - Describe the steps in the process.
> - Describe things the audience should avoid during the process.

One of the issues that you might face when presenting a speech of demonstration is the method of delivery. Will the presentation be live or asynchronous? This is something that you will have to consider because this will impact the choices and ways that you deliver your presentation. For example, it impacts they way you use transitions. Transitions are much more important in an asynchronous presentation because people often fast forward through presentations, so it becomes important that you recap and mark where you are in the presentation. There are other issues to consider, such as delivery. Chapter 12 will outline some of these challenges and address issues with online presentations. Make sure you consult this chapter before designing your asynchronous "how to" presentation.

There are many examples of asynchronous demonstration presentations on YouTube and even many TED Talks that use this same format. We encourage you to watch a few of these before you get started if you plan to deliver a speech of demonstration.

Speech of Explanation

A speech of explanation is a type of informative speaking that deepens the audience's understanding of some complex subject. Topics that might be addressed in an explanatory presentation include scientific topics, health topics, financial topics, complex theoretical issues, and technological topics, just to name a few.

Explanatory presentations introduce unique problems for the speaker. You must deal with the issues of organization and support, but you also must address special challenges in terms of audience analysis. As mentioned in other chapters, all good presentations require thorough audience analysis. However, when faced with presenting difficult information, you must step back and analyze your audience in different ways. Ask the following questions:

- What type of previous knowledge do these particular audience members bring to this situation that may enhance or impede their ability to process the material?
- What obstacles (e.g., previously held ideas) may interfere with this audience's ability to process this information?
- What are the challenges inherent in this information that might make the information difficult for an audience to process (e.g., vocabulary, amount of material, etc.)?

By answering these questions, you have better insight into the needs of your audience. To be an effective speaker in this complex situation, you must have a thorough understanding of just what it is about the information you are presenting that may make it difficult for a specific audience to understand. Your goal is to anticipate what difficulties the information may present for your audience and then to design a presentation that overcomes those obstacles.

There are several common obstacles that may interfere with an audience's ability to understand a difficult presentation or information. These difficulties may be inherent in the material itself, or your audience may present distinguishing factors that make them unique and therefore, a challenge to reach. According to Kathy Rowan, Professor of Risk Communication and *Fellow* of the American Association for the Advancement of Science, audiences experience difficulty understanding ideas or topics for three primary reasons:[5]

1. **Difficulty understanding the definition of a concept or term.** For example, your audience may have heard the term "statistically significant" but may have trouble explaining exactly what the concept means and how it should be used. Other problems in understanding the use of a concept or term may surround the misuse of terminology. For example, many people outside of meteorology don't know the difference between asteroids, meteorites, and meteors. Lay audiences often misuse these terms when describing activity that surrounds our planet. Sometimes, these misunderstandings can impact how an audience understands a presentation.
2. **Difficulty understanding a phenomenon, structure, or process.** Some presentations are difficult to understand because they describe processes or structures that are hard for an audience to envision. Either the amount of the material is difficult to process, the relationship between elements in the presentation is hard for the audience to see, or there is a large amount of material. For example, audiences may have difficulty understanding how the process of immigration works in the U.S. This is a complicated process with many facets. Picturing and following all of the components in this process is difficult for an audience to navigate with limited understanding of system.[6] Therefore, organizing the material in such a way that the audience can follow and grasp the essential parts in the process is imperative and explaining how they relate to each other is also vitally important.

3. **Difficulty understanding phenomena that are hard to believe.** Sometimes, information is hard to understand because the ideas surrounding the information are counterintuitive to our experiences. Audiences may have trouble understanding aspects of quantum mechanics, for example. Ideas may also be hard to believe because of competing ideas that we hold dear. For example, many people believe that you can catch a cold from going outside with wet hair. This simply is not true. The common cold is caused from a virus, and your hair has little to do with it.[7] The obstacle to understanding here is a pre-existing belief.

Each of these three difficulties or obstacles has a set of unique strategies that can help illuminate your ideas for an audience. The remainder of this chapter discusses each of these three difficulties in more detail, followed by a discussion of strategies that can impact audience understanding.

Difficulty Understanding the Use of a Concept or Term

Sometimes, the difficulty in understanding information involves the concepts or definitions that surround a particular phenomenon. We often misuse certain terminology in ways that make it difficult for us to understand larger issues. For example, suppose that you are planning to present material on some aspect of climate change. After conducting your research, you decide that audience members' primary obstacle to understanding your presentation will be their previously held ideas about what climate is and what it is not. Now that you understand this obstacle, you can plan to overcome it.

Effective Elucidating Explanations
- Provide definition of the concept.
- Provide examples.
- Provide nonexamples.

Research has shown that for audiences to understand content in which concepts or definitions may be difficult, it is best to use an **elucidating explanation.** Elucidating explanations explain a concept's meaning or use by providing the definition of the term and explaining what is essential in that definition and what is not. Let's continue with the example of climate. Many people think that climate and weather are the same thing. According to NASA, climate is a pattern that is exhibited over time in a specific region.[8] Usually, scientists are looking at patterns lasting 30 years or so when they think about climate. It is the average weather over time and space.[9] So when you hear we hit a record low or high on the local weather, they are talking about climate.

When making a presentation that requires an elucidating explanation, here are some steps to follow:

1. **Provide a definition of the concept.** Begin by providing the audience with a definition that lists all of the essential characteristics and features of the definition. Let's examine the following example of a cactus. "Cactuses are a species of plants that grow in hot, dry regions. Most are stem succulents. They never have leaves and cannot remove water from cold soils, so they are dormant in the winter and grow in the summer."[10] The essential characteristics of the definition are made clear: they grow in hot dry regions, are stem succulents, etc.
2. **Address associated meanings, if necessary.** Sometimes, concepts have associated meanings that make a true understanding of the definition difficult. For example, audience members often consider radiation dangerous. However, not all radiation is harmful. Radiation is simply the process of emitting radiant energy in the form of waves or particles. The term *radiation* refers to the electromagnetic radiation that includes radio waves, X-rays, and even the energy from sunlight, light bulbs, and candles. By addressing the associated meaning—dangerous—along with providing a definition, you give the audience a much better understanding of the concept of radiation.[11]
3. **Provide examples.** While it may seem obvious to provide an example of the definition you are presenting, research on explaining information suggests that you should provide

several examples. Continuing with the example on cactuses, you could also provide the audience with the following examples to further illuminate the definition: "The giant saguaro cactus looks like a bare tree with thick, upturned branches, while the flat prickly pear resembles a pancake."

4. **Provide nonexamples.** Multiple examples will help convey your message but so will the use of nonexamples. Often, your audience may have difficulty deciding which examples fit the definition of your concept. By presenting examples and commonly held nonexamples, you can enhance understanding. Nonexamples resemble the concept by sharing some aspects of the criteria but fall short of having all of the criteria. By presenting some of these nonexamples, you help audience members clearly understand the difference. Continuing with the cactus example, you could use the following nonexample: "Most people commonly believe that the yucca plant is a cactus. While it may resemble cactuses, the yucca plant group has pointed, stiff, narrow leaves that grow along the stem or in clusters at the end of the stem. Remember, cactuses do not have leaves."[12] So, a yucca plant is not a considered a cactus.

Sometimes, the entire goal of your presentation is to explain the definition of a concept or term. If this is the case, use a topical organizational pattern utilizing all three of the steps for elucidating explanations. For example, if the entire goal of your presentation is to explain to your audience exactly what is and what is not considered climate, you would simply use a topical pattern.

Other times, explaining a concept or definition may be a smaller part of a larger topic or purpose. Imagine that you have been asked to address a problem with pests in your garden club. As part of this presentation, it might be important to differentiate the difference between venomous and poisonous species. This differentiation would probably be a small piece of a larger presentation, so just weave in the three steps of an elucidating explanation into your larger presentation. The larger presentation topic, in this case, garden pests, should dictate the pattern of organization.

Understanding Complex Structures or Processes

Sometimes, what makes a particular topic difficult is the structure, processes inherent in the topic, or the shear quantity of information on the topic. Because of these difficulties, it becomes problematic for an audience to see the big picture. An audience may have a problem understanding the scientific method, the carbon budget, the process of viral marketing, or the history of hashtags. In each of previous examples, audience members struggle to envision the processes or structures that accompany these topics.

Even when the topic is straight forward, the amount of material can be overwhelming. Imagine how all the pieces of a college curriculum fit together. Imagine having to deliver a presentation on the required freshman curriculum, general education requirements, and requirements for graduation to a crowd of college freshman. This is a lot of information to process, and it is difficult to keep track of all the moving parts for the audience.

Complex structures or processes can best be explained using **quasi-scientific explanations.** Effective quasi-scientific explanations have two important characteristics: First, they help audiences attune to important features of the message. Second, they help organize the information so that audiences see relationships in the material and keep track of it. Simple devices you can use to achieve solid quasi-scientific explanations include organizing analogies, visual aids, clear organizational structure, repetition, and transitions.

> Complex structures or processes can best be explained using quasi-scientific explanations.

Analogies and metaphors are good ways to organize the information for your audience. Organizing analogies take your material and relate it to something with which the audience is already familiar. Ongoing research programs in various disciplines from science to marketing have indicated that individuals understand unfamiliar concepts better when the material is presented through the use of an analogy or metaphor.[13]

Choose familiar objects or actions for the analogy. The audience must be able to make an immediate comparison and connection without needing additional information or explanation.[14] The analogy should also be short and simple.

In a recent issue of *Popular Science,* the author of an article about the human brain used this analogy so that audiences could understand the amount of electricity circulating throughout the brain.

"Every single neuron contains about 0.07 volts of electricity. A human boasts 86 billion of those stimulating little cells, which puts the charge inside your head at about 6 billion volts. That's like having 477,777,777 car batteries hooked up to your noggin."

The initial sentence that described the volts in a single neuron didn't mean much. But once the example was multiplied by the amount of neurons in our brain and then compared to 400 million plus car batteries, it had much more meaning. This example demonstrates how powerful an analogy or metaphor can be.

It is important to tailor the comparisons and metaphors for your audience. If your audience isn't familiar with knitting, for example, using a knitting analogy to explain a concept won't be very effective.[15] Know your audience so you know what will work for them.

Diagramming the process or topic for your audience is another tool that you might find useful. Diagrams, charts, and visual representations aid audiences in processing information. Visual aids become particularly important with quasi-scientific explanations and are absolutely necessary. Whether the difficulty results from the amount of information or the relationships between the information, visual representations help the audience organize the material and see relationships. See Chapter 9 for assistance for creating an effective visual aid.

Having a clear organizational structure is another tool you have to explain your information. Be systematic when choosing an organizational pattern. Think about why you are choosing that structure. Be ready to answer the question, "How does this pattern make my material more clear?" Don't choose a topical pattern just because it is easy. Really think about what you are trying to convey and examine other patterns that help your audience see how parts of the whole fit together.

Repetition is the fourth important device in a quasi-scientific explanation. As explained throughout this text, audiences do not have the luxury of going back to hear what you said previously like they do when reading a text. Remind them of what you told them. They will appreciate it, and it increases the likelihood that your explanation will be effective and that your audience will retain it.

> **Effective Quasi-Scientific Explanations**
> - Use metaphors and analogies.
> - Use a clear organizational structure.
> - Use visual aids.
> - Use repetition.
> - Use transitions.

The final device is the transition. Transitions are essential in quasi-scientific explanations. Although they are important in any presentation, quasi-scientific presentations require you to use transitions more frequently and thoughtfully. Although we discussed transitions in Chapter 6, it is important that we go into more detail here.

Linking transitions are the tools that link ideas and concepts together for your audience. They signal to the audience where you have been and where you are going. Assume that you are delivering a presentation on an effective graduate school application. The presentation has three main points or parts: GREs, writing samples, and letters of recommendations. The following linking transition signals to the audience that you are leaving main point number one and moving to main point number two. "GREs are not the only important aspect to a graduate school application; the writing sample is also extremely important."

Signposts help your audience focus on the elements that are most important to the presentation and let your audience know exactly where they are in the presentation. Signposts can include the following: in conclusion, to begin, the most important part, first, second, or third. There are many other types of signposts but these give you an idea.

Internal summaries and internal previews help with repetition. These provide a summary or preview in the middle of your presentation. While it is important to preview your main points or primary ideas before you begin your presentation and review them at the end, you may need to provide these summaries/previews during the body of your presentation as well. This is particularly important when the material is dense.

Research shows that when the types of devices just discussed (organizing analogies, strong organization, visual aids, repetition, and transitions) are used, audience members are better able to envision the processes discussed, and their problem-solving abilities regarding the material are improved.[16] All of these strategies are necessary in an effective quasi-scientific presentation.

Hard-to-Believe Phenomena

Occasionally, a topic is difficult for an audience to understand because the theories or ideas that encompass that topic are hard for an audience to believe. The difficulty with the material isn't related to any particular term or a complex collection of information, but rather, the idea itself is counterintuitive to particular audiences and other ideas they hold.

People develop lay theories around events and experiences that are familiar to them. They do not develop lay theories around phenomena that do not hold personal importance. Thus, people do not hold lay theories about new findings regarding nanotechnology or mathematical Knot Theory. They do hold lay theories about household safety, disease management, and nutrition.[17]

Effective Transformative Explanations
- State the lay theory.
- Acknowledge the reasonableness of the lay theory.
- Show limitations with the lay theory.
- Explain the scientific theory or positions.

Lay audiences struggle to understand how Earth can be weightless or why getting a chill doesn't cause a cold. With each of these ideas, we have developed lay theories that we use to explain our world. Some of these theories are passed down from generation to generation, so they are deeply ingrained. In many cases, these lay theories are wrong. In fact, these nonscientific or lay theories are the source of our confusion and often lead to dangerous consequences. For example, many people believe that if you get the flu shot, it can cause you to get the flu.

If you believe the material you are presenting to your audience is hard to understand due to some preconceived notion or lay theory the audience holds, you will want to use a **transformative explanation.**

An effective transformative explanation contains four elements. First, the explanation should contain a statement of the lay theory to which the audience currently subscribes. Second, the strengths and reasonableness of the lay theory should be acknowledged in the explanation. Third, transformative presentations create dissatisfaction with the current lay theory by explaining its weaknesses. Finally, present the scientific explanation and provide a justification as to why it better explains the phenomenon in question.[18]

Give audience members credit. They have no reason to give up their beliefs until another theory proves otherwise. That is your job in a transformative explanation. Below, each of the steps in an effective transformative explanation is further explained along with an illustrative example on leprosy. According to the CDC there are many myths surrounding this disease.[18]

1. **State the lay theory.** Present the lay theory that the audience holds or currently believes to be true. For illustration purposes,[19] we use the belief that some individuals hold that you can get the flu from the flu shot. At step one, you simply state what the audience currently believes about the flu vaccine.
2. **Acknowledge the reasonableness of the lay view.** In this step, you want to show that the current view does have some merit for explaining the situation. You don't want to offend audience members by attacking their current beliefs, explain why their current views are plausible. You might say,

many people get the flu or flu like symptoms after getting the vaccine, so it is easy to see why people believe that the vaccine actually causes the flu.

3. **Show dissatisfaction with the current view.** Here you want to show audience members what is wrong with their current view. For example, you might state, "according to the CDC there are two types of flu shots. One vaccine uses inactivated viruses that are not infectious and the other type of vaccine has no flu virus in it at all. This second type of vaccine is commonly called the recombinant flu vaccine. So, the vaccine can't be causing the flu." In this way, you point out problems with the nonscientific or lay view.

4. **Explain the scientific theory or position.** In this step, you lay out the true explanation for audience members and provide them with the evidence that will help them accept the less conventional notion. Continuing with our example, "When people believe they have the flu after getting the vaccine, there are typically four things that could be going on. First, some people get sick with other respiratory infections that aren't related to the flu virus at all. They simply think they have the flu. Second, the flu vaccine takes two weeks to provide protection from the virus so some people get exposed to it before they get the vaccine or during the unprotected period. Other people catch a strain of flu virus that the vaccine cannot prevent. And still other people get the flu because the vaccine is never 100 percent effective. So, while the vaccine may not cause the flu it may not prevent someone from getting it either."[19] By providing audience members with this information, you increased their awareness about the flu shot and its possible side-effects.

One important factor related to transformative explanations is that the steps do not have to be presented in order within your presentation. As long as all four steps are present and adequate, your presentation will be effective. Each of the steps can serve as a main point.

Chapter Summary

The one thing all of these presentations have in common is that they communicate new or novel information to an audience. If there is nothing new in your presentation, it may not be necessary. So make sure you do your homework in relation to what your audience already knows to ensure you are actually presenting new information.

Informative speaking is a vital skill for you to develop. As this chapter has demonstrated, informative speaking is just as important and can be just as challenging for the speaker as persuasive speaking is. Informative speaking includes speeches of awareness, speeches of demonstration, and speeches of explanation. Each of these types of presentations contains its own set of challenges, and this chapter presented recommendations for overcoming those challenges.

References

[1] Schneider, M. 2017. "Most-Watched Television Network Rankings of 2017 Winners and Losers." *IndieWire*. http://www.indiewire.com/2017/12/highest-network-ratings-2017-most-watched-hbo-cbs-espn-fx-msnbc-fox-news-1201911363/.

[2] Farkas, D. K. 1999. "The Logic and Rhetorical Construction of Procedural Discourse." *Technical Communication* 46(1): 42–54.

[3] Van der Meij, H. 1995. "Principles and Heuristics for Designing Minimalist Instruction." *Technical Communication* 42(2): 243–261.

[4] Van der Meij.

[5] Rowan, K. E. (2003). "Informing and Explaining Skills: Theory and Research on Informative Communication." In O. J. Greene & B. R. Burleson (Eds.), *Handbook of Communication and Social Interaction Skills*. Mahwah, NJ: Lawrence Erlbaum Associates Publishers.

6   O'Neil-Hart, C. 2017. "Why You Should Lean Into How-To Content in 2018." *Think with Google*. https://www.thinkwithgoogle.com/advertising-channels/video/self-directed-learning-youtube/.

7   Carroll, A., and R. Vreeman. 2009. *Don't Swallow Your Gum!* New York: St. Martin's.

8   "What's the Difference Between Weather and Climate? 2015. *NASA*. https://www.nasa.gov/mission_pages/noaa-n/climate/climate_weather.html.

9   "What Is the Difference Between Weather and Climate?" National Oceanic and Atmospheric Administration U.S. Department of Commerce. Accessed February 5, 2018. https://oceanservice.noaa.gov/facts/weather_climate.html.

10 "Cactus." n.d. Retrieved from http://eduscapes.com/nature/cactus/index1.htm

11 Rowan, K. E. 1990. "The Speech to Explain Difficult Ideas." *Communication Teacher* 4(4): 2–3.

12 "Cacti or Not? Many Succulents Look Like Cacti, but Are Not." *CactiGuide.com*. Accessed February 5, 2018. http://cactiguide.com/cactiornot/.

13 Thagard, P. 1992. "Analogy, Explanation, and Education." *Journal of Research in Science Teaching* 29(6): 537–544. doi: 10.1002/tea.3660290603.

14 D"Arcy, J. 1999. "Bridging the Knowledge Gap." *Security Management* 43(7): 31–34.

15 Sullivan, C., and C. M. Smith. 2006. "5 Tips for Writing Popular Science: Learn the Art of Conveying Complexity to the General Reader." *Writer* 119(7): 23–25; Rowan, K. E. 2003. "Informing and Explaining Skills: Theory and Research on Informative Communication." In J. O. Greene & B. R. Burleson (Eds.), *Handbook of Communication and Social Interaction Skills*, 403–438. Mahwah, NJ: Lawrence Erlbaum Associates Publishers.

16 Rowan, K. E. 1992. "Strategies for Enhancing the Comprehension of Science." In B. V. Lewenstein (Ed.), *When Science Meets the Public*, 131–143. Washington, DC: American Association for the Advancement of Science.

17 Rowan, K. E. 2003. "Informing and Explaining Skills: Theory and Research on Informative Communication." In J. O. Greene & B. R. Burleson (Eds.), *Handbook of Communication and Social Interaction Skills*, 403–438. Mahwah, NJ: Lawrence Erlbaum Associates Publishers.

18 Rowan.

19 CDC. 2018. "World Leprosy Day." Centers for Disease Control and Prevention, January 26, 2018. https://www.cdc.gov/features/world-leprosy-day/index.html.

Chapter 9

Visual Communication

Objectives

After this chapter you will be able to:

- Apply assumptions from learning theory to create effective visual aids.
- Understand the elements of effective visual aids.
- Apply the Assertion–Evidence Method of slide creation.
- Apply ethical practices to the development of visual aids.
- Present effectively using visual aids.

We often hear about global warming in the media and the impact it will have on our environment. We hear stories of how our coastlines will change, how the weather will become extreme, and how all of this warming will affect wildlife and agriculture. Regardless of where you stand on this issue, the changes that might occur seem sort of abstract. How will these changes actually materialize? It's hard to imagine what these changes will look like and just what kind of impact global warming will have.

In early winter of 2017, a photo hit social media that provided a window into this possible future. A National Geographic photographer, Paul Nicklen, posted a picture of an emaciated polar bear to Instagram and that post went viral.[1] The world had heard about the plight of the polar bear due to melting sea ice, but this picture made it real. Through this post, a global audience could see, first hand, what it looked like for a polar bear to be trapped with no source of food. They could see the emaciation, the boney frame, and the despair in the bear's eyes as it searched for food. The photographer said he wanted "to make a scientific data point something real"[2] and this picture did just that.

The photo allowed the world to see, firsthand, what climate change means for wildlife. The audience was able to empathize with the bear and other creatures that may be impacted by a warming climate. The story of this polar bear would not have been so impactful if the audience had not also been presented with the photograph. The old adage, "a picture is worth a thousand words" was definitely true in this case. It made many people engage in a conversation about global warming and its impact.

The story, however, doesn't end here. Many critics joined the discussion to argue that the photographer didn't know the reasons for the bear's demise. It could have been starving due to disease or its age. Others called the picture a public relations ploy and argued that the photographer behaved unethically by posting this picture while implying that it could be due to global warming. A single bear and its story is simply not enough evidence to make any type of conclusion.[3]

What do you think about the picture and the context in which it was framed? Was it ethical for the photographer to use the image in the way that he did?

Let's Talk

1. What do you think about the photo used by Paul Nicklen in the example above? In your mind, was it moving? Did it make an abstract idea more concrete for you?
2. Some people found the graphic and accompanying video disturbing. Some critics felt that it was too sad and aroused too many negative emotions? Do you agree or disagree? Where is the line on using graphics that illicit emotion?
3. Do you think it was ethical for the photographer to post the video and make the possible link to global warming? Why or why not?
4. Can you think of a visual aid that you have seen presented in the media, in a class, or in a presentation that was impactful?

Introduction

There will be moments in your own presentations, where you will want to make an abstract idea come to life for your audience. You will want to **show** an audience something rather than just **tell** them about it. This may happen through a picture like the example just discussed, or it could be illustrated in a graph, in a table, or with a model. Using visual aids during a presentation can have a big impact if they are used well. This chapter will examine different types of visual aids and discuss methods for creating and utilizing them effectively.

Cognitive Theory of Multimedia Learning

Before we can begin to discuss how to develop and use a visual aid, it is helpful to think about how we learn information. One theory that can shed some light on this topic is the Cognitive Theory of Multimedia Learning. This theory claims that we learn more effectively through words and pictures or visuals. Words alone are not as effective as words and visuals used together.

However, it isn't as simple as that. We can't just add a series of visuals to our presentations and hope that we will be more effective. There are three underlying principles that support this theory and should guide visual aid construction. First, people have two channels that they can access when processing information. One of these channels is for processing verbal or auditory messages, and the other is for processing visual messages. Second, each of these channels is limited in its capacity.[4] This means that these channels can be overloaded if we simultaneously present too much information in one or both of these channels. Third, we process information in an active way. Meaning that we select, filter, and organize new information in relation to information we already know.

So according to the Cognitive Theory of Multimedia Learning, when we attend to a presentation, there are five things that happen as we process the information:[5]

1. We **select** relevant words for processing
2. We **select** relevant images for processing
3. We **organize** selected words into a verbal model
4. We **organize** selected images into a pictorial model
5. We **integrate** these verbal and pictorial models with each other and our prior knowledge.

Because we are limited in our processing capacity, it is important that we think about this process as we design our presentations and think about ways that we could lighten the cognitive load for our audience. The process of selecting, organizing, and integrating is complex. In addition, many of our audience members are listening to our speech in a second language that is not their native or first language. This challenge adds even more complexity to processing. Plus, the information that many of us are addressing in our presentations is complex in nature—again adding to the cognitive load. Attention to load becomes extremely important when we think about designing visual aids. So, how can we design and present visual aids in ways that make it easier for our audience to process our main ideas? The following section provides some key guidelines for designing visuals that will have the most impact.

General Guidelines for Designing Effective Visuals

Keeping in mind what we have learned about the Cognitive Theory of Multimedia Learning, we can use the following guidelines to help create effective visuals.[6]

Regardless, of what you are developing (i.e., chart, graph, model, picture, etc.) the following guidelines should be utilized to produce the most effective graphics that audiences can easily process.

1. Never divide your audience's attention. Don't combine a lot of text and a graph or image on a single slide. This overloads the visual channel and makes processing difficult for your audience. Present the graph or image and explain it with a verbal narration.

2. Visuals should be simplified. Eliminate any interesting but extraneous material in your graphic. This means that pre-made graphs and charts published in research articles aren't good choices for visuals. These are too small and usually have too much information and text on them to be effective in an oral presentation. It is easy to take the data and create a new table or graph that is easier for your audience to read and process.
3. Signaling is highlighting key parts of a chart, visual, or model for your audience. Research shows that highlighting important aspects of a visual with color, arrows, or any other type of marker helps your audience focus on the important details that are vital to understanding your message. This prevents a graphical element from overwhelming your audience.[7]
4. Graphics and brief explanatory text should not be separated. Although text should be limited, if it necessary to explain part of a visual, make sure it is close to the element it describes.
5. Divide your information when possible. Don't put everything in one chart or on one slide. Audiences are better able to process your information when it is presented in small pieces.
6. Explain your visuals as you present them to your audience. Sometime speakers rely on the visual to communicate everything. It is easier for the audience to process any visual aid, if the speaker adequately explains it while it is presented.

Before we start to apply these findings from the theory, it is important to note that visuals aren't always necessary in a presentation. As a speaker, it is extremely important that you consider where you need extra support in the form of a visual aid. If you don't need it, don't use it. Presentation aids are hard to construct well, and it takes practice to deliver a presentation effectively with visuals. So, don't use gratuitous visuals. If they enhance your message, provide a sense of vividness that you couldn't achieve with words alone, and/or help your audience understand better, use them. If they don't, leave them out.

Creating Effective Slides

Most likely you will be expected to develop presentation slides for talks or speeches you deliver. Slides are the most common type of presentation aid used because software has made them so easy to produce. Because they are the most popular, they are also the most misused. There are two primary problems with presentation slides that are produced from software like PowerPoint and Keynote. First, many people throw text on slides and simply use these slides as their speaking outline and claim they use presentational aids. However, as you have read earlier in this chapter, a text heavy slide is not effective and can actually impede learning and cognitive processing for your audience because the audience reads the slide instead of listening to the speaker. The slide in Figure 1 overwhelms the audience with text.

Figure 1

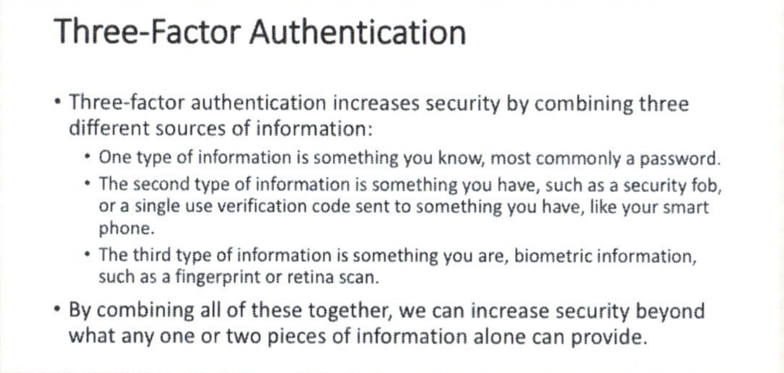

Three-Factor Authentication

- Three-factor authentication increases security by combining three different sources of information:
    - One type of information is something you know, most commonly a password.
    - The second type of information is something you have, such as a security fob, or a single use verification code sent to something you have, like your smart phone.
    - The third type of information is something you are, biometric information, such as a fingerprint or retina scan.
- By combining all of these together, we can increase security beyond what any one or two pieces of information alone can provide.

This slide has a phrase headline instead of an assertion/sentence, and it has too much text. Slide software programs encourage this type of slide. So, it is important to think about what you are putting on the slide. Don't fall prey to a template.

A second issue with these slides comes from the software that we use to create them. PowerPoint and Keynote have been criticized heavily for their reliance on templates.[8] These templates tend to use headers and bullet points to organize and guide the layout of material. The relationship between the ideas on the slide is not clear when bullet points are used. What you have is just a list of ideas, terms, etc. The audience can't see how pieces fit together. This is extremely important when audiences are learning material for the first time. As the Cognitive Theory of Multimedia Learning explains, we are always trying to integrate new material we have just learned with our existing knowledge. If these relationships aren't made clear to us, it becomes more difficult. See the example slide in Figure 2. The bullet list simply provides a list, but the audience can't tell how these items fit together.

> The relationship between the ideas on a slide is not clear when bullet points are used.

Figure 2

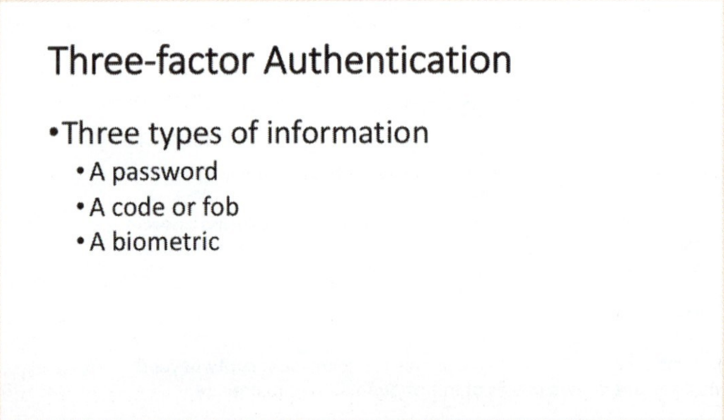

Three-factor Authentication

- Three types of information
  - A password
  - A code or fob
  - A biometric

This slide uses the bullet template and it fails to describe the relationship between these ideas. In addition, the phrase headline does little to explain the point of the visual aid.

In order to avoid some of the problems associated with the default templates provided by popular software packages, we advocate using the Assertion–Evidence Method for building slides. This style of building slides was first used by managers at the Lawrence Livermore National Labs.[9] They rolled out this method at an industry conference and blew everyone away, and others in their industry soon adopted the method. It is now the design structure of choice in STEM industries and has utility in other areas as well.

The Assertion–Evidence Method asks the speaker to use visual evidence along with a full sentence headline to tell their story. That is the key thing to remember as you begin to use this method.

The Assertion–Evidence Method

As an overview, the Assertion–Evidence Model begins with a single sentence headline with no more than two lines at the top left of the slide. This headline makes an argument, assertion, or key insight in the presentation. The bottom of the slide follows up with visual evidence to support that headline. This visual evidence can be a photo, drawing, diagram, chart, graph, film, equation, or table. Figure 3 provides an example of the Assertion–Evidence Method that this book advocates. It improves upon the slides shown in Figure 1 and Figure 2 by simplifying the language, making a statement about the topic, and providing visual evidence that supports the headline. The following sections cover the specifics of how to create a headline and the corresponding visual evidence.

The Headline

The headline is a complete thought or assertion about a point in your presentation. It is not a phrase, and it is written as a full sentence. It is also a declarative statement and cannot be written as a question. The headline identifies an insight, a feature, or a result that the visual then supports. The slide just gets you started. It is up to the speaker to add the rest of the story in their narration or speech. The method advocates simplicity. Slides should only contain what is essential while the speaker fills in the detail with their verbal message.

The Assertion–Evidence Model recommends that the headline be no longer than two lines. Research on this method has found that when text is more than two lines, more than half the people in a room fail to read all of it. However, most of the people in the room report reading the lines when they are only one or two lines long.[10] Typically, headlines should use 28 point font. PowerPoint headers use 44 point font. You will find it difficult to write a meaningful headline that is only two lines with font this large. Twenty-eight point font is usually large enough the see from the back of the room.[11] The font, Calibri, is highly recommended by technical artists for use on headlines. It is narrow and allows more blank space along its edges making it easier for audiences to read. If you prefer to use a different font, just remember that it should be sans serif.[12] This is a font without feet or curls at the bottom. Sans serif fonts are easier for an audience to read.

Place the headline in the left corner of the slide. People from western countries read from left to right, and eye tracking software indicates that they usually begin at the left when reading slides, webpages, etc. PowerPoint typically centers headers which slows an audience down. As a speaker, you want to make everything as easy on your audience as possible so that they can focus on your message.

Headlines in all capital letters are more difficult for audiences to read. Title case headlines (This Study Indicated ...) also slow audience reading time and take up valuable space. Capital letters take up to 35 percent more horizontal space. This will make it harder for you to fit your headline on two lines. Use sentence case for the headline (This study indicated ...). It's the easiest to read and provides the most real estate for your headline.[13]

Figure 3

This slide demonstrates the Assertion–Evidence Method for building slides. This slide makes an assertion and has visual support. You can also see how it improves on the previous two slides.

The Visual Support

Once you have decided on a headline, it's time to consider your visual support. As mentioned earlier, the visual support to your headline can take the form of photos, diagrams, movie clips, equations, charts, graphs, or tables. You can be as creative as you want in terms of using visual support.[14] In the section that follows, we cover a few things to consider when designing your visual.

Photos

As the opening example indicated, photos can have a big impact on a presentation. They can elicit emotion from an audience and be instrumental in telling a story. However, the photo should be important to telling your story. It shouldn't be just for decoration or entertainment. The photo should have a purpose in advancing your message.

When choosing photos, make sure they are high resolution and easy for the audience to see. Remember, they will be displayed by a projector that is much lower in resolution. Check the quality of the photo as well. Photos that are too light or too dark can't be seen well by your audience, and a projector may exacerbate these issues.

Be ethical in your use of photos by providing citations and giving credit to the photographer who took them. While it is fine to enhance your image with editing tools for quality, it is not ok to edit a photo to show something that didn't really happen. Make sure that your photo really depicts what you are claiming it depicts.

Don't settle on the first picture you find. Keep looking until you discover the right one that enhances your message. Sometimes we get lazy when looking for visuals for our slides. Your visual is as important as your verbal message, so don't underestimate the importance of your slides. Make sure you have the right photo to make the point you hope to make.

Never use a photo with a distracting watermark. Watermarks are there to protect the owner of the photo from copyright infringements. Even for a classroom presentation, you should not display a photo with a watermark. It is unethical to use someone's property without paying for it. You can search Google Images with advanced features to locate copyright free images. There are also many sites that provide free photos for use; see the box below for other places where you can find free images.

Sites for Free Images
The following websites provide access to copyright free images:
- Creative Commons—this site provides all types of creative content, including pictures, music, and film.
  - https://creativecommons.org/use-remix/pi
- Pixabay provides access to images.
  - https://pixabay.com/
- StockSnap
  - https://stocksnap.io/
- Pexels
  - https://www.pexels.com/

As a rule, stay away from clip art. It usually appears unprofessional. Sometimes, it can be funny or clever, but it never enhances your credibility as a speaker. Unless clip art is directly associated with your topic, don't use it.

Creating Graphs and Charts

Many times, a chart or graph is the only way to present data to your audience. It seems like they should be easy for us to use, but they aren't as easy to implement well in a presentation as it seems. One issue to consider is that the charts and graphs you find in written documents and on webpages are usually too detailed to be useful for a presentation. They were designed for a medium that allowed the reader ample time to absorb details of the graphic's message. Once they are projected on the screen, the details become too small for your audience to read. As a general rule, do not use graphs and charts that have been produced by someone else in your presentations. By taking the time to create them yourself, you can make sure that they communicate the message you want your audience to receive. You can implement good signaling and make sure that they are easy for your audience to process during your presentation.

A thorough tutorial on building effective charts and graphs is beyond the scope of this book. The following sections discuss the appropriate tools for telling specific types of stories using graphs or charts.

Graphing Trends

When the story you want to tell your audience evolves over time, you will want to use a line chart or graph. These types of charts are good at describing trends demonstrating how things changed or did not change over a specific time period. The line graph is the most basic tool for describing trends over a specific time period.

The major mistake that most people make when constructing a line graph is using too many lines. You end up with something that looks like spaghetti. It becomes hard for an audience to tease them apart when they are listening to a presentation. A good rule for line charts is to leave it to four lines. Anymore than that and things get crazy and hard to interpret when projected.[15]

Audiences from Western cultures tend to see lines that go up as positive and lines that go down as negative.[16] This is especially true when you have been talking about upward trends and then there is data with a negative slope. Negative slopes or trends aren't always bad. Think about losing weight. Losing weight in reference to a new diet regime isn't negative; it's positive even though the trend line goes in the opposite direction or is negatively sloped. Some data visualization researchers suggest flipping your variable in this case.[17] Instead of graphing weight, track pounds lost and your line will actually go up and be positive. This is positive association and is sometimes more comfortable for audiences and easier to process quickly. Figure 4 and Figure 5 demonstrate this idea and show how you can easily flip the data to be more aligned with the audiences' expectations.

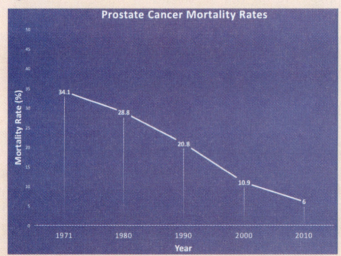

Figure 4

This slide shows a negative trend that the audience may associate with negative or bad outcomes. Even though this data is positive, the slope of the line may indicate otherwise for them.

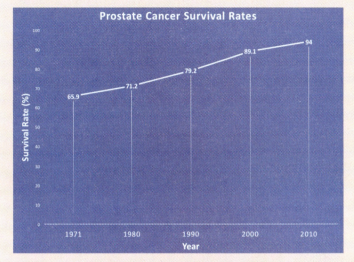

This slide takes the same data as in Figure 4 but states it in terms that can be displayed using a positively sloped graph. So, instead of showing deaths going down, it shows survival rates going up.

Graphing Parts of a Whole

If the story your data tells is parts of a whole, there are many different ways you may choose to chart this for your audience. Let's start with the most simple, pie charts. **Pie charts** demonstrate part of a whole and describe how that whole breaks out. So, you may look at a freshman class and then break down that whole by major. Maybe the freshman class has four different majors. When you have a small number of groups within a whole, a pie chart is an acceptable way to demonstrate that story. However, people can't estimate very well past four segments. Once a group has more than four subdivisions, the pie chart isn't very accurate at depicting those relationships. That is because, we aren't very good at judging angles. So, you end up with multiple segments that have to be labeled in order for an audience to get the sense of what the data means. Some data display experts argue what's the point of the graph if it has to be so heavily labeled? It might as well be a table at that point.[18] Experts assert that if you have more than four segments in a pie chart, you should use a stacked bar chart instead. The bottom line is this; if you can pull something meaningful out of your pie chart without labels, use it. If not, consider something else.

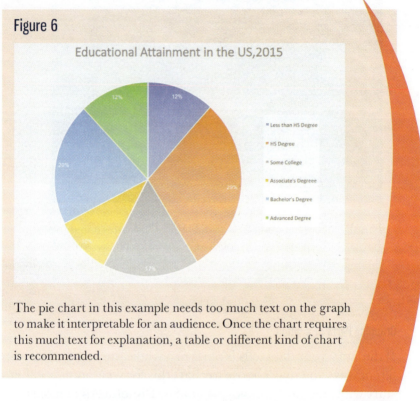

Figure 6

The pie chart in this example needs too much text on the graph to make it interpretable for an audience. Once the chart requires this much text for explanation, a table or different kind of chart is recommended.

A **bar chart** is a good substitute for a pie chart if you have too much data or segments.

People can compare lengths better than angles, so stacked bar charts are better ways for audiences to visualize your data.[19] The drawback is that people fail to recognize that they are part of a whole. You can demonstrate this with a simple trick in Excel where you switch columns and rows to arrive at a chart that uses the block or rectangle as a whole rather than a circle. Then it becomes easier for your audience to visualize how that data makes up the whole.[20] You can actually get around two issues. You address the angle issue with pie charts, and your columns allow an audience to visualize the data as part of a whole. Figure 7 demonstrates this.

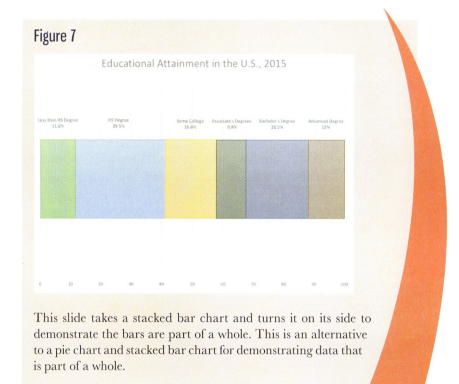

This slide takes a stacked bar chart and turns it on its side to demonstrate the bars are part of a whole. This is an alternative to a pie chart and stacked bar chart for demonstrating data that is part of a whole.

A Heat Map

Another way to tell a story when you are describing parts of a whole is using a map. Geolocation is more and more important in our everyday lives, and it can communicate graphically how trends move across a space. Heat maps are particularly well suited for demonstrating things geospatially. Although you can find heat maps online to use in your presentations, you can build your own, and similar to graphs you make yourself, they are easier for your audience to follow. The benefit is that you can tailor them to your own needs, and they will focus just on the area that is essential to the story your data is telling.

You an actually install an app from Office for Excel, and you can build some simple maps that way. There are easy tutorials all over the internet that can help you build your own heat map. You can also download PowerPoint files of editable maps and use PowerPoint to create pictures of data and demonstrate spatially how it is spread throughout a geographical space. Maybe you want to show how income or education is distributed or how industry is concentrated in a particular region. Using these maps allows you to customize and make a strong visual argument for your audience.

Effectively designing useful charts and graphs is important, but presenting them is just as important. It takes time to let the audience absorb the information in your graphs and charts. Make sure you allow sufficient time to work through graphs and charts and all of their elements in your presentation. There is a reason you choose to include them, so make sure your audience has time to process them.

Video

Sometimes, the only way you can communicate your message is through a video. What is important here is that it works when you pull it up. You don't want to wait for the video or play a commercial. You have many choices on how to upload or embed a video in PowerPoint. Some of these options allow you more control over the video and how it appears in your presentation. If you will not have an internet connection during your presentation, you will want to take a screen capture of the video and upload it that way. There are many tutorials online that can easily teach you how to upload a video to your PowerPoint. Just make sure that it is ready to go when you are, and the method you choose fits your circumstances.

Using Color

Be thoughtful as you think about the colors you want to use on your slides. Use either a dark type against a light background or a light type against a dark background. Color can have different meaning for different cultures. So, it is important to consider this when choosing your palate for your slides. Warm colors such as red, orange, and yellow are unsettling for Western audiences. Blue is a universal color and preferred across many cultures. Other positively rated colors across cultures include green and white.[21] If you are presenting in another part of the world, it is important that you consider the colors used in your presentation and check for cultural meaning and preferences. Once you have selected a color palette, it is important that you ensure it can easily be seen once projected.

Color can be a powerful tool in terms of signaling on a graphic. You can use color to highlight certain aspects of examples.

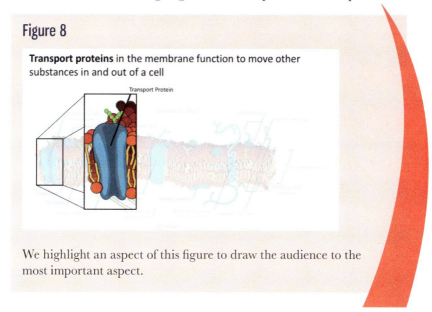

We highlight an aspect of this figure to draw the audience to the most important aspect.

In Figure 8, we highlight an aspect of this figure to draw the audience to the most important aspect. We used a transparency feature to send the rest of the graphic to the background so that the audience only focuses on the essential elements in the visual that we have highlighted. Color can also help audiences follow a pattern and point out important aspects of photos. It can also be instrumental in graphs as it highlights the essential argument that a speaker may want to make.

Templates that use patterns or wild backgrounds should be avoided. These obstruct the audience's view of your graphics and can make your visuals more difficult to interpret. The slide should contain as much free space as possible so that you have plenty of room to design your slide. Slides that use templates with big arrows and stripes waste precious design space. You are better off starting with just a plain slide with a single background color when using the Assertion–Evidence Method.[22]

Leave Room for Your Elements to Breath

It is important that the different elements on your slides have enough room. If they are crowded together, it becomes difficult to read and interpret for the audience. See Figure 11. The image along with the text allows "breathing" room around each element. This makes it easier for the audience to see.

Use Supporting Visual Graphics Ethically

Graphs and charts can easily be manipulated to show exaggerated patterns or relationships. Make sure that your graphs accurately represent the data that you have to share. Sometimes misrepresentation of data is an honest mistake, and sometimes people purposefully manipulate the visualization of data to mislead an audience.

One easy way to mislead an audience is to use the effects that software provides for making charts 3-D. Research shows that we are bad at determining volume. All 3-D effects use volume and that makes it difficult for an audience to evaluate that type of chart.[23] So, avoid using any of the 3-D effects that come with your software packages.

Another way a chart can mislead an audience is not starting the axis with zero. This can make the length on bars deceptive. Look at Figure 9. The difference between the bars of columns on this chart aren't very different, but because the axis does not start at zero, the difference between the two looks exaggerated. Figure 10 displays the data more ethically and accurately.

Visual Communication   Chapter 9

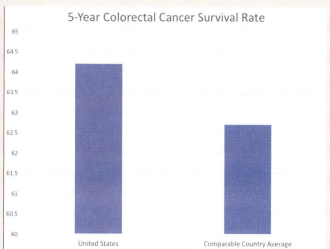

This slide exaggerates the differences between these two bars because the axis does not start at zero.

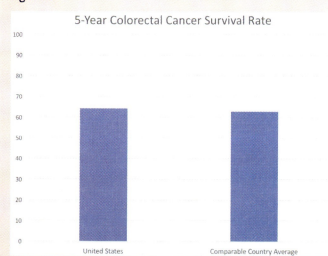

This slide starts at zero and displays the data more accurately.

Presentations That Matter   245

Pictures and graphics can be very emotionally charged. Make sure that you don't go over the top in terms of emotion when using a visual. For example, you can deliver a very emotional presentation on animal rights, whether you are discussing the treatment of horses in racing environments or dogs and the Yulin Dog Festival. However, showing graphic images of these abuses is overwhelming for an audience. Think about a visual and how it might impact an audience before you incorporate it into your presentation. If it arouses too much emotion, it probably isn't ethical to use. Ask friends and family for their feedback before using something that might make your audience extremely uncomfortable.

As discussed above, there are many ways to support your headline visually when constructing a slide remember to keep these tips in mind and you will create a visual aid that will communicate the message that you intend.

Benefits of the Assertion-Evidence Method

As previously mentioned, the Assertion–Evidence Method for slide development has many benefits over the templates that come with popular software. First, the amount of text on your slide will be limited and so you won't be tempted to read your slides to the audience. We learned earlier in the chapter that reading text to an audience impedes the audience's ability to process the information because of the competition between the auditory and visual input systems. This method alleviates this problem.

We know that this method for slide construction increases audience's recall of the material covered on the slide. Your audience will actually remember more of your presentation when you use this method.[24]

There is also evidence to suggest that the Assertion–Evidence Model allows the presenter to gain a better understanding of their own information. So, this format actually helps the presenter see connections between their own material that they otherwise might not have noticed. Being more comfortable with your material will just enhance the overall presentation.[25]

General Guidelines for Presenting Visuals Effectively

Creating effective visuals is one piece of the puzzle, but you must also be effective at presenting with them. The following section provides some tips that can help you use visuals more effectively during your presentation.

They Take Longer to Create Than You Think

Effective visual aids take longer to design and create than you think. They aren't a last minute detail that you can throw together the night before your presentation. Think about what you are tying to communicate. What point should the visual make? Once you have a clear direction, design them following the guidelines discussed above. Create them then get feedback from your friends and colleagues. Find out what areas might need clarification. Finally, test them from the perspective of your audience. If possible, project them in the actual room where you will present them and sit where the audience will be. That way, you can address any details that you might need to sharpen. This process is a long one, so make sure you allow sufficient time to create an outstanding visual aid.

> This process is a long one, so make sure you allow sufficient time to create an outstanding visual aid.

Slow Down When Presenting Graphs and Charts

Take a breath and slightly slow the pace when presenting graphs and charts. It is important that you explain what is on each axis and thoroughly describe the rest of the graph. Slow down your rate of speech and pause as you move through the explanation so that your audience can completely understand the graph and absorb it. It is never a good idea to just flash a graph at your audience. They need time to absorb the material it was designed to present.

Know How to Use Your Clicker

If you use a remote clicker/slide advancer, make sure you are familiar with how it works before you begin your presentation. It is usually better to use your own so that you can practice in advance. However, you may face a situation where you need to borrow one from someone. Make sure you figure out how it works before the presentation begins. If you yell out during the presentation with something like, "How do you work this thing?," it will detract from your credibility.

Present the Visual Only When Discussing It

A presentational aid should only be visible while you are talking about it. Once you move on to another idea, you should blank the screen or remove the item. Presenting a visual of something that you are no longer talking about can be distracting for an audience. They may focus on the visual instead of your talk, and you always want to be the center of attention. The "appear" function in PowerPoint can also help in this regard. With the appear function, you can uncover only part of the slide and build to the conclusion.

Using Video

Video is like any other visual aid. Cite it unless you created it yourself. Make sure that you set the video up for your audience. You never start a video or end a video without an explanation. You want to explain what is coming so they can prepare for it, and you want to explain what they saw and how that fits with the presentation after the video concludes.

Cite Your Visuals

If you use a visual someone else created, you must provide a citation. Put the citation in small font at the bottom of the slide or poster. Sometimes it may be relevant to tell an audience where the visual is from, but you do not need to cite it like you do with other references in the presentation.

Rehearse with Your Visuals

It is harder to deliver a speech and manage your visuals than you think. It takes practice to move through it smoothly. If possible, practice in the venue in which you will speak. Practice using and explaining the visuals. Go out into the audience and see how the visual aid will look once projected. Sometimes they look fantastic on our computer screen, but they look very different once they are projected. Make sure you know what your audience is going to see, so you aren't surprised during the presentation.

You Are the Main Event

Sometimes we forget that we are the main event when delivering a presentation. The audience came to see you, so make sure you are front and center and don't hide behind your visual aid. Look at the audience and make eye contact while you present your visual aid. Don't read slides to them and let the visual simply enhance what you are saying.

Keep these guidelines in mind as you prepare for your presentation as they can help you make an impact on your audience. Delivery is important, and you don't want to lose credibility with your audience just because the presentation of the visuals doesn't go smoothly.

Creating Effective Posters for Poster Presentations

Sometimes the visuals that you are asked to make aren't presented as part of a traditional presentation but are presented in what is called a poster session. If you aren't familiar with poster sessions, they look like something similar to a science fair, but the posters and presentations are usually a bit more polished. A poster presentation combines a narrative, graphics, and an oral presentation.[26] Chapter 13 talks more about the oral aspect of a poster presentation, so we are only going to address the poster and its design in this chapter.

We all think it is pretty easy to throw some ideas up on a poster, but it is actually much more complicated to deliver a great poster. If it is done well, a poster effectively communicates your ideas visually while engaging your audience in a conversation about your ideas or research.[27] Typically, in a poster presentation, there are times when you will not be at your poster to explain it to your audience. So, many times the poster has to speak for itself. That is asking a lot from a single visual.

Although posters are a unique type of presentation, they should still follow the guidelines for effective presentational aids presented at the beginning of this chapter. They should **tell the story** of your research or design project. In the following section, we outline some important things to consider when designing a poster.

Poster Layout

Make sure that the flow of your poster is intuitive for your audience. Most modern languages are read from left to right, so it makes sense that your poster should flow that way. If you are presenting at a conference where the audience will be used to other patterns of movement, provide cues or graphics to direct them through your material, like arrows to guide them through the poster.

Although the abstract is central to the story you are trying to tell, don't use the limited real estate that you have on the poster to post the abstract. If you are part of a conference, abstracts will be posted in the conference program or proceedings. You can also print the abstract on a hand-out that you provide for the audience.

Poster Text

All posters should have a succinct title that communicates the main message of what you are presenting. The rest of the text on the poster should be minimal, and it should be placed close to any corresponding graphic. The font you choose should be easy to read and consistent throughout the poster. Headings should be bold and uniform so that the audience can easily move through your ideas and know exactly where they are in your story. In the following paragraphs, we list the common headers and discuss key strategies for implementing them well.

Sections or Headers on a Poster

Title

The title is very important in a poster session because it will attract your audience to your poster. As people pass posters, they scan titles and choose those that are catchy for closer examination. Your title should also encapsulate the main idea of your presentation. Consider these two titles:

- "The correlation of humidity and diagnosis of joint pain among older adults"
- "No relationship found between rain and joint pain for older adults"

The first title is fine, but it fails to tell the entire story. The second title tells your audience what you studied, among whom, and most importantly, what you found.

Make sure your title tells your entire story in a clear and succinct manner.

The words you choose for your title are important, but how you present them on your poster is equally as important. Your title should be easy to read for your audience. That means it needs to be simple and large enough to read from several feet away. To ensure it is easy to read, begin with a san serif font. This means a font that doesn't have feet or curves at the bottom of the letters. Sans serif fonts are easier for audiences to read at a distance.

Second, use sentence case rather than title case or all CAPS. The sentence case is easiest for audiences to read.[28]

- This is sentence case.
- This is Title Case.
- THIS IS ALL CAPS

Finally, titles should be somewhere between 144 and 256 font points. Test your title out to see if you can see it from two feet away easily.[29]

Introduction/Background

The background provides enough information to situate your project within the larger research landscape and help your audience understand your poster. In a paper, this section is typically several paragraphs. On a poster, it should be four to eight sentences. Use figures and graphics to replace words when you can.

Hypothesis/Research Questions/Goal

This is the element that drives your entire project. So, make sure that you clearly communicate your guiding question on your poster. Sometimes in papers, we have multiple hypotheses or research questions. In the poster, you may decide to cover just one or some of these. Whatever you decide, make sure the hypotheses or questions are clear for your audience.

Methods

The method section tells your audience how you did what you did. This is an important aspect for your audience to understand. Again, it is important to remember that this is not the paper, so you do not need to be as detailed as you are when writing. If there are ideas that you can communicate with graphics, use them in order to keep this section from getting too wordy.

Results

Your research project or study will probably contain more than one result. Be specific about each finding and use graphics, charts, and tables rather than descriptive text to keep this section from becoming overwhelming.

Conclusions

In this section, you succinctly summarize your results, and you will answer the big "so what" questions. Now that we know this, what does that tell us about what you are studying? How do these results change or reinforce what we already knew in this area?

References

If there are key references that guided your research, list them—but do not provide a large list of sources or provide a complete bibliography. Three key references are enough. If you do choose to use some references on your poster, use a smaller font size and consider placing them at the bottom. Remember, there is usually a paper that will accompany a poster, and the bibliography will be presented there. You can also provide a bibliography on any handouts you give at your poster session.

Acknowledgments

If you received help or assistance from anyone to conduct the research or present the poster, it is important that you give credit at the bottom of the poster. If you received funding from some agency or school to conduct your research, make sure you acknowledge them at the bottom of the poster. Sometimes research is conducted as part of a course; acknowledge that and any help you may have received from a faculty mentor. If you had any assistance from others to collect or analyze data, it is important to mention that here as well. As with the references, use a smaller font, and put it at the bottom of the poster.

Poster Graphics

Borders

To help your audience process your poster, it is helpful to place each section in its own box or border. Borders will help your audience distinguish between the various sections. Look at the example in Figure 11. You can easily see each section, and you know exactly where it begins and ends. These visual cues help audiences work through the material and process it more efficiently.

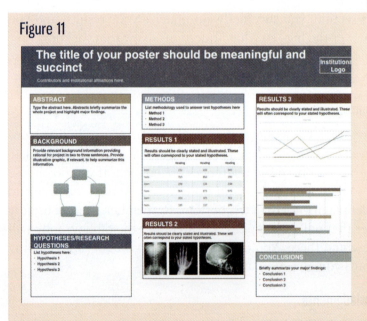

Figure 11

This is an example of a poster with all the headers and sections. Notice how each section has ample room around it to make it standout to the audience.

Surround Your Sections with Free Space

Each section of your poster should be surrounded with "dead space." This means that you give each of your sections space around it to breath. You don't want sections touching each other. This crowds the poster, and it becomes hard for the audience to read.

Glossy vs. Matte Prints

Although glossy paper enhances the color contrast on posters, it is more expensive. It can also be harder to read if there is a glare. Most posters are presented in rooms with overhead lights that aren't too bright, so it should be ok. However, if you are presenting outside on a bright day, the gloss could be problematic. So, consider these choices when printing your poster.

Chapter Summary

This chapter provides some guidelines for creating and using visuals well during your presentations. The Cognitive Theory of Multimedia Learning provides a good set of premises to use for creating visual aids. These guidelines assure that you don't overload the processing capabilities of your audience. If you decide to use a presentation aid in your presentation, it cannot be an afterthought. You need to plan and use the theories outlined in this chapter. The Assertion–Evidence Method can have a big impact on your audience and affect how they process, learn, and remember what you had to say. Regardless of what type of visual aid you use, you must rehearse with it and become comfortable using them during your presentation.

References

[1] Stevens, M. 2017. "Video of Starving Polar Bear 'Rips Your Heart Out of Your Chest.'" *New York Times,* December 11, 2017. https://www.nytimes.com/2017/12/11/world/canada/starving-polar-bear.html?rref=collection%2Ftimestopic%2FPolar%20Bears&action=click&contentCollection=timestopics&region=stream&module=stream_unit&version=latest&contentPlacement=2&pgtype=collection.

[2] Stevens.

[3] Stover, D. 2017. "Yes, That Dying Polar Bear Is Connected to Climate Change." *Bulletin of the Atomic Scientists,* December 18, 2017. https://thebulletin.org/yes-dying-polar-bear-connected-climate-change11363.

[4] Mayer, R. 2015. "Cognitive Theory of Multimedia Learning (Mayer)." *Learning Theories* (blog), September 10, 2015. https://www.learning-theories.com/cognitive-theory-of-multimedia-learning-mayer.html.

[5] Mayer.

[6] Mayer, R., and Moreno, R. 2003. "Nine Ways to Reduce Cognitive Load in Multimedia Learning." *Educational Psychologist* 38(1): 43–52. https://doi.org/10.1207/S15326985EP3801_6.

[7] Mayer and Moreno.

[8] Tufte, E. 2006. *The Cognitive Style of PowerPoint: Pitching out Corrupts Within* (2nd ed.). Cheshire, CONN: Graphics Press LLC.

[9] Alley, M. 2013. *The Craft of Scientific Presentations—Critical Steps to Succeed and Critical Errors to Avoid.* U.S.: Springer. http://www.springer.com/us/book/9781441982780.

[10] Alley, M., M. Schreiber, K. Ramsdell, and J. Muffo. 2006. "How the Design of Headlines in Presentation Slides Affects Audience Retention." *Technical Communication* 53(2): 225–234.

[11] Alley, M. 2013. *The Craft of Scientific Presentations—Critical Steps to Succeed and Critical Errors to Avoid.* U.S.: Springer. http://www.springer.com/us/book/9781441982780.

[12] Alley.

[13] Alley.

[14] Alley.

[15] Evergreen, S. D. H. 2017. *Effective Data Visualization: The Right Chart for the Right Data.* Los Angeles: SAGE Publications.

[16] Evergreen.

[17] Evergreen.

18. Evergreen.
19. Evergreen.
20. Evergreen.
21. Aslam, M. M. 2006. "Are You Selling the Right Colour? A Cross-Cultural Review of Colour as a Marketing Cue." *Journal of Marketing* 12(1): 15–30. doi: 10.1080/13527260500247827.
22. Alley, M. 2013. *The Craft of Scientific Presentations—Critical Steps to Succeed and Critical Errors to Avoid*. U.S.: Springer. http://www.springer.com/us/book/9781441982780.
23. Evergreen, S. D. H. 2017. *Effective Data Visualization: The Right Chart for the Right Data*. Los Angeles: SAGE Publications.
24. Alley, M., M. Schreiber, K. Ramsdell, and J. Muffo. 2006. "How the Design of Headlines in Presentation Slides Affects Audience Retention." *Technical Communication* 53(2): 225–234.
25. Garner, J., and M. Alley. 2016. "Slide Structure Can Influence the Presenter's Understanding of the Presentation's Content." *International Journal of Engineering Education* 32(1): 39–54.
26. Hess, G. R., K. W. Tosney, and L. H. Liegel. 2009. "Creating Effective Poster Presentations: AMEE Guide No. 40." *Medical Teacher* 31(4): 319–21. doi: 10.1080/01421590902825131.
27. Hess, Tosney, and Liegel.
28. Carter, M. 2013. *Designing Science Presentations* (1st ed.). Amsterdam, Netherlands: Elsevier.
29. Carter.

Chapter 10

The Persuasive Process

Objectives

After this chapter you will be able to:

- Define persuasion.
- Identify the three targets of persuasion.
- Explain the psychological process of persuasion.
- Understand the major components of the persuasive theories presented in this chapter.

In September 2017, Congress was hotly debating a new healthcare bill written by Senators Bill Cassidy and Lindsey Graham that would repeal and replace Obamacare. Opponents of the bill frequently pointed to analyses that indicted millions of Americans would lose their insurance coverage, and insurance premiums would rise. Another key issue for both supporters and opponents of the bill was the insurance coverage of individuals with pre-existing conditions. Under the Obamacare law, insurance companies were not allowed to deny coverage or charge higher rates for those with a pre-existing condition such as diabetes or a heart condition. This was a widely popular component of Obamacare, and Graham and Cassidy along with fellow Senators had previously said that they would not take away this protection from any repeal of Obamacare.

A few days before Congress was set to vote on the bill, a strong plea for senators to vote no on the bill came from a surprising place. Instead of delivering his typical monologue at the beginning of his show, late night talk show host Jimmy Kimmel used his time to deliver a harsh critique of the bill and of one of its authors, Senator Cassidy. Jimmy Kimmel's infant son was born with a serious heart defect that required him to have open heart surgery a few hours after his birth, and he will require two additional surgeries as he grows. Fortunately for Kimmel, he had health insurance, but his experience showed him just how important adequate health coverage is. Knowing just how much his son's future medical bills would be, Kimmel recognized the importance of the Obamacare provision that forbid insurance companies from putting life-time spending caps on individuals.

As he spoke, Kimmel referred back to Senator Cassidy's appearance on Kimmel's show the previous spring in which Cassidy told Kimmel that he would never vote for a new healthcare law that took away protections for those with preexisting conditions or put a cap on life-time benefits. Kimmel acknowledged that he was not a policy expert, but he had done a lot of research and investigating to understand what was in the proposed bill. Using facts and research that he had gathered from a variety of sources, he explained that the Graham Cassidy Bill did not, in fact, protect people with pre-existing conditions, and it allowed for life time caps on spending. Cassidy, Kimmel argued, had, in fact, lied and was not pushing for a law *that would protect some of the most vulnerable people in the country. Kimmel explained that children like his son would be hurt by these laws and as adults with a preexisting condition and a long history of high medical bills could be denied coverage.*

Kimmel became very emotional as he told his viewers that his son would be okay even if this bill became law because Kimmel personally had the financial means to pay for his needed medical care. Kimmel told his audience that it was wrong that another child, born to a family without the financial means of the Kimmel family, would not be given the medical care and treatment she needed, only because her family could not pay. A child could be denied lifesaving medical treatment now or in the future because of a medical condition. Kimmel ended his monologue urging senators to vote no and his audience to contact their Senators to let them know they were opposed to the bill.

Let's Talk
1. What was the goal of Jimmy Kimmel's monologue?
2. What was the target of his persuasive appeal?
3. How effective do you think his persuasive message was?

Introduction

Persuasion is the process of influencing someone to change his or her beliefs, opinions, or actions through communication. You engage in persuasion when you try to convince your friends to go the new Italian restaurant for dinner instead of your usual Mexican place. In the work place, people use persuasion to sell products, pitch new ideas to management, ask for a raise, and get coworkers to buy into their ideas. While we are all very familiar with persuasion, as both the persuader and the one being persuaded, you may be less familiar with the specific techniques that can be used to increase the likelihood that your persuasive efforts are successful. In this chapter, we will look at the targets of persuasion, the psychology of persuasion, and the persuasive process.

Targets of Persuasion

Before we discuss the targets of persuasion, it is important to understand that persuasion is a goal-directed activity. In contrast to informative speaking where you are providing information to an audience, persuasive speaking has a goal of enacting some type of change in your audience. Because of the goal of change, persuasive speaking has a higher ethical threshold. When you are trying to change the way a person thinks or acts, you have an obligation to argue your case with truth and facts and to be sure that you are not advocating that someone engage in behavior that could cause harm.

Take, for example, Mark Blaxill, a member of the executive leadership of the nonprofit Health Choice, an organization that aims to raise awareness about natural ways to prevent chronic illnesses. In May of 2017, there was a measles outbreak in Minnesota. Blaxill spoke to a group of concerned parents, many of whom were Somali-American, about the outbreak and urged parents not to vaccinate their children despite the urgings of the public health department. During his presentation, he cited studies that have since been discredited that linked vaccinations to autism. By presenting incorrect and false information to parents who were rightfully concerned about their children's well-being and safety Blaxill was advocating for a position that could actually harm the children, as unvaccinated children were at a much higher risk of contracting measles. Parents who believed what Blaxill was presenting were not really given the opportunity to make an educated decision based on facts and data as they were not given factual information. In this case, Blaxill behaved unethically as a speaker and in the process put children's health at risk.[1]

When you are engaged in persuasive communication, your goal is to influence or change your audience's beliefs, attitudes, or behaviors. **Beliefs** are a person's convictions of what is "true" or "false," When you hear the terms true or false you might think that when it comes to facts, there is no need for persuasion as facts are facts. The reality is that people can interpret facts differently which can lead to different beliefs. Additionally, not all beliefs that people have are rooted in facts and evidence. In the previous example, the speaker, Mark Blaxill, holds a belief that vaccines can cause autism despite evidence to the contrary. Persuasive efforts aimed at changing belief focus on getting the audience to accept or deny that something is true.

Attitudes go beyond a person's belief about the truth of something and are a person's assessment of something as far as it being good or bad or right or wrong. An attitude is a person's evaluation of a thing or idea. In the case of vaccines, a person might have an attitude that vaccines are bad, or that it is wrong to vaccinate children. On the flip side, a person might have an attitude that vaccines are a good thing, or that it is right to vaccinate children.

Behaviors are the actions that a person takes. Of the three targets of persuasion, behavior can be the most difficult to change as behavior requires the most action from a person. It is one thing to have an attitude that regular exercise is a good thing, but it is another thing for a person to actually make the time to go work out. In many professional settings, behavior change is often the goal whether you're a nutritionist trying to persuade clients to change their diets or a salesman trying to get a potential client to choose to do business with your organization.

When you are thinking about persuasion, in addition to thinking about which factor you are targeting, it is also important to consider how a person's beliefs, attitudes, and behaviors are linked. One's beliefs often influence a person's attitudes. In the case of vaccines, a belief that vaccines can cause autism will lead to negative attitudes towards vaccines. In turn, those attitudes will often influence one's behaviors. If people hold negative attitudes towards vaccines, they might opt not to vaccinate their children or to delay vaccination.

In the inverse, one's behavior can also influence attitudes and beliefs. For example, if I join a gym and start to exercise, I may develop more positive attitudes towards exercise as a result of my behavior. I may also develop beliefs about the benefits of exercise if I experience them first hand. Generally, one's beliefs, attitudes, and behaviors are consistent. When they are not consistent, a person experiences **cognitive dissonance.** Cognitive dissonance, a concept identified by psychologist Leo Festinger,[2] is the psychological discomfort one feels when his or her beliefs, attitudes, and behaviors are not consistent.

> Cognitive dissonance is the psychological discomfort one feels when his/her beliefs, attitudes, and behaviors are not consistent.

An example of cognitive dissonance can be found in the practice of using reusable bags rather than plastic bags when you are shopping. You may hold a belief that plastic bags are harmful to the environment because they end up in landfills. You may also hold an attitude that plastic bags are bad and that it is important to take steps to protect the environment and reduce the amount of trash in landfills. When you go to the store, though, you often forget to bring your reusable bags, so you go ahead and use plastic bags. When this happens, you might feel uncomfortable or guilty as your actions are not matching your attitudes about using reusable bags. When a person experiences cognitive dissonance, he or she will work to alleviate his or her discomfort. This can happen in one of two ways. People can change their attitudes or beliefs to be in line with their attitudes, or they can change their behavior. In this case, you may either start to remember to bring your reusable bags, or you might change your attitude about how important using reusable bags really is. In persuasion, highlighting these inconsistencies when they exist can be a powerful way to motivate change.

When you are attempting to persuade someone, it is important to both identify your persuasive goal and the target of your persuasion. It is also important to know what the person or audience's current beliefs, attitudes, and behaviors are. Imagine that you work in finance, and your goal is to get your audience to diversify their investment portfolios. If your audience has negative attitudes towards investment or beliefs that investing money is risky or that the best place to save money is in a traditional savings account, your task of changing their behaviors is going to be difficult. In order to reach your goal, you will have to spend some time during your presentation trying to change their beliefs and attitudes as well before you can get them to take your recommended actions.

The Psychology of Persuasion

Now that we know what persuasion is and what types of things it is trying to change, we will look at the psychology of persuasion and how the brain processes persuasive messages. As you know, not everyone responds to the same persuasive message in the same way, and some messages are more successful than others. Understanding how persuasive messages are processed and acted on can be very helpful in planning a persuasive strategy.

The most important thing to recognize about persuasion is that it is a process. Sometimes the process is relatively short and a change can occur after just one message, but oftentimes, it takes multiple messages over a period of time for change to occur. Generally, the larger the goal of your persuasive efforts, the more extensive your persuasive communication efforts will need to be.

In the early 1950s, a team of researchers at Yale led by Carl Hovland set about studying how attitudes changed. Hovland had worked during World War II on efforts to increase U.S. troop morale through propaganda efforts and wanted to better understand what made some propaganda more effective than others. The initial efforts of the research team focused on three key factors that influence the persuasive process; the source of the message, the message itself, and characteristics of the person or people being persuaded.[3]

Out of the initial work of the Yale team arose the work of William McGuire who was most interested in what factors influenced the reception and rejection of the message by the audience. His research led him to develop the Yale Model of persuasion which describes a six-stage process that message receivers go through in the cases of successful persuasion when the persuasion is aimed to change behaviors.[4] The six steps are outline here:

1. Exposure—The first stage in persuasion is exposure to the message. This is the easiest step as it just requires that the audience hear or see the message. This could involve an audience being present for your sales pitch or seeing a politician's campaign speech on television.
2. Attention—Just because a person is exposed to a message does not mean then he or she does anything more with that message that have it in their presence. The second stage of persuasion is when the audience pays attention to and considers the persuasive message. As we will discuss later, the level of attention receivers give to a message varies, and this level will have a profound influence on the next stage.
3. Comprehension—This is the stage where the receiver processes the message and understands the arguments and the goal of your persuasive message.
4. Acceptance—In the acceptance stage, a stage that McGuire also refers to as the yielding stage, the receiver accepts or agrees with the message.

5. Retention—This stage is when an attitude, belief, or intention and desire to engage in the target behavior remains consistent. In some cases, a person may in the moment agree with a message but over time revert back to their original attitude or belief. The tendency for people to change newly develop attitudes and beliefs is one of the reasons that persuasive messages might be needed to reinforce or strengthen them.
6. Action—The final stage of persuasion is when the message target engages in the desired behavior.

As you can see, it becomes increasingly more difficult to get an audience to each stage in the process. This model also illustrates the link between attitudes and behavior and explains why behavior change is more challenging to achieve than changing attitudes.

While this model is helpful in illustrating the process of persuasion, it does not provide information about what factors move message receivers through each stage. Additional work by psychologist and communication scholars provides more insight into this. After you are able to get an audience to pay attention to your persuasive message, the next critical stage is for that audience to process the message to gain an understanding that allows the receiver to evaluate the message. It can be difficult to get past the attention stage because people are constantly being bombarded with all types of messages. Your audience might sit in the room while you are talking but be distracted by thinking about a previous meeting that went badly or an upcoming project and not be able to pay attention to what you are saying.

Because humans are exposed to so much input, they are frequently unable to fully consider and take in all aspects of a message. Because of this, the brain has developed methods to help people determine how much mental capacity to expend when processing a message. The **Elaboration Likelihood Model (ELM)** is based on the idea that there are two basic ways that people process messages via either the central or the peripheral route. When a person elaborates on a message, the message is processed via the central route. In the central route, a person carefully considers and evaluates the arguments and logical appeals in the message.[5]

In contrast, when a person does not elaborate on a message, the message is processed via the peripheral route. In the peripheral route, instead of carefully considering the logical content of the message, a person relies on heuristic or peripheral cues. **Heuristic cues** are mental short cuts that enable a person to quickly evaluate and make a decision about whether or not to accept or agree with a message. Heuristic cues for a persuasive message might include the appearance of the speaker, the number of arguments, or how much the speaker is liked. The field of advertising relies heavily on heuristic cues and assumes that people will use things like visual images, enjoyable music, or a celebrity endorser to make a decision.

The next question is what would make someone more or less likely to elaborate on a message. The key factor is his or her motivation and involvement with the subject. When the subject is personally relevant or interesting to the receiver, he or she is more likely to engage in central processing. If you are talking to a group of prospective students about why they should attend your university, the topic is very important to them, so they are going to be more motivated to listen to your message and process it centrally.

When the subject is less relevant or the stakes of the issue are not that high, people are more likely to engage in peripheral processing. Messages about which car to buy carry much higher stakes than which brand of gum to purchase. If you are talking to this same group of students and trying to persuade them to follow your university on social media, an action and decision that carries far less weight than where to attend college, they are going to be less motivated to process your message and will likely use the peripheral route. Additionally, people who are distracted, tired, or bored are also more likely to use the peripheral route to process messages, even if the message is personally relevant.

What does the ELM mean for you as a speaker as you prepare and deliver your persuasive messages? As always, it is important to consider your audience. If your topic is something that is relevant and important to your audience, you will want to focus on building the strongest case possible and making sure that all of your evidence and facts are strong. If your topic is less relevant or important to your audience, you will want to think more about what heuristic cues you can include in your message. This is not to say that you should ignore the logical case you are presenting. But, knowing that a lot of your audience may be processing your message using the peripheral route, you will want to be sure that you include elements that will appeal to them. This could include listing your credentials, using impressive looking visual elements, making reference to well-known people who also support your idea, or appearing as a very capable speaker.

When thinking about the psychology of persuasion, another important thing to consider is how big of a change you are asking your audience to make. For many persuasive issues, you can imagine where a person stands on an issue as being on a continuum. Take, for example, the issue of the second amendment and gun rights. At the farthest right on the continuum are those who believe that the second amendment means that there should be absolutely no restrictions on an individual's ability to own and carry a gun. At the complete left of the spectrum are those who believe that the second amendment does not apply to individual rights regarding gun ownership and believe that all guns should be banned. Along the path of that continuum are people with a range of attitudes towards the issue. For example, someone might be a strong supporter of the right for individuals to own guns but support universal background checks while another might be in favor of limiting the types of guns or the number of guns that an individual can own.

A theory that helps to explain the likelihood that a person will accept a persuasive message based on this continuum is **Social Judgement Theory.**[6] Social Judgement Theory was proposed by the team of Sherif, Shefit, and Hovland, a name you might recognize from the earlier discussion of the Yale Model of Persuasion. The basic premise of this theory is that people use their current attitudes as a benchmark to compare all new ideas to. When presented with a message asking them to adopt a new attitude, people consider their current attitude and place the new attitude on the continuum of attitudes based on how close or far away they perceive the new attitude as being from their current attitude.

In the prior example of gun control, imagine that Ryan's attitudes about gun control fall on the mid-right of the continuum. He is a strong supporter of the individual right to bear arms but does believe that there should be universal background checks so that no one can purchase a firearm without one. When presented with an appeal to support a new law that would ban the sale of assault rifles in the United States, Ryan would consider how close or far away this position was from his current stance. It is important to recognize that this placement is personal. While you can make an educated guess of where a position would fall in relation to someone's attitude, it is that person's perception that determines where they place a given position or attitude.

> Every person has a range of what attitudes and ideas are within a range they find acceptable.

Social Judgement Theory also explains how people evaluate how acceptable an idea is based on where it is on their personal continuum. Every person has a range of what attitudes and ideas are within a range they find acceptable. This range is the **latitude of acceptance.** People also have a range of ideas outside of the latitude of acceptance that they find completely unacceptable or unworthy of consideration. This is known as the **latitude of rejection.** There is a third range, which is the attitudes and ideas that a person has not yet considered and has not formulated an opinion on as far as either accepting or rejecting. This is known as the **latitude of noncommittal.**

Within the latitudes of acceptance and rejection, there is a range of ideas from the most acceptable which is where the person currently stands to least acceptable that is still permissible. This may not be a person's ideal, but he or she still agrees that this position or idea is something that could be okay. Similarly, the latitude of rejection is the least acceptable position. In terms of persuasion, if you are arguing for a position that falls in your audience's latitude of rejection, you will have very little chance of success. If you are arguing for a position within the latitude of acceptance, the persuasion is fairly easy as your audience already agrees with you.

So does this mean persuasion is impossible? No. Remember there is a latitude of noncommittal. In terms of persuasion, this is what you could call the sweet spot. Because your audience has not already rejected this idea, they will be at least open to hearing your position without immediately rejecting it. When the minds of your audience are not already made up, you have the opportunity to change your audience's attitude and shift your position into their latitude of acceptance.

Let's look at another example. Imagine that you work in HR for a large telecommunications company. You have proposed that the company implement some type of flex time policy that would allow employees more freedom in setting their work schedules. Some options on the table are allowing employees to set their own working hours as long as 40 hours are logged each week and allowing employees to telecommute from home or another location for up to 20 hours a week. If your supervisor has an attitude that a traditional 9–5 work week is where all employees are on the clock, any proposal that advocates for flexible work schedules each day would be outside his latitude of acceptance and in his latitude of rejection. Perhaps, though, he has not previously considered or taken a position on where employees need to be during designated hours. In this case, a proposal that would allow for telecommuting during traditional office hours would be in his latitude of noncommittal. In this situation, you would put together a persuasive argument that could lead to him adopting your proposed policy.

Another key concept in Social Judgment Theory is **ego involvement.** Ego involvement refers to how important an issue is to a person and his or her life. For example, if you consider Ryan who held positive attitudes related to the right to bear arms, this might be very important to him. He may own several guns or be member of the National Rifle Association (NRA). Because of this, his attitudes about this issue are important to him and central to his self-image. Because of his high-ego involvement with the issue, he is more likely to have strong feelings about all positions on the issue and therefore will have a very small to non-existent latitude of noncommittal, making it much more difficult to persuade him to accept a position outside of his attitude of acceptance.

In contrast, when an issue is less important to a person and less central to his or her identify, there is a low level of ego involvement. In situations like these, people have an attitude or position on the topic but often have not taken the time to consider and evaluate all of the possible positions on the issue. This leads to a larger latitude of noncommittal and more opportunity for successful persuasion. Take for example the issue of self-driving cars. There are some people at either end of the continuum who have strong opinions about whether this is a technology that should be pursed or not and under what circumstance if any they should be allowed. Many people, though, who are less familiar with the technology and the developments that have made self-driving cars more of a reality may not have given a lot of thought to the issue. This leads to a larger latitude of noncommittal and more opportunity to persuade someone in either direction about the issue.

As we think about persuasion being a process, we can look at not just the way that audiences move through the stages or persuasion but also how people move towards the final goal of persuasion. Imagine that a nutritionist is trying to get a client with dangerously high cholesterol levels to adopt a healthier, all natural, vegetarian diet. The client's current diet contains a large amount of red meat and highly processed foods. The client believes that meat is the only effective source of protein and has expressed negative attitudes towards vegetarian diets referring to them as fads and something that women who are into yoga adopt. Given the client's current beliefs and attitudes, moving him to a completely vegetarian diet during the first attempt may not be possible. Instead, the nutritionist could focus on making small changes in his beliefs about the health benefits of different types of food and changing his attitude about a healthier diet. Overtime, as these beliefs and attitudes change, the nutritionist may be able to work towards the ultimate goal of a complete diet change.

When you are thinking about your persuasive goals, you may need to consider the possibility of a long-term approach. If your audience's current stance on this is far from where you desire them to be, you may need to establish smaller persuasive goals. After meeting each smaller goal, you can work to move your audience to change again in your desired direction.

Chapter Summary

Persuasive communication is something that you will frequently engage in whether it is in your personal or professional life. As this chapter described, persuasion is a communicative process in which your goal is to change another's beliefs, attitudes, or behavior. When thinking about persuasion, it is important to consider that the psychological aspects of persuasion and the ways people think about issues influence the likelihood of your persuasive efforts being successful. Persuasive theories can provide powerful tools for crafting effective persuasive messages, so use these when you think about your audiences and what types of information and strategies might be used to persuade them.

Case Study Conclusion

When Jimmy Kimmel urged his audience and Congress to reject the proposed healthcare bill, he targeted attitudes, beliefs and behaviors. His message was very powerful and shared widely on social media because he was able to appeal to a wide variety of audience members. In terms of the success of his appeal, the Graham–Cassidy bill did not pass the Senate, and the protections provided by Obamacare remained intact. We can't say that this one monologue alone accounted for this outcome. However, persuasion is a process, and the more appeals an audience experiences, the more persuasive strength they garner.

References

[1] Adler, E. 2017. "Speaker Says Vaccines and Autism May Be Linked, a View Denied by Public Health Officials." *Star Tribune,* May 2, 2017. http://www.startribune.com/speaker-says-vaccines-and-autism-may-be-linked-a-view-denied-by-public-health-officials/420859653/.

[2] Festinger, A. 1957. *A Theory of Cognitive Dissonance.* Stanford, CA: Stanford University Press.

[3] Demirdöğen, Ü. 2010. "The Roots of Research in (Political) Persuasion: Ethos, Pathos, Logos and the Yale Studies of Persuasive Communications." *International Journal of Social Inquiry,* January 2010. https://www.researchgate.net/publication/268257788_The_Roots_of_Research_in_political_Persuasion_Ethos_Pathos_Logos_and_the_Yale_Studies_of_Persuasive_Communications.

[4] McGuire, W. J. 2000. "Standing on the Shoulders of Ancients: Consumer Research, Persuasion, and Figurative Language." *Journal of Consumer Research* 27(1): 109. http://www.uky.edu/~ngrant/CJT780/readings/Day%205/McGuire2000.pdf.

[5] Cacioppo, J., and R. Petty. 1986. "The Elaboration Likelihood Model of Persuasion." *Advances in Experimental Social Psychology* 19: 124–192. http://www.psy.ohio-state.edu/petty/documents/1986ADVANCESPettyCacioppo.pdf.

[6] Hovland, C., and M. Sherif. 1961. *Social Judgment: Assimilation and Contrast Effects in Communication and Attitude Change.* New Haven, CT: Yale University Press.

Chapter 11

Persuasive Speaking

Objectives

After this chapter you will be able to:

- Distinguish between speeches of fact, value and policy.
- Structure a persuasive presentation using the appropriate organizational pattern.
- Apply tips for using reasoning effectively.
- Understand the role of appeals in persuasive speaking.
- Consider the role of ethics in persuasive speaking.

During his congressional testimony, Dr. Lu, a former astronaut, explains that there are millions of asteroids that orbit around the Earth and that they hit the Earth all the time. He goes on to explain that we aren't aware of it because they are small. Big ones hit the earth about every 100 to 200 years. According to Dr. Lu, most of the world is unpopulated so it is unlikely that one of these big asteroids will hit a densely populated area, but if one did, it would be devastating. In our lifetimes, we can expect a major asteroid to hit earth. He argues, we might get lucky, but there is always the chance that the next big one may hit a populated area, and that would be devastating. Think dinosaurs!

As Dr. Lu's testimony continues, he argues that the technology exists today to stop an asteroid from impacting the earth. With enough notice, he says, it's actually pretty easy to change the course of an asteroid. All you have to do is nudge them with a space craft, and you can actually tow an asteroid. Even a change in their velocity of a millimeter per second will alter their course, thereby, missing the Earth.

In his statement he says the problem here is not that we can't deflect an asteroid. The problem is that we don't know where all the asteroids are. Dr. Lu argues that for every 100 asteroids that exist, we know about one of them. There are a lot of unchartered asteroids out there. If we don't know about them, we can't deflect them.

So, in his appearance before a congressional panel, he makes the argument that we need to start mapping these asteroids in a more systematic way. The problem is that the equipment we need to map them doesn't exist. Building that equipment would cost a fortune, over 300 million dollars to be exact, and no one is willing to pay for it, especially not the government.

He gave this same presentation to many people over the course of several months. Finally, it became clear to him that he should use this talk to persuade people to donate to this mission and raise the money himself. He has been raising money for this spacecraft called Sentinel that will help spot asteroids for several years. He has been extremely successful. Over a period of several years, he has built a foundation called the B612 Foundation, where the Sentinel and other mapping equipment are being designed and implemented.

In a TED Talk, Dr. Lu, tells this entire story of the asteroids and how he began his persuasive quest to convince people to donate to this mission. This is an interesting example of persuasion, and many of the things we will discuss later in this chapter appear in his presentation. Please take a look at his talk by searching for Dr. Lu and TEDexMarion or visiting the following link: https://www.youtube.com/watch?v=KAlF4xxRTwI After watching this presentation, think about the following questions.

> **Let's Talk**
> 1. How did Dr. Lu attempt to persuade the audience? Did he use logic, emotion, or credibility as a persuasive tool?
> 2. Was this a speech of fact, value, or policy?
> 3. Ultimately, how effective do you think his appeal was?

Introduction

We've talked about a lot of persuasive theory in Chapter 10. In this chapter, we will actually put those definitions and theories into practice and see how these components operate in a presentation.

Types of Persuasive Speeches

As mentioned earlier in the text, when you are engaged in persuasive communication, your goal is to influence or change your audience's beliefs, attitudes, or behaviors. Beliefs, attitudes, or behaviors are actually the targets of your persuasive appeal. We can actually define speeches by their target. Speeches that target beliefs are called **speeches of fact.** Speeches that target attitudes are called **speeches of value,** and speeches that target behaviors are called **speeches of policy.** In the following sections we are going to discuss each of these speech types in more detail.

Speeches of Fact

Speeches of fact involve the truth or falsity of a claim or position. They often involve questions about the existence or nonexistence of something or that something causes something else. There are some things that we know for sure. For example, the Earth is round. The majority of reasonable people believe this to be true. However, for many other "facts" there is some debate. Consider this example. A current debate centers around the dangers of artificial intelligence. Some expert scientists like Stephen Hawking believe that artificial intelligence will cause the end of the world as we know it.[1] Others, like Eric Schmidt at Google, disagree arguing that there are safeguards in place that would not allow this to happen.[2] However, you could likely find support for either of these positions. You could find data to support each side and experts who support one side or the other. So, in order to get an audience to agree with your position on AI, you would have to be pretty persuasive.

When you are discussing a topic where we can't agree on the facts, like the example of AI, you are dealing with a question of fact. Here are some examples of questions of fact:

- The earth is warming as a result of human activity.
- Nuclear waste can be stored safely in deep underground rock formations.
- Hydraulic fracturing of bedrock to extract natural gas is environmentally sound.
- Allowing citizens to carry concealed handguns in public places will deter crime.

Think about all of the examples provided above and the positions of your friends and family. You probably know people who are on each side of these issues. That is what makes something a question of fact—there is some debate about the facts. There isn't much debate about the fact that smoking cigarettes causes cancer or that wearing seatbelts increases safety when riding in cars. If the prevailing science and data agree on the facts, it isn't a question of fact. So, before you begin planning a persuasive presentation on a question of fact, make sure you are really dealing with a question of fact. Ask yourself, is there a debate surrounding this issue? If there is, it is probably a question of fact. If there is not, it is probably not.

> ### One-Sided vs. Two-Sided vs. Two-Sided Refutational Messages
>
> Is it better for a persuader to present only their side of an argument, both sides of an argument, both sides of an argument and let the audience come to the correct conclusion, or present both sides while refuting the other side of an argument?
>
> In some ways, it makes sense to ignore opposing arguments, since in bringing them up you may inadvertently persuade someone to adopt the opposing position.
>
> In contrast, it may seem that if you discuss both sides of an argument without directly refuting the opposing position, your listeners should see you as objective and support your position over the opposition.
>
> As it turns out, many studies have concluded that presenting both sides and then offering a refutation of the opposing position by showing its weaknesses is stronger than simply presenting your own side and much stronger than presenting both sides without a refutation. So when presented with a choice, the two-sided refutational message is the best option.[3]

Strategies for Effective Speeches of Fact

One way to build a presentation on a question of fact is to organize your material in a **refutative pattern.** This organizational pattern allows you to advance your own arguments by demonstrating why they are effective while acknowledging and refuting the arguments of the opposition. This pattern is the most persuasive that you can use.[4] When we present both sides of an argument and refute our opponents' position, we have the best chance of being persuasive. This is called a two-sided rebuttal, and it can easily be accomplished by using the organizational pattern of refutation.

This pattern is only used in persuasive presentations. To be successful using this speech pattern you should include the following:

1. State the point or argument you are going to refute.
2. List the errors of the opposing argument. Support it with evidence such as facts, figures, examples, and expert testimony.
3. State your alternative argument and provide evidence to support it.
4. Explain how your argument or position disputes that of the opposition.

The following brief outline argues that homeopathy is not an effective alternative to main stream medicine. This outline demonstrates how this pattern can be used.

Main Point 1: According to the American Institute of Homeopathy, homeopathic medicine is a "holistic, natural approach to the treatment of the sick" (this is the arugment that will be refuted).

- Homeopathy proposes that the more diluted a medical substance is, the more potent it actually becomes. Maximum effect is said to be obtained when a solution has been diluted to the point where the medical ingredient is no longer detectible. (By explaining the basic principles of homoeopathy, the speaker has further clarified the position being refuted.)
- This principle has no sound theoretical scientific basis or clinical evidence to support it. Many reviews of homeopathy by scientific and health organizations have found limited evidence for the effectiveness of homeopathic remedies for any specific health issue. (Cite evidence from credible sources.)
- Homeopathic practitioners argue that their products are safe and that their approach reduces unwanted side-effects associated with taking larger doses of a medical ingredient.
- Concerns about the safety of homeopathic products because of poor manufacturing have been raised by the FDA, and some homeopathic medicines are based on substances that are known to be dangerous for human consumption. Additionally, individuals seeking homeopathic solutions to serious health issues may go without treatments clinically proven to be effective. (Cite recent research.)

Main Point 2: In order to address health issues, patients should consult with qualified medical professionals following evidence-based guidelines and treatments rather than homeopathy (this is the alternative argument).

- Evidence-based medicines and medical procedures go through rigorous testing before being approved for use as treatments for illnesses.
- Evidence-based medicine has to demonstrate that it benefits patients above and beyond what would be expected from a placebo.
- Conventional medical practitioners and drug manufacturers have to disclose the risks and benefits of medical procedures and medications so patients can make informed decisions about their care based on actual evidence. (Cite your evidence.)

Sometimes, you simply are not able to use the refutative organizational pattern. For some reason it may not be possible to present both sides of a question of fact and refute them. There might be situational constraints like time available for your presentation or other issues. If you choose not to use the refutative design, you have other options.

Another popular organizational pattern for a presentation on the question of fact is a causal pattern. **Causal patterns,** as you will remember from Chapter 6, use two main points. The first main point presents the cause, and the second main point the effect. The persuasive point of the arrangement is to convince your audience of the causal link between the two.

- **Thesis Statement:** Sunscreen usage has caused an increase in vitamin D deficiency.
- **Main Point 1 (Cause):** Sunscreen blocks the body's absorption of natural sunlight.
- **Main Point 2 (Effect):** The body makes vitamin D when your skin is exposed to sunlight, so constant use of sunscreen prohibits this process.

Speeches of Value

If your speech evaluates a topic, it is what we call a question of value. Speeches of value go past is and isn't and place a value on a topic or claim. So, claims that something is the best, ideal, harmful, or unethical are all examples of value. Below are thesis statements on questions of value:

- No-kill animal shelters are unethical.
- Government funding for NASA is worthwhile.
- Flipped classrooms provide the best learning environments.
- Low carb diets are the healthiest.

The thing that all of these thesis statements have in common is that they have a positive or negative evaluation connected to them. Questions of value are hard to argue because they don't always appeal to logic in the same way as questions of fact do. What is important to remember is that to argue a question of value is more than to offer your opinion. Questions of value should use evidence and support to make their claims. You must build a case for your position as in any other situation. So, if you want to argue that low carb diets are healthy—you can't just say you tried it and feel better; you have to present data that shows the health benefits. The speech must go past your opinion. You have to present evidence that your claim is actually true.

> If your audience finds your criteria useful and compelling and you can demonstrate that your claims match that criteria, you will likely be persuasive.

Strategies for Effective Speeches of Value

An important thing to note is that questions of value do not call an audience to action. They merely argue the right and wrong, good or bad of a question. Your audience may become engaged in your topic as a result of your speech, but that isn't the purpose of your presentation, and a speech of value will not advocate or suggest action on the part of your audience.

Questions of value can be organized in a topical design where you simply go point by point providing supporting evidence to support each claim. Another way they can be organized is by establishing some sort of criteria and then judging your claims by that criteria. If your audience finds your criteria useful and compelling and you can demonstrate that your claims match that criteria, you will likely be persuasive. We use this method a lot when we have criteria for awards. The award for student of the year lists the criteria, and you supply an application arguing why you and your accomplishments match that criteria better than anyone else's.

Say that you want to argue that a low-carb diet is the optimal diet. First, you will want to establish criteria for the optimal diet. The following outline provides an example of what this pattern could look like:

- **Thesis Statement:** A low-carb diet is an excellent diet for a healthy lifestyle.
- **Main Point 1:** An excellent diet should meet the following criteria:
  - It should be nutritious.
  - It should be affordable.
  - It should help manage diseases such as diabetes, obesity. etc.
- **Main Point 2:** A low-carb diet meets all of these criteria.
  - A low-carb diet provides a healthy mix of recommended daily vitamins.
  - There are many affordable low-carb options in the market.
  - Low-carb diets can improve serious health conditions, such as metabolic syndrome, diabetes, high blood pressure, and cardiovascular disease.

Of course, you will need to provide support for all of the claims you make including your criteria. It will also be important that you make the conclusion for your audience. In your conclusion emphasis how the diet measures up and then draw the conclusion that the diet is a good one.

Questions of Policy

If your question involves a behavior, you are working with a question of policy. If you are asking your audience to do something like vote for your candidate, buy your technology, or engage in a particular medical recommendation, you have a question of policy. Most of the time when we talk about persuasion, people think about a speech regarding a question of policy. People want to get their audience members to do something. So typically, a speech of policy is what students in a course like this look forward to.

Speeches of policy surround questions of what we should or should not be doing. Should we update our immigration policies, or should we provide more funding to NASA for space exploration. Here are some example thesis statements for speeches on questions of policy:

- All college classrooms should have a technology use policy.
- Exercisers hoping to increase muscle mass should increase their protein intake.
- High speed internet should be freely available to all citizens.
- Putting astronauts on Mars should be NASA's number one priority.

Questions of policy often include questions of value and questions of fact in addition to the question of policy. However, once you make a request of an audience member in terms of behavior, you have moved into a question of policy.

Strategies for Effective Policy Speeches

Persuasive speeches of policy convince an audience that there is a problem that needs to be addressed, pose a solution that will adequately address that problem, and argue that this solution is feasible or practical.

Need

Speeches of policy convince audiences that there is a problem that needs to be addressed. Sometimes an audience knows about a problem but doesn't really know what to do about it. Other times, an audience may not even know a problem exists.

But framing the problem for an audience is a big part of the process in a persuasive appeal involving a question of policy. If you can't accurately define and frame the problem for your audience, it is unlikely they will engage in your solution because they won't see the need to.

Solution

The solution directly addresses the need or problem. This portion of the presentation lays out the solution in detail. It must adequately describe the solution so that the audience can determine whether the solution is adequate or not. So, here you must persuade the audience that your solution can actually solve the problem.

Practicality

An audience will not only evaluate the solution but will also decide if it is practical. Yes, you may have developed an idea that will solve the parking problem at your university, but are students going to be willing to pay $1,000.00 a year to park? Probably not. So, when we say the solution is practical, we are looking to see that it is affordable and something that people will be able to do and easily implement. You may have found a cheap way to increase the amount of protein in people's diets, but are people really going to be willing to eat insects?

Once you develop your solution, run it by many people to make sure that it is something that will be reasonable. If you aren't close enough to the problem, sometimes that is difficult for you to figure out, and you may need to run your solution by a couple of experts or individuals who are really connected to the problem.

Organizing Speeches of Policy

Speeches of policy can be organized in many different ways. The simplest way is through a **problem solution organizational pattern.** This pattern of organization is straightforward where main point one describes the problem, and main point two offers the solution.

Problem Solution

- **Thesis:** Today, I am going to ask you to join the Plastic Pollution Coalition and just say **"No straw, please."**
- **Main Point 1 (problem):** Plastic straws are one of the worst polluters on our beaches.
  - They are poisoning our water supplies.
  - They can be extremely harmful to wildlife.
- **Main Point 2 (solution):** By joining a national movement, you can help prevent this source of pollution.
  - Just say no to straws.
  - Ask your servers to switch to straws upon request.

A spin on the problem solution design pattern is the **problem cause solution pattern.** In this pattern the speaker also addresses the causes of the problem. Here is an example (of course, supporting evidence and citations should be provided):

Problem Cause Solution

- **Thesis:** Today, I am going to ask you to join the Plastic Pollution Coalition and just say **"No straw, please."**
- **Main Point 1 (problem):** Plastic straws are one of the worst polluters on our beaches.
  - They are poisoning our water supplies.
  - They can be extremely harmful to wildlife.
- **Main Point 2 (cause):** Over 5 million plastic straws are used in the U.S. everyday.
  - Plastic straws are not recycled.
  - Many are made from polystyrene.
- **Main Point 3 (solution):** By joining a national movement, you can help prevent this source of pollution.
  - Just say no to straws.
  - Ask your servers to switch to straws upon request.

A final method for arranging your speech of policy is **Monroe's Motivated Sequence.** This design was created by Professor Alan Monroe at Purdue University and is still used today in advertising. In fact, you can see it demonstrated in infomercials and on some of the home shopping channels.

Monroe's Motivated Sequence is a type of problem solution design, but it paints a visual picture of your policy speech. It includes five steps. Some of these steps occur in the introduction, and others occur in the conclusion. These include attention, need, satisfaction, visualization, and a call to action.

Monroe's Motivated Sequence

Attention Step This is like any other attention gaining device. You have to grab the audience's attention and pull them in to your topic. Get them interested in your problem from the first words out of your mouth.

Need Step Here you detail the problem and convince your audience that the issue you have identified deserves to be addressed. You must use logical appeals and supporting facts and figures to persuade them that the problem is significant.

Satisfaction Step In this step you present your plan for addressing the problem. Specifically, spell out what you plan to do to address the situation. Your plan must be adequately developed and explained to your audience.

Visualization Step This is where you show your audience what it will be like if they adopt your solution. How will things change? Describe it. What will the new statistics look like after the implementation of your change? This is a very persuasive tool, and often students skip this step.

Call to Action This is where you explain what you will need from your audience to implement your solution. Do you need a signature or a donation? Are you asking them to change a behavior? Whatever it is, be specific. Make the call to action easy for them to engage in. If you want them to write the president of the university—provide the email address or the mailing address and stamped post cards so they can jot down a note after class and just drop it in the mail.

Let's take a look at this pattern in action. Presented below is an abbreviated example of a speech that used a Monroe's Motivated Sequence Design on the topic of driverless cars.

- **Attention Step:** On April 2, 2018, California began issuing permits needed for fully driverless cars.[5] This means that fully driverless cars are on California roads as you read this. Many other states are right behind them.
- **Need:** According to the Department of Transportation, over 35,000 people died on U.S. roadways in 2015 as a result of motor vehicle accidents. Ninety-four percent of all car accidents are caused by human error.[6] As these statistics indicate, our roads aren't safe.
- **Satisfaction:** These horrible statistics could be diminished with more driverless cars on the roads. With driverless cars we could remove human error from the equation.
- **Visualization:** If we put driverless cars on the road, 90 percent of traffic fatalities would be eliminated in the U.S. 300,000 people's lives will be spared over the course of a decade. Driverless cars can save $190 billion in health care associated with accidents.[7]
- **Call to Action:** Today, I want to encourage you to reach out to our lawmakers and urge them to write policy that continues to push the envelope on driverless technology. We need to continue to allow test vehicles on our streets and provide incentives to companies who are developing technology that could change driving as we know it and make our roads safer.

Questions of fact, value and policy focus your persuasive messages while the organizational structures presented in the previous section provide an outline for your thoughts and arguments. Now, it's time to think about how to build your arguments and the type of evidence you will use.

Types of Persuasive Appeals

Now that we have a better understanding of how to target our arguments and organize them, it becomes important that we look at the types of arguments and appeals we use in our presentations. As we have learned in the previous chapter, quality of argument is important. By examining appeals, we can begin to learn about crafting better argument.

The beginnings of the formal study of persuasion can be traced back to ancient Greece. Ancient philosopher Aristotle is known as the Father of Rhetoric. **Rhetoric** is the art of effective persuasion through writing or speaking. Rhetoric sometimes holds a negative connotation as people use the word rhetoric to refer to empty arguments and claims. You may have heard someone speak disparagingly about a politician's rhetoric or accused lobbyists of using rhetoric to support their position. Rhetoric itself, the art of persuasion, is not a bad thing. But, when people use incorrect information, faulty logic, or their persuasion for negative purposes, it can cast persuasion in an unflattering light. As we have mentioned earlier, persuasive speaking has a higher ethical threshold and in this section we will focus on using strong, factual, and ethical claims to meet persuasive goals.

One of the fundamental ideas that Aristotle taught is that there are three basic categories of persuasive appeals you can use when building a persuasive argument. It is pretty incredible to consider that his ancient ideas are still the primary method we utilize to craft persuasive strategies today. The three types of appeals that Aristotle identified are **logos,** appeals to logic, **ethos,** appeals to credibility, and **pathos,** appeals to emotion. In the following sections, we will look at each category and ways to develop and use these appeals in your persuasive messages.

Appeals to Credibility

Earlier, in Chapter 3 you read about the importance of establishing your credibility as a speaker in order to build trust and confidence with your audience. When it comes to persuasion, your credibility as a speaker is even more essential. Ethos or appeals to credibility, are persuasive appeals that ask your audience to agree with you because of who you are. Credibility is comprised of two components, a speaker's trustworthiness and a speaker's expertise. An audience needs to perceive a speaker as both having knowledge of the topic and believe that what the speaker says is true to perceive a speaker as credible.

There are several ways to build your ethos when you are speaking. First, we will look at ways to build up the perception of your expertise. The most important way is to be knowledgeable about your topic. This includes things like knowing how to pronounce terminology associated with the topic. Nothing will hurt your credibility more than mispronouncing a word you should know. During the 2016 Republican presidential primary candidate, Ben Carson, mispronounced the name of the Islamic terrorist group Hamas as hummus during a presentation at the forum sponsored by the Republican Jewish Coalition. This quickly led to widespread ridicule and questions about his understanding of Middle Eastern affairs.[8]

You can also establish your expertise by sharing your credentials with your audience. These can be formal things like education, training, or job titles, as well as more informal things like personal experiences you've had or research you've done. It is important to remember though that your performance while speaking is often more important in your audience's mind than your stated credentials. People routinely evaluate speakers who present with confidence as having more expertise that those who do not have a confident style.[9] As you learned in Chapter 3 on delivery, speakers who maintain eye contact and have good posture are also seen as being more credible as they are viewed as being more competent which lends the speaker an air of expertise.

Establishing your trustworthiness is a less exact process than establishing your expertise but it can be even more important because audiences will discount an expert they do not trust.

An interesting thing to note about trustworthiness is that people will often make an assessment about someone's trustworthiness within seconds of meeting someone. In fact, the brain makes a decision about how trustworthy a face looks before a person even fully perceives the face.[10] This means that if you are speaking to a group of people who do not know you, there are subconsciously deciding whether they think you can be trusted or not as soon as you enter the room. One simple way you can enhance your perceived trustworthiness is to smile, as people rate more frequent smilers as more trustworthy.[11] There are other things that influence initial impressions of trustworthiness that you cannot control. For example, studies have shown that people rate those with brown eyes as more trustworthy than those with blue eyes. Researchers hypothesize this is because faces with blue eyes tend to be more narrow and the eye shape less round, subconscious indicators that the face is less innocent.[12]

This is not to say thought that trustworthiness is merely a function of how a person looks and nonverbal behaviors. Being honest and conveying correct information while you are speaking is important. If your audience is knowledgeable about your topic and you tell them incorrect information, you will damage their trust in you. Addressing opposing points of view and opposing arguments can also increase your perceived trustworthiness. Your willingness to acknowledge rather than try to hide the opposition demonstrates to your audience your commitment to providing them with the truth. Use facts and figures and other supporting evidence from trustworthy sources and make sure validate that information. Check the information you share with your audience for accuracy.

Building Ethos
- Be knowledgeable about your topic.
- Share your credentials and expertise.
- Use eye contact and good posture.
- Be ethical in presenting information.
- Use supporting evidence from trustworthy sources.
- Double check and validate the evidence you use.

Appeals to Emotion

The next category of appeals is pathos, or appeals to emotion. As much as many of us would like to think that we make decisions based on facts and good reasoning, the truth is that we are often persuaded or make decisions based on feelings and emotion. In Chapter 7 on narrative you read about the persuasive power of stories. One of the primary reasons they are so powerful is because stories can promote an empathic and emotional response.[13]

When making appeals to emotion, one should consider the **valence** of the emotion. High valence emotions are positive emotions such as happiness, pride, and excitement while low valence emotions are negative emotions like fear and guilt. We will first look at ways to appeal to positive emotions.

Positive Emotions

The goal of an emotional appeal is to invoke a feeling in the audience so that the emotion motivates them to either agree with you or engage in the desired behavior. When appealing to positive emotions, the motivation for your audience is experience those emotions. The field of advertising is highly skilled at appealing to people's positive feelings. Take for example, Nike, one of the largest athletic wear brands in the world. Their advertisements rarely focus on the features of their products, but instead show people engaged in physical activity. Advertisements encourage potential consumers to play like a champion and "just do it." As viewers experience feelings of excitement and feel inspired, they are motivated to buy Nike products. The advertisers have established a connection between those products and the positive feelings inspired by the advertisement.

In September of 2016, Elon Musk, the founder of Space X, spoke to members of the International Astronautical Congress about his plan to colonize Mars within the next 20 years. Throughout his presentation he tried to persuade his audience that his plan would not only work, but would be extremely beneficial to the human species. While he was directly addressing a group of scientists, he also had a much larger audience across the globe of people wanting to learn more about his ambitious plan.

Throughout his presentation he appealed to his audience's sense of excitement and adventure, asking them to envision what life on another planet might look like.

Humor

Another technique to appeal to positive emotions is through the use of humor. Humor can increase the persuasiveness of a message in a few ways. First, people enjoy laughing, and a happy audience is more likely to agree with a message.[14] The use of humor has also been found to increase and audience's recollection of your message, making it more likely that they will remember and continue to consider your arguments.[15] Finally, humor can reduce and audience's resistance and reaction to persuasive messages.[16]

One needs to be extremely careful when using humor during a presentation though. One of the biggest risks of using humor is that it may fall flat. It can be difficult to predict what an audience will find funny. This is especially true when speaking to a diverse audience. Different cultures, ages, and types of people find different things funny and may be offended by certain attempts at humor. Offending those you are trying to persuade is an almost sure way to have your persuasive efforts fail.

Negative Emotions

Fear Appeals

Persuasion often uses appeals to negatively valenced emotions, such as fear and guilt. Fear is a very powerful emotion and in persuasive situations arousing fear in your audience can make them more likely to agree with an idea that they see as being able to protect them from a threat. The American Cancer Society has a created a series of presentations with speaker notes and slides that physicians and public health professionals can adapt and use when addressing groups or putting on workshops. For the presentation on skin cancer, the speaker attempts to arouse fear in the audience by talking about the risks, the prevalence of skin cancer and the consequences of developing cancer including death. The goal in the presentation is to raise enough fear in the audience so that they will adopt the recommended preventative behaviors including using sunscreen daily and avoiding tanning beds.[17]

When using a fear appeal like the one just described, speakers need to proceed with caution. If a message is too fearful, rather than adopting the recommended behaviors, the audience may simply avoid or ignore the message to alleviate the uncomfortable feeling of being frightened. The **Extended Parallel Processing Model** or **EPPM,** helps to explain why some people avoid or ignore frightening messages. Much like the ELM that was discussed in the previous chapter, the EPPM proposes that there are three possible ways that people will respond to a frightening message; a fear control response, a danger control response, or no response.

There are four key factors that determine which type of response the receiver will engage in. The first is **self-efficacy.** Self-efficacy is a person's belief that he has the ability to take the actions needed to reduce the threat. **Response efficacy** is a person's perception that the recommended behavior will work to minimize the threat. Another important factor is the audience's perception of their **susceptibility** to the threat which is their assessment of how likely it is that they will be personally harmed by the threat. The final factor that influences the response is the audience's assessment of the **severity** of the threat.

Effective Fear Appeals: Applying the EPPM
- Persuade your audience that they are susceptible to the threat.
- Convince your audience that the threat is severe and has negative consequences.
- Explain how your recommended action/behavior will address and alleviate the threat.
- Show your audience that they are able to engage in the recommended action/behavior.

In order for an audience to engage is any type of response to a fear message, they must first perceive that they are susceptible to the threat. If they do not believe they are susceptible, they will have no response to the message. Take for example the issue of identity theft where someone's personal information is stolen by computer hackers. Cyber security experts may use fear appeals to try and persuade people to protect their information by using strong passwords that are frequently changed. Before an audience will process the message, they must first believe that this is a threat that could personally harm them. For a variety of reasons, people may assume that they are not vulnerable to the threat. Perhaps they feel that already take enough safety measures or they might not believe that identity theft is a widespread problem. Messages about the prevalence of the problem and examples of individuals similar to audience members are ways to convince an audience they are susceptible to the threat.

People also make assessments about the severity of the threat. If they do not perceive that the threat will cause a large amount of harm, even if they are susceptible to it, they will not respond to the message. In the case of identity theft, speakers can provide information about the consequences of identity theft including financial loss and poor credit scores. In some situations, the challenge for the persuader is to convince the audience that the consequences are something to be concerned about. For a younger audience, such as a group of high school students, the concept of a credit score might not be something they are actively concerned about, so a speaker would need to spend some time explaining the negative impacts of this.

If the audience perceives the threat as both serious and something they are susceptible to, the next step is evaluating their perceived ability to minimize that threat. This perception comes from the final two factors, self-efficacy and response efficacy. The audience will consider the recommended behavior and determine if they think that the behavior will work to minimize the threat. They will also consider their personal ability to engage in the recommended behavior. Those listening to the cyber security expert would consider how easy or difficult it would be to easily change their passwords on a regular basis.

Some might think this will be too difficult as it would be too hard to keep track of the frequent changes and will have difficulty accessing their accounts. The audience will also evaluate how effective they think that changing passwords will be in protecting their identity. If an audience member thinks this solution is too simple or that hackers will be able to find other ways to steal information, they will have low feelings of response efficacy.

If the audience has either low response or self-efficacy, they are likely to engage in a fear control response. Rather than trying to minimize the threat, they will try to minimize the uncomfortable feeling of fear. Because they do lack confidence that they can personally reduce the threat, it is easier to ignore the threat and not think about it. If the audience has both high response and self-efficacy, they will be more likely to engage in a fear control response and take actions to reduce the threat.

Guilt Appeals

Another negative emotion that you can appeal to is guilt. Guilt is the negative feelings people have when they believe they have committed some type of wrong that has violated an accepted moral standard.[18] What is interesting about guilt is that person can experience it as a result of past behavior as well as the result of anticipating a future action. Because guilt is an uncomfortable emotion, people will engage in behaviors to eliminate the negative feelings. The best way to eliminate feelings of guilt are to either to engage in behavior that makes up for a past wrong or engage in a behavior that will prevent anticipated guilt.

In 2017, Purdue launched a campaign around campus to reduce the usage of plastic drinking straws. At several locations around campus where drinks are sold, a small sign was placed next to the straws with image of a sea turtle. Text on the sign informed readers of the hazard that plastic like he straw the reader is about to reach for poses for turtles and other sea creatures. The sign asks the reader to please stop using plastic straws. The reader of the sign now has to make a conscious choice of whether or not to use a straw. If she does, she will experience the guilt of knowing that her straw could one day end up in the stomach of an adorable sea creature like the one starting at her in the sign. Research has shown that a guilt appeals are especially effective in motivating pro-social behavior like not using plastic drinking straws.[19]

When using emotional appeals, you should also be cognizant of the potential ethical issues that may arise. Because emotions are so powerful, people may agree with a position based on their feelings and emotions, rather than facts. Think of the example at the beginning of the chapter of Mr. Blaxill and his talk encouraging parents not to vaccinate their children against measles. In addition to using incorrect and false information to support his claim, Blaxill created a sense of fear in his audience. While many of the parents were already frightened about the prospect of their children catching the measles, he created an even greater sense of fear about the possibility of their children developing autism. By not balancing the emotional appeal with facts and logic, Blaxill was manipulating his audience. When appealing to emotions, it is important that the emotional appeals are supported with logical and factual arguments as well.

Appeals to Logic

The final category of appeals, logos, or appeals to logic are appeals that ask the audience to use the rational side of their brains to process and evaluate arguments. When you have a highly motivated audience who is using the central route to process your message, it is especially important to have strong logical appeals and to build your case through arguments and facts such as statistics, examples, and testimony from experts. Studies have shown that while ethical and emotional appeals can play a large role in persuasion, the strength and relevance of your logical arguments have the strongest effects in most situations.[20]

Think back to Elon Musk who had the challenge of persuading his audience that his Mars plan was feasible. While he used emotional appeals to get his audience to support his ideas, his presentation also relied heavily on logical appeals. For most of his 50 minute talk, he presented scientific evidence to support his claims of how a shuttle could make it to Mars and how Mars' atmosphere could be transformed to support life. Additionally, he addressed the cost of the multiple missions and provided a thorough financial analysis for raising funds from his company Space X, private citizens, and the government. Without building his extensive logical case, the majority of his audience would dismiss his idea plan as nothing more than a dream.

Inductive Arguments

When a speaker is working to build a persuasive case, there are some formal persuasive structures and strategies that can be used to help frame the argument. One strategy is to reason from specific cases and examples, which is also known as **inductive reasoning.** The U.S. Composting Council is a nonprofit organization whose mission is to promote the practice of composting throughout the U.S. One of their strategies for increasing composting is advocating for legislation that bans yard waste from landfills. As part of their advocacy efforts, members frequently go and speak at public meetings, to local and state legislatures, and community groups. As they build the case for why yard waste should be banned, they frequently point to other communities where bans have been implemented and have had a positive effect on the environment. They also include examples of communities without bans and describe the negative impacts on the environment. From these multiple examples, the audience is asked make the broader conclusion that a ban on yard waste in landfills would be a positive thing for a community or state.

When reasoning from examples, you as the persuader need to consider a few things about your argument and the example cases you are using. First, you need to be sure that you have included enough examples and cases that allow your audience to draw a reasonable conclusion. Imagine that you have decided that airbags should be removed from vehicles because you believe they are dangerous and actually cause more harm than good.

If during your presentation you only provide examples of someone who was killed in an accident when the airbag deployed, your argument will not be strong. On the other hand, if you are able to include multiple stories of people who have been killed or seriously injured by their airbags deploying, you have built a stronger case.

It is also important that your examples are representative. In the case of banning yard waste from landfills, examples from a community that is vastly different in terms of size and climate, will be less convincing than examples from more similar communities to where you are presenting. If you are arguing against airbags, your examples need to be cases that are likely to occur in other situations. If all of your examples are from unusual circumstances or when the passenger neglected to take other safety precautions such as wearing a seatbelt, your argument will be less convincing.

Another thing to consider when arguing from example is that many times, examples need to be combined with other types of evidence such as statistics or expert testimony. If someone is going to be convinced that airbags do more harm than good, then they will want to know the number of injuries and fatalities that occur each year as a result of airbags. Additionally, providing just those numbers may not provide enough context, so you will may need to provide the percentage of accidents with bad outcomes or the total number of accidents.

Deductive Arguments

Another strategy for making an argument is to argue from a broader premise to a specific case. This is known as **deductive reasoning** and can be thought of as the inverse of inductive logic. When using deductive reasoning, you begin with an overarching premise that you want your audience to accept. Once this has been accepted, you being to apply that premise to a specific case.

Another strategy for making an argument is to argue from a broader premise to a specific case.

Let's look at an example of how this type or argument would work. As science and technology have advanced, new questions and issues have arisen. One of those issues is how information gleaned from genetic testing should and can be used by organizations. For example, if genetic testing reveals that a person has a higher likelihood of developing cancer or Alzheimer's, should insurance companies or employers be allowed to use that information to deny coverage or not hire someone? Some would say that no, organizations should not be able to use this information in this way and if they do, this would constitute genetic discrimination. Someone arguing against this practice might first start with the argument that discriminating against someone because of who they are or physical traits such as sex or race is wrong. This is a premise that many agree with and laws in the United States are in place to protect people from this type of discrimination.

Once the speaker has established that discrimination is wrong, the next step is to apply that principle to the specific case of using DNA tests to make decisions about hiring or insurance coverage. One could argue that people's genetics are something they are born with. Not hiring someone because their DNA indicates they are more likely to develop a medical condition is no different than not hiring someone because they have a disability or have a certain skin color. In deductive reasoning, you are asking your audience to go back to an idea they support and transferring that support to the specific situation you are addressing.

One of the challenges in using deductive reasoning successfully is demonstrating how the larger principle applies to the specific case. In terms of genetic discrimination, opponents may argue that making hiring decisions based on genetic testing is different than making decisions based on skin color because skin color has no bearing on potential work performance whereas developing a medical condition could. If your audience does not see how the specific case relates to the broader premise, your persuasive efforts are far less likely to be successful.

Faulty Logic

When talking about logic, we must also discuss logical errors, more formally known as **fallacies.** Often when building an argument, a speaker may intentionally or unintentionally use faulty to logic to build the case. You need to be able to recognize these errors so that you avoid using them as the persuader and so you recognize them when you are being persuaded.

Those who formally study logic and argumentation have identified and named over 100 types of logical fallacies. While we do not have the time and space to look at every type of logical fallacies, we will look at a few of the most commonly used ones.

> ### Inculcation Theory—Messages as Vaccinations
>
> In the 1960s McGuire noted that sometimes even very weak persuasive arguments, over time, can make people more resistant to counter persuasive attempts. Vaccines in medicine work by introducing a radically weakened version of virus that doesn't actually make people sick yet still encourages the body to produce antibodies against the virus. This production of antibodies helps a person to resist a strong attack by the virus at a later time.
>
> Persuasive messages can work the same way. For instance, a parent might tell a child that someday someone will try to get them to smoke (a threat or forewarning) because it will make them look "cool" (a weak attack), but, in reality, it will only make your child "smell bad," which is not very cool (a counterargument). Even though this argument is not particularly strong, it serves to reinforce an existing belief, and, over time, encourages the child to even think of other arguments (called counterarguments) to help them resist future persuasion attempts. This, and similar techniques, have been used in a variety of contexts, including health campaigns, political campaigns, and advertising.

> ### Inculcation Theory—Messages as Vaccinations Continued
> The basic process goes like this:
> - Pose a threat or forewarning of a future persuasive attempt that must be resisted.
> - Provide a weak attack against the belief that is to be preserved.
> - Provide a refutation of the weak attack.
>
> There are several variations on inoculation messages, but this type of technique is one of the most effective strategies known for improving a person's ability to resist future persuasive attempts they may encounter.[21]

Slippery Slope

A slippery slope fallacy argues that one action will lead to a series of sequential actions that will end in something catastrophic. What makes this a faulty argument, is that there is no evidence to support that the chain of events will occur. Sometimes a slippery slope argument is used to argue against stem cell research. Stem cell research involves extracting cells from human embryos that have been created at fertility clinics, but not used. These stem cells have shown promise in treating a variety of medical conditions including neurological conditions, diabetes, and paralysis. Opponents of embryonic stem cell research argue that an embryo is a human life and destroying an embryo for research is equivalent to taking a life. Opponents will also argue that if research on existing embryos is allowed that additional embryos will be created solely for the purpose of research that will destroy them. Once this has occurred they argue, there is nothing to stop researchers from starting to killing and harvesting cells from more mature fetuses, new born infants, or even from the disabled or elderly. In arguments like this, opponents are going from using already created embryos that will not be implanted to killing adult humans for research purposes.

False Dilemma

A false dilemma incorrectly poses that there are only two possible choices, when in reality, there are often multiple choices or the two choices can coexist. In 2017, multiple players in the NFL either knelt or held hands during the National Anthem to protest racism and police violence against people of color. As the number of players engaging in the protest increased, public debate over whether or not the players should be protesting increased. Many opposed the protests because they felt that kneeling during the anthem was a sign of disrespect to the flag and the military. In making a case for their position, some made statements such as those who supported the protests were unpatriotic. In making this argument, they were presenting a false dilemma that someone either supported the players or the country. The reality is that many supporters of the protest were patriotic and supported the players' right to free speech.

Hasty Generalization

A hasty generalization is made when the speaker makes a broad assumption based on one case or limited evidence. Hasty generalizations are the basis for many of the prejudices and stereotypes that exist. When you are using inductive reasoning this is a fallacy you need to be very careful to avoid. Drawing a conclusion based on just one or two examples can lead to a logical error. In 2014, Sara Kovac wrote an opinion piece on why she is not an organ donor. One of her arguments was that it is possible to recover from brain death. To support this claim, she referred to the case of a young man from Oklahoma who was declared brain dead after a serious ATV accident and after almost 30 days recovered and woke up from the coma. By pointing to this one very rare case, in which there is no certainty that his original diagnosis of brain death was correct, Kovac made a logical error in drawing a general conclusion that recovery from brain death is likely enough that one should stay on life support rather than donate his or her organs.

Correlation vs. Causation

With this fallacy, the persuader incorrectly attributes one factor as leading to a particular outcome when there is no evidence of the factor actually causing the outcome, and instead the two events occurred together. A common occurrence of this fallacy involves many dedicated sports fans or athletes who have lucky shirt they wear on game day or a specific pre-competition ritual such as eating a certain meal or listening to a lucky song. People will incorrectly attribute a win to the lucky item or their pre-game activity rather than the actual performance during the competition.

The correlation vs. causation fallacy is often made when people are arguing that something is either good or bad because it leads to an outcome, when the reality is that other factors are causing the outcome. An example of this can be found in arguments to support providing breakfast for low income school children. Before looking into the fallacious arguments that are used, it is important to note that feeding children so that they are not hungry during the day and are getting proper nutrition is a good thing in itself. In order to be sure that the funds and resources are being allocated for these programs, solid arguments need to be made. Many in support of breakfast programs point to studies that have shown that students who eat breakfast perform better at school. While this is a true fact, further investigation into issue shows that students who do not typically eat breakfast before school are also more likely to be from a lower socio-economic status and are more likely to be tardy or absent form school, both factors that could contribute to poor academic performance.[22] This evidence shows that it not the lack of breakfast that leads to poor performance, but a variety of other factors.

Ad Hominem

An ad hominem fallacy is when someone lodges a personal attack against the person supporting the opposing view point rather than attacking the argument or issue itself. By attacking the person, the persuader is often hoping that a dislike or negative view of the opposition will translate into not supporting the opposing position.

A great example of an ad hominem attack is from 2015 when Sea World went after former orca trainer John Hargrove. Sea World, who had received a lot of negative press and resistance after the release of the documentary *BlackFish,* was trying to refute claims made in the documentary that its captive orcas were mistreated. Hargrove appeared in the documentary and stated publicly that Sea World severely mistreated its captive whales. In response, rather than refuting the specific claims that Hargrove made about policies and procedures in the parks, Sea World released a video of an intoxicated Hargrove using racial slurs and started a website called The Real John Hargrove which included several stories and comments of people attacking Hargrove's character.[23] While some of the attacks on Hargrove may have been accurate, the line of reasoning is a fallacy as Hargrove's actions have nothing to do with Sea World's treatment of orcas.

Appeal to Authority

Many times, when people are building a persuasive case they will provide testimony from different experts and authorities. This itself is not problematic. When this fallacy occurs is when the only evidence for the claim is that an authority said it and that authority is either wrong or more commonly does not have expertise on the given topic. When you are citing and quoting experts, it is important to determine if that person is an actual authority on the subject.

An example of a fallacious appeal to authority can be found in people who use the advice of celebrities when it comes to matters of nutrition and health. Actress Gwyneth Paltrow also runs a popular lifestyle website called Goop is which she gives advice about a variety of topics including fashion, style, decorating, diet, and health. Many times, the recommendations her site publishes have been shown to be incorrect or unproven and those who cite her and her writing are using faulty logic. In 2015, Goop published an article telling people to avoid chemical-based sunscreens because the chemicals could lead to hormone and endocrine imbalances. Paltrow fans and Goop readers trusted this advice and used it to support using only mineral based sunscreen.

Further investigation of the claims made in the article revealed that no scientific study has ever found damaging effects from chemical based sunscreen.[24] Paltrow, who has no education or training in this area was cited as an authority due to her celebrity status.

Faulty Analogy

Making arguments from analogies is an effective and clear way to present an argument to an audience. Typically, you present a set of facts and argue that because they are alike in these ways, they must also be alike in these other ways. In presentations, people often use arguments of analogy in speeches of policy. Typically, people argue that if a solution worked in this case, it should also work in another case. That is true as long as the cases are similar in important respects. What happens many times is that the two cases are not similar enough to be compared. When this happens, we say that it is a faulty analogy. Just because a particular university solved their parking on campus doesn't mean that same plan will work on your campus. You have to think about where the two universities are located, how they receive their funding, how many students they have, if they are private or public, etc. If these important characteristics are different from one university to another, it is unlikely that the policy they implemented would also work on your campus.

Building Your Persuasive Argument

When you enter into a persuasive situation, your task is to build the most effective persuasive message possible. You may be wondering what types of arguments to use. The simplest answer is to use all three types of appeals as you want to hit your audience with arguments that build your own credibility, create an emotional response, and are based in sound logic and reasoning. If you build your argument using only one type of appeal, it will be much easier for your audience to reject your appeal.

When building your persuasive argument, you also need to consider your audience and their likely level or involvement with your message and motivation to listen to and process what you are saying. If you are speaking to an audience with lower motivation, the ELM tells us that they will be rely more on peripheral cues to make a decision. In these situations, it is advantageous to include ethical and emotional appeals as the audience will spend less time considering any logical arguments you make. In contrast, if you are speaking to a highly motivated audience, it is essential that you have strong logical arguments that cannot easily be picked apart. While a highly motivated audience will certainly care about the credibility of the speaker, if they speaker's arguments and facts do not hold up, they will not be persuaded.

How to Approach a Hostile Audience

In everyday life it is difficult to face an audience that we know disagrees with our position. In fact, we think it is just about the most nerve-wracking task you can undertake. But if you think about it in advance and learn everything you can about your audience and their position, you can plan for it and make it much more enjoyable for yourself and the audience. Here are some tips to consider when facing an audience who doesn't agree with your position.

1. **Building Identification:** Identification is the process of demonstrating what you have in common with the opposition. What are the values, experiences, etc. that you and the

audience share? If you can identify those, point those out and move from a place of agreement to disagreement, they will be less likely to resist. Sometimes, we forget that we want the same things as our audience, but it is how to get there that we disagree on. Reminding ourselves and the audience of the goals we have in common makes it easier to move forward.[25]

2. **Show Respect:** Acknowledge your respect of them as an audience. Just because you disagree on this particular issue doesn't mean that you have no respect for your audience. Show your respect to them by the way you deliver your message, with the integrity that you use when presenting your material, and with sincerity in which you approach the topic.

3. **Keep Goals Moderate:** As we discussed in the previous chapter, when people have small latitudes of noncommitment, there just isn't anywhere to move in terms of persuasion. They are going to reject any of our ideas and arguments that run counter to their own because their latitude of rejection is so large. So don't hope to persuade them in just one presentation. Remember, persuasion is a process. Take very small steps. Maybe you just want them to listen to your position in your first attempt. Then you can take incremental steps building to some larger goal.

4. **Use Humor and Likability:** This isn't a time to be defensive. You want to be as likable as possible. Likability can sometimes moderate persuasive appeals.[26] If you are someone who can use humor well, a little levity won't hurt here either. However, inappropriate humor will hurt your credibility, so use it sparingly.[27]

5. **Building Relationships:** If you have the opportunity to research your audience well, you may be able to talk to a few of the audience members before hand. Hearing their concerns and incorporating their feedback helps build a bridge between your position and that of the audience. You may be able to call on these individuals during the presentation to demonstrate your sincerity in trying to reach common ground, and many times they will lend some support.

Chapter Summary

This chapter has provided a lot of concrete information on implementing your persuasive argument. We started with the target of your persuasive message and discussed questions of fact, value, and policy. The chapter then provided methods for organizing each of these. We then presented a discussion of how to weave appeals to ethos, pathos, and logos into your presentation. The chapter also discussed faulty reasoning and some things that you should avoid. Finally, we provided some tips for addressing argument order and hostile audiences. Keep in mind this recommendations as you craft your persuasive presentations.

Case Study Conclusion

Professor Lu has been very successful in his efforts to raise money for his asteroid identification program. He has used a fear appeal perfectly. He aroused enough fear, showed us what needed to be done, and convinced us it could easily be done if we would make a simple donation. His B612 Foundation is currently on the cutting edge in terms of this research, and they are working diligently on this problem. This is a very nice example of how to deliver a speech on a question of policy using both facts and emotions.

References

[1] Osborne, H. 2017. "Stephen Hawking AI Warning: Artificial Intelligence Could Destroy Civilization." *Newsweek*, November 7, 2017. http://www.newsweek.com/stephen-hawking-artificial-intelligence-warning-destroy-civilization-703630.

[2] Shermer, NM. 2017. "Artificial Intelligence Is Not a Threat—Yet." *Scientific American*, March 1, 2017. https://www.scientificamerican.com/article/artificial-intelligence-is-not-a-threat-mdash-yet/.

[3] O' Keefe, D. J. 1999. "How to Handle Opposing Arguments in Persuasive Messages: A Meta-Analytic Review of the Effects of One-Sided and Two-Sided Messages." *Communication Yearbook* 22:209–249.

4   O' Keefe, D. J. 2016. *Persuasion: Theory and Research* (3rd ed.). U.S.: Sage Publications.

5   Hafner, J. 2018. "California Approves Fully Driverless Cars on Public Roads for Testing." *USA Today*, February 27, 2018. https://www.usatoday.com/story/money/nation-now/2018/02/27/california-approves-fully-driverless-cars-public-roads-testing/378703002/.

6   Atherton, K. 2016. "What You Need to Know About the New Federal Rules for Driverless Cars." *Popular Science*, September 21, 2016. https://www.popsci.com/read-federal-rules-for-driverless-cars.

7   LaFrance, A. 2015. "Self-Driving Cars Could Save 300,000 Lives Per Decade in America." *The Atlantic*, September 29, 2015. https://www.theatlantic.com/technology/archive/2015/09/self-driving-cars-could-save-300000-lives-per-decade-in-america/407956/.

8   Wang, Y. 2015. "Ben Carson Pronounces 'Hamas' like 'Hummus' at Event Hosted by Republican Jewish Group." *Washington Post*, December 4, 2015. https://www.washingtonpost.com/news/morning-mix/wp/2015/12/04/ben-carson-pronounces-hamas-like-hummus/?utm_term=.f16766c9a810.

9   Tenney, E., J. Small, R. Kondrad, V. Jaswal, and B. Spellman. 2011. "Accuracy, Confidence, and Calibration." *Developmental Psychology* 47(4): 1065–1077. https://agelabs.appstate.edu/sites/agelabs.appstate.edu/files/TenneyEtAl.pdf.

10 Sifferlin, A. 2014. "Our Brains Immediately Judge People." *TIME*, August 6, 2014. http://time.com/3083667/brain-trustworthiness/.

11 Nagle, J., S. Brodsky, and K. Weeter. 2014. "Gender, Smiling, and Witness Credibility in Actual Trials." *Behavioral Sciences & The Law* 32(2): 195–206. doi: 10.1002/bsl.2112. Schmidt, K., R. Levenstein, and Z. Ambadar. 2012. "Intensity of Smiling and Attractiveness as Facial Signals of Trustworthiness in Women." *Perceptual and Motor Skills* 114(3): 964–78. https://www.ncbi.nlm.nih.gov/pubmed/22913033.

12 Sifferlin, A. 2013. "Trust: Is It All in the Eyes?" *TIME*, Jan. 11, 2013. http://healthland.time.com/2013/01/11/trust-is-it-all-in-the-eyes/.

13 Green, M., and T. Brock. 2000. "The Role of Transportation in the Persuasiveness of Public Narratives." *Journal of Personality and Social Psychology* 79(5): 701–721. http://www.communicationcache.com/uploads/1/0/8/8/10887248/the_role_of_transportation_in_the_persuasiveness_of_public_narratives.pdf.

14 Chamorro-Premuzic, T. 2015. "Persuasion Depends Mostly on the Audience." *Harvard Business Review*, June 2, 2015. https://hbr.org/2015/06/persuasion-depends-mostly-on-the-audience. Yan, C., J. Dillard, and F. Shen. 2010. "The Effects of Mood, Message Framing,

15. and Behavioral Advocacy on Persuasion." *Journal of Communication* 60(2): 344–363. https://academic.oup.com/joc/article/60/2/344/4098457.

15. Blanc, N., and E. Brigaud. 2014. "Humor in Print Health Advertisements: Enhanced Attention, Privileged Recognition, and Persuasiveness of Preventive Messages." *Health Communication* 29(7): 669–677. doi: 10.1080/10410236.2013.769832.

16. Young, D. 2008. "The Privileged Role of the Late-Night Joke: Exploring Humor's Role in Disrupting Argument Scrutiny." *Media Psychology* 11(1): 119–142. https://doi.org/10.1080/15213260701837073.

17. "Ready to Use Cancer Presentations." 2017. American Cancer Society. https://www.cancer.org/health-care-professionals/resources-for-professionals/cancer-presentations.html.

18. Coulter, R., and M. B. Pinto. 1996. "Guilt Appeals in Advertising: What Are Their Effects?" *Journal of Applied Psychology* 80(6): 697–705. doi: 10.1037/0021-9010.80.6.697.

19. Renner, S., J. Lindenmeier, D. Tscheulin, and F. Drevs. 2013. "Guilt Appeals and Prosocial Behavior: An Experimental Analysis of the Effects of Anticipatory Versus Reactive Guilt Appeals on the Effectiveness of Blood Donor Appeals." *Journal of Nonprofit & Public Sector Marketing* 25(3): 237–255. https://doi.org/10.1080/10495142.2013.816595.

20. Banas, J., M. Turner, and H. Shulman. 2012. "A Test of Competing Hypotheses of the Effects of Mood on Persuasion." *Communication Quarterly* 60(2): 143–164. doi: 10.1080/01463373.2012.668845.

21. McGuire, W. J. 1961. "The Effectiveness of Supportive and Refutational Defenses in Immunizing and Restoring Beliefs Against Persuasion." *Sociometry* 24: 184–197.

22. Golding, R. "Causation vs. Correlation." 2015. *SENSE about SCIENCE USA*, August 19, 2015. http://senseaboutscienceusa.org/causation-vs-correlation/.

23. Pedicini, S. 2015. "SeaWorld Steps Up Offense Against Former Trainer John Hargrove." *Orlando Sentinel*, March 31, 2015. http://www.orlandosentinel.com/business/tourism/os-seaworld-trainer-video-john-hargrove-20150331-story.html.

24. Harrington, R. 2015. "6 Terrible Health Tips from Gwyneth Paltrow." *Business Insider*, October 23, 2015. http://www.businessinsider.com/gwyneth-paltrow-goop-bad-health-advice-2015-10.

25. Burke, K. (1969). *Rhetoric of Motives*. Berkley University of California Press.

26. O' Keefe, D. J. 2016. *Persuasion: Theory and Research* (3rd ed.). U.S.: Sage Publications.

27. O' Keefe.

Chapter 12

Virtual Presentations

Objectives

After this chapter you will be able to:

- Articulate the differences between asynchronous and synchronous presentations.
- List the advantages and disadvantages of virtual presentations.
- Use basic techniques to record a successful virtual presentation.
- Understand the challenges of virtual presentation environments.

In 2016, political science professor Robert Kelly was being asked to come on to a BBC news program to talk about the recently ousted South Korean President. Because Kelly lives and works in South Korea, he used his computer to participate in the interview. The interview started out smoothly with Kelly sitting at his desk in what looked like his office. Midway through the interview, the door opened, and Kelly's four-year-old daughter entered the room and danced up to her dad to see what was happening. Without stopping his presentation, Kelly pushed his daughter towards the door without pausing what he was saying or looking at her. Instead of solving the problem, his infant son also wheeled into the room in his walker. Kelly ignored his children and continued to discuss the political situation, looking directly at the camera. At this point, Kelly's wife crawled into the room to retrieve the children, crouching down low as she tried to avoid being on film. She managed to snag her children, but the baby's walker got stuck in the door, and viewers could hear his daughter crying in the hallway. Again, Kelly did not flinch or acknowledge the chaos behind him until the end of his segment when the BBC host laughed and said "There is a first time for everything, and I think you have some children who need you." Kelly probably never imagined when he agreed to appear on the BBC that he would become somewhat famous. Shortly after his segment aired, the clip went viral, and people around the world laughed at the interview gone wrong.[1]

Let's Talk
1. What factors did Kelly not consider when he was planning for his interview?
2. How did the distractions while he was speaking influence Kelly's ability to get his message across?

Introduction

Not all presentations take place where the speaker is in the room with the audience. As technology continues to advance and the world becomes smaller and more connected, more presentations occur over the phone, via the internet, and with the speaker and audience in different places. While presentations that take place in a mediated context share many of the same fundamental principles of a face-to-face presentations, there are some unique issues and concerns that you need to consider in order to deliver a successful presentation. The ultimate goal of any presentation is to tell your story in a way that is compelling and informative. In this chapter, we will talk about why virtual presentations matter, the different types of virtual presentations, and things to consider when delivering and recording a virtual presentation so that your story is effectively delivered.

Why Virtual Presentations Matter

The primary reason you need to be aware of virtual presentations is because they are becoming increasingly common. Since the invention of radio and television, people have been able to communicate to widespread audiences. The technology was not available for the average person to use, and few people could have imagined that one day an individual could stream themselves on the internet to people around the globe or take questions from an audience member more than a 1,000 miles away. Television and radio were intended for mass audiences, so the types of presentations that the majority of people give in their personal and professional lives were not appropriate for these mediums.

The idea that people could use technology to conduct meetings and give presentations began in the early 1960s when AT&T developed the idea for what they called the Picture Phone. When callers used this special device, they could see a picture of the person they were speaking to. Although primitive by today's standards, this was the first time that an image was transmitted directly through a phone. In the 1990s, the capacity for video conferencing continued to increase, but it required specialized equipment and expensive infrastructure and networking.[2]

In the 2000s the internet exploded, which vastly increased the possibilities for virtual meetings and virtual presentations. Now, people and organizations have access to free technologies such as Google hangouts or virtual meeting programs like GotoMeeting or Skype that allow anyone with a screen and an internet connection to virtually meet with anyone around the globe. The advancement of technology along with increased access means that more and more people experience both giving presentations and being the audience for virtual presentations.

Another reason you should consider virtual presentations and take the time to learn how to do them well is because of the factors that make them unique from traditional face-to-face presentations. An obvious difference is that the audience, or the majority of the audience, is not in the same room as the speaker. As we will discuss later in the chapter, presenting to an audience you cannot see provides a unique set of challenges. Another key difference is the potential permanence of the presentation. When a presentation is posted to a public forum or website, it can be shared and viewed multiple times. If your presentation is used for internal purposes, it may be archived and made available to employees and clients for a long period of time. Because of this, it is even more important to be accurate and clear in what you say.

If you include incorrect information or improperly give credit to a source, there is a recorded account of what you have said that others can go back to.

The way an audience participates and provides feedback to the speaker can also be very different than a face-to-face presentation. In a traditional face-to-face presentation, the audience is providing continuous feedback through their nonverbal communication. A speaker who is paying attention and reading the audience can tell if an audience is confused, bored, or angry. If you have prerecorded your presentation, you will have no way to know how your future audience will respond. Even when you are presenting live, it can be difficult to have a good idea of how your audience is responding to what you are saying. If you are giving a presentation using some type of virtual meeting software, you may be able to see your audience while you are speaking. Often though, especially if you are speaking to a larger audience, you will be unable to see your audience, so you cannot rely on their nonverbal cues for feedback.

This does not mean that there are no forms of feedback for virtual presentations. Following a prerecorded presentation, audience members can contact the speaker directly to comment on the content. If the presentation is shared in a public space such as YouTube, viewers can post comments. While the speaker cannot incorporate that feedback in the presentation that has already been shared, he or she can adapt future presentations or decide to share additional information with the audience. In a live presentation, there are more options for immediate feedback. Many virtual meeting tools allow speakers to do things like take polls during the presentation, or viewers and listeners can press a button to raise a hand or applaud to show their agreement or support for an idea.

Another difference between traditional face-to-face and virtual presentations is the interaction with the audience. Depending on the format of your presentation, there will be different ways that you as the speaker can interact with the audience and get them involved in the presentation. If your presentation is pre-recorded, your interaction will take place after the audience has viewed it. It is always a good idea to include your contact information at the end of your presentation so those who have questions or comments can send them to you. Some presentation tools have a chat feature where participants can type and send comments to both the presenter and other participants. Depending on the size of your anticipated audience, it can be helpful to have a moderator who monitors the discussion feed and lets you know if a question or comment needs to be addressed.

Types of Virtual Presentations

When thinking about virtual presentations, there are two basic types you need to know: asynchronous and synchronous presentations. **Asynchronous Presentations** are presentations where the presenter and the audience do not experience the presentation at the same time. In other words, the presenter will record the presentation and the audience will view or listen to that recording at a different time. **Synchronous Presentations** are presentations that the presenter and audience experience simultaneously. In a virtual setting this means that the presenter is speaking, and the audience is listening or watching live. Some presentations are initially given synchronously and then are made available for future viewing making them a hybrid of synchronous and asynchronous styles. When preparing for a virtual presentation, it is important to know what type of presentation you are giving so you can adequately plan.

Asynchronous Presentations

Asynchronous presentations are not dependent on the speaker and audience experiencing the presentation at the same time. There are several common types of asynchronous presentations including video presentations that are recorded and posted online or sent directly to audience members. If you have ever taken an online course where your instructor has posted a lecture or you have watched an online video so that you could learn how to change a tire or frost a cake, you have experienced an asynchronous presentation. More and more companies are using virtual presentations to conduct employee trainings. These prerecorded sessions can be accessed and viewed whenever they are needed. Podcasts, which have been increasingly growing in popularity, are another example of prerecorded content that is made available to the audience to listen whenever they would like.[3]

One of the benefits of an asynchronous presentation is that you have time to prepare and record your presentation prior to it being seen by your audience. This also means that your audience will most likely hold you to a higher standard in terms of your delivery and production. If you are stumbling over your words or have lost your place in your presentation and there is a long pause, your audience may wonder why you did not take the time to record your presentation again. Because of the importance of being accurate in what you say, it can be helpful to write out a manuscript of your presentation.

Another advantage of asynchronous presentations is that the audience is not tied to a certain time to view it. This is particularly valuable if you have a dispersed audience who are living in different time zones across the country or around the world. Asynchronous presentations can also be made available for a long timeframe. In the case of a training video, for example, it can be used multiple times. This can save you, the presenter, time, and in turn, this can save your organization money.

Asynchronous presentations are not dependent on the speaker and audience experiencing the presentation at the same time.

For the audience, one of the benefits of an asynchronous presentation is that they can go back and watch it again or watch parts of the presentation again. As you learned in Chapter 8, how-to videos have become increasingly popular on YouTube. If you are watching a video to figure out how to set up your new programmable thermostat, you can pause, rewind, and re-watch as needed. Some college instructors will post their lectures online for students so students can go back and listen to parts that they found confusing or just need to hear again.

Synchronous Presentations

During a synchronous presentation, the audience is listening and watching the speaker as the speaker is presenting. Examples of virtual synchronous presentations include virtual meetings and webinars. In these situations, the audience is seeing or hearing your presentation as you present. A common example of a synchronous presentation is a virtual meeting when the meeting participants are in different locations. Live webinars where participants call or log-in to listen to your content are another example. Sometimes synchronous presentations will be recorded and made available after the live presentation, effectively turning a synchronous presentation into an asynchronous presentation.

One of the advantages of a synchronous presentation is that there are ways to receive immediate feedback from the audience, and it is also possible for the audience to participate in ways such as asking or responding to questions. The possibility for interactivity can keep your audience more engaged and involved during the presentation. The presenter can use the feedback to adapt and change the presentation while speaking. For example, you may notice that something seems to be confusing to the audience. After noting this, you could find a way to clarify the information or think of a new way to explain it.

One disadvantage of a synchronous presentation is that it is time bound, and the speaker and audience must be participating at the same time. This can become more challenging when participants are located in several different locations in different time zones. Another disadvantage as compared to an asynchronous presentation is that it is live so you cannot rerecord if you make a mistake. This means you need to be prepared and ready to go. It also means that if there is a mistake or error, you need to be able to continue with your presentation as you cannot stop and start again.

Special Considerations

Technology

One of the most challenging parts of a virtual presentation can be the technology. Challenges can arise both from understanding how the technology works as well as technical difficulties, when the technology does not work as expected. Because technology is always changing and evolving, we will not take the time to discuss how to use specific technologies here. Instead, we will discuss some basic guidelines and tips to ensure that your technology does not trip you up.

When selecting a technology to use, you will want to consider which features you want and need for your presentation. Does your face need to be on the screen, or does you audience only need to hear your voice? Are you going to use visual aids such as slides, or will you just be showing your face? Do you want only your slides or computer screen to show and not have your face appear on screen? These are all decisions you will need to make. After making them, be sure that the tools you are using allow you to present in your desired way.

One of the most important things you can do is test the technology before the presentation. If you are using a virtual meeting tool or skype, take the time to log in before your presentation to make sure you can get onto the system and are familiar with how to control the audio, share your visuals if you plan on doing this, and how to see or interact with the attendees of the presentation. Running through your presentation in the virtual setting is a great way to ensure you are comfortable using all of the tools within the platform. Take some time before you record to see if your lighting, camera angles, and audio levels are what you want them to be.

You also need to have a backup plan for how you will handle any technical failures or challenges. If the internet is down and you cannot join the virtual meeting with your laptop, you may have the option of dialing in on your phone. This will not allow you to be on camera, but you can at least deliver your presentation. If you are hosting a webinar and multiple attendees are having trouble logging on to the system, you will want to have a plan in place for how you will handle the situation.

Recording the Presentation

When you are recording a presentation or streaming it live, there are things you need to consider in terms of production. This does not mean that you need a professional videographer or extensive editing skills in order to produce a quality video. There are some key things you can do to improve the quality of your recording, which in turn will help you share your story more effectively.

Lighting

Any professional photographer will tell you that lighting is the key element to a great image. Things to consider are having enough light as well as the position of your light. Whether you are filming yourself using a web camera or someone is filming you, you want the main source of light to be behind the camera. If your main source of light comes from a window, for example, set up the camera in front of the window so that the light is hitting you from the front. Having your main source of light behind you will cast shadows and make it difficult for your audience to clearly see you. You should also make sure that there is enough light in the filming area so that your audience can clearly see you on video.

If possible, avoid having overhead or ceiling lights be your main source of lighting. These can cast shadows on the face and cause dark circles around the eyes. If you wear glasses, check to make sure that there is not a glare from the lights. This glare will distract the audience and limit the amount of eye contact they perceive.

Positioning the Camera

Another thing you need to consider is where the camera will be positioned. You already know that it should be in front of the light source, but you also want to consider how close or far away you want the camera shot to be. Some of this will depend on what type of presentation you are doing and how much of your audience will need to see. If your audience does not need to see your entire body, a shot of you from your elbows or shoulders up is a great option. You don't want to be zoomed in so close that the top of your head is cut off. Be close enough or zoom in the camera enough that it feels like you are close to the screen and not too far away or removed. A good rule of thumb is to imagine the screen is cut into thirds both vertically and horizontally. Instead of centering the image, place your subject into one or two of the thirds. This provides more visual balance and interest in your shot.

Thirds Rule

Subject Centered   Using Rule of Thirds

If you are using a phone or tablet device to record your presentation, you will want to film in landscape instead of the vertical position. The wider landscape shot is the size you need to fill a frame if you share your video online. If you shoot in the vertical format, your video will have two black stripes on the side when your audience views it.

Camera Stability

It is essential that your camera is held steady throughout your presentation. A shaky or wobbly camera will lead to a shaky and wobbly video. If you are using a free-standing camera or even your phone, your best bet is to use a tripod. If you are using a camera built into your computer, be sure that it is resting on a table and even surface.

Audio Quality

Nothing can ruin a virtual presentation more quickly than poor audio quality. Before filming, you should always test your microphone to make sure it is working. Check to see if you are sitting too far away from it or too close. Talking too closely into a microphone can make your voice sound overpowering. It can also magnify the sound of your breathing which can be both annoying and distracting to your audience. If you notice a lot of static or squeaking during your test recording, you will want to find a new way to record your audio. An inexpensive external microphone can be a great investment if you anticipate doing frequent virtual presentations. If you are recording using your computer, using earbuds or headphones with a built-in microphone is a good option.

> Nothing can ruin a virtual presentation more quickly than poor audio quality.

Related to the issue of audio quality is minimizing any type of background noise. Whether you have prerecorded your presentation or are delivering it live, you want to be sure that there is no distracting noise in the background such as other people talking or a television program. Be sure to find a quiet place to record your presentation. While delivering a synchronous presentation, it is a good idea to post a sign on the door letting people know that a recording is in progress so they do not walk in on the middle of your presentation. Another audio issue is ambient noise that you may not notice but can be amplified in the background of your audio. These are noises such as fans, air conditioners, or other machines. Turn off what you can and place your microphone away from any sources you cannot turn off.

Background

Another thing to consider is what is in the background of your camera shot. It can be easy to forget that the camera is not just capturing you, the speaker, but also anything around or behind you. A solid, neutral background such as a plain wall is a great option. If that is not possible, you will want to make sure that the background is not too distracting A wall filled with pictures and posters, for example, could distract your audience or provide too much contrast. You also want to be careful that there is nothing offensive or potentially embarrassing in the background. For example, if you are working from home and skype into a business presentation to give your sales update, be sure that a pile of dirty dishes or laundry is not in the shot.

Delivery Factors

While the basic rules of good delivery still apply in any type of presentation, being on camera requires special considerations. One thing you need to consider is where you should look while you are recording. In a live presentation, you know to make extended eye contact. When you are not looking at your audience because they are not in the same room with you, you may not be sure where to look. If you are delivering your presentation directly to your audience, you will want to look directly into the camera, imaging that the audience is sitting just on the other side of the camera or screen. This can be tricky when using a camera that is built into your computer or laptop. People have a tendency to look into the middle of the computer screen, a location where they often have notes or visual aids. The problem with this, is that the camera is generally at the middle top of the computer, and this is where your eyes should be directed. If you are giving a presentation in which you are interviewing someone or someone is interviewing you, you will want to look at that person rather than directly at the camera.

Another delivery factor that you need to consider is what you are wearing. Just like any presentation, you will want to be sure that you are dressed in a manner appropriate to the situation.

Because you will be on camera, you also need to consider the color and pattern of your clothing. Shirts with large colorful patterns or stripes should be avoided as they can be distracting. You also want to avoid wearing all white or black as these can cast shadows and reflect or absorb the light. Neutral or light shades tend to look best on camera. In terms of accessories, you want to avoid large jewelry or ties with bold patterns that will again distract your audience.

When giving a virtual presentation, you also need to be aware of your vocal quality. We discussed earlier the importance of having a high-quality audio in terms of the quality of your recording. We are now talking about the way your voice sounds. When delivering a live presentation or prerecording a presentation, it is important to still sound conversational and natural. This can be challenging when you have a prepared manuscript. While you will be reading from that script, you do not want it to sound like you are reading to the audience instead of talking to them.

The way that you move and gesture during a virtual presentation will also be different. When you are on a camera, any movement or gesture you make is magnified, especially if you are recording a close up shot. There is only so much room on the screen, and a lot of movement of your hands or swaying or walking back and forth will take up a lot of space and be visually distracting. Nervous or adaptive gestures such as twirling a pen or fiddling with your hair will become even more noticeable on camera. If you are using your computer to record your presentation, it may make the most sense for you to sit in front of the screen. Be aware that when sitting, you may appear to have lower energy than when you are standing. You may want to arrange your camera so that you can stand and present. Otherwise, be sure you are presenting with strong energy.

> **Nervous or adaptive gestures will become even more noticeable on camera.**

Time

Just like any presentation you give, the length of your presentation is important. It is always important to be respectful of your audience's time. If you have promoted a webinar as lasting for 30 minutes, you need to be sure that you are done within that timeframe. If you are giving a presentation during a meeting, you will want to treat your timing the same as you would if you were attending the meeting in person.

Another thing to consider when creating virtual presentations is the attention span and overall attention of your audience. Because you are not in the same room with your audience, it is easy for them to multitask while you are speaking. Someone who is attending a webinar may be listening to the speaker but also checking his email. This phenomenon, known as divided attention, is always a potential challenge when you are speaking but becomes a greater challenge when audiences are not in the room with you. For an asynchronous presentation such as a video, there is also the possibility that your audience will lose interest and simply stop watching or skip forward to the information they want. Often, audiences have other options. If the video someone is watching to learn how to program the thermostat is too long or confusing, he or she can quickly search for another video and find one that is more appealing.

There are several things that you can do to keep your audience focused on your presentation. One is to keep your presentations short and to the point. It is important to include all needed information, but consider how you are conveying that information and avoid including unneeded information. If you can convey your idea in ten minutes, do so rather than recording a 20-minute presentation that rambles more and gets off track.

You also want your information to be needed, informative, compelling, and interesting. If the information you are sharing with your audience is information that they need and will be useful to them, they are more likely to attend to your presentation rather than doing other work or responding to emails. To help audiences see the utility of your information, you can outline the relevance for them. Additionally, conducting an audience analysis before your presentation can help you to determine what information will be the most useful to your audience. If you are including visuals, which we will discuss next in the section, it is also a good idea to change the visuals frequently so your audience does not get bored looking at the same thing.

Consider ways to engage your audience and get them to interact with your content. Even if it is not practical or feasible to have audience members respond to questions, you can include questions followed by a pause. If I am delivering a presentation on better investment options, I could ask the audience to quickly list their financial goals. Even if those goals are not shared, by engaging in this activity, the audience has participated with the content and is more likely to be mentally involved with the presentation.

Using Visual Aids

Virtual presentations can also present a challenge in using visual aids. You may be wondering how you can show your visuals to your audience, what types of visuals work best in virtual presentations, or if you even should use visual aids. As we think about using visual aids in virtual presentations, it is important to consider the Cognitive Theory of Multimedia Learning that was discussed in the "Visual Communication" chapter. Remember that the primary function of a visual aid is to increase audience understanding. When deciding what, if any, visual aids to use during a virtual presentation, you should go through the same process you would if you were giving a traditional face-to-face presentation.

Once you have decided to include visual aids, you want to be sure that you have the appropriate technology and/or tools to display your visuals in a professional way to your audience. For some virtual presentations, you will be showing or teaching your audience how to do something, and you will want to use actual objects. You will need to film your presentation in a way that the audience can clearly see the components of the task so they can emulate your actions. If your presentation is on basic first aid techniques and you are teaching your audience how to bandage a cut, the camera should be close enough so that your audience can clearly see where you are placing the bandage and how you are wrapping the bandage. If your camera shot is too far away, the audience will not have a clear image of what to do.

In other presentations, you may want to use images and presentation slides. This is a very viable option for virtual presentations, but you need to be sure you have the appropriate technology to share your visuals in a professional way. It is usually not a good idea to project your slides on a screen like you would during an in-person presentation and film yourself standing near the screen. It is difficult to record both the screen and the speaker clearly. Instead, you will want to use your technology to share or capture your screen so that your visuals are clearly displayed on the screen for the audience. You can then use your mouse to point to different features on your visuals or use animation such as arrows or circles to help focus your audience on key parts of the visual.

Many programs have an option where you can toggle between a camera shot of the speaker and your images or slides. They may also have an option where the screen can be split between the visual and the speaker. This style of filming is known as a talking head video. Based on what the Cognitive Theory of Multimedia Learning tells us, it is better to toggle between the views than to have the image of you speaking competing for attention with your visuals. Cognitively, your audience cannot effectively pay attention to both the images and words on the visuals and watch and listen to you speak. Additionally, you do not want your visuals to compete for your attention. When you are not talking about your visual, you do not want it to be on the screen. You also do not want the majority of your slides to be comprised of text. As you previously learned, your audience will start to read your slides instead of listening to you.

Chapter 12   Virtual Presentations

Toggling between Viewing Modes

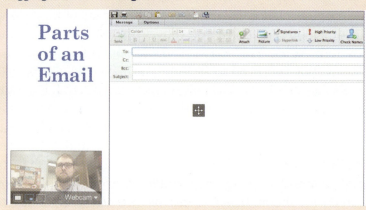

When you aren't referencing the slide, you should toggle the viewing mode back to full camera.

Chapter Summary

In this chapter, we discussed how common virtual presentations have become and why it is important to learn how to deliver a virtual presentation effectively. The chapter then highlighted some of the major differences between virtual and face-to-face presentations and discussed the two types of presentations, synchronous and asynchronous. The chapter then provided several technical aspects to consider when preparing for, delivering, and making your virtual presentation available. Finally, the chapter described how to effectively include visual aids in your virtual presentation.

Case Study Conclusion

When Kelly was getting ready to go on television to discuss the current political situation in South Korea, he made one critical error. By not locking the door or asking his wife to keep his children out of the room, Kelly left himself open to the possibility that his presentation would be interrupted. Even though Kelly continued to stay on message and discuss the political situation, the audience was distracted by everything that was going on behind him. When his interview went viral, it was not because of his unique insight or intelligent commentary but because of the mayhem his young children caused during his interview. When preparing to present in a virtual space, take the time to consider how you can avoid any unwanted distractions from taking away from your presentation.

References

[1] Chappell, B. 2017. "Overtaken by Events: Kids Burst Onto Scene of Live BBC TV Interview." *NPR*. https://www.npr.org/sections/thetwo-way/2017/03/10/519641281/overtaken-by-events-kids-burst-onto-scene-of-live-bbc-tv-interview.

[2] Laskow, S. 2014. "The First 'Picturephone' for Video Chatting Was a Colossal Failure." *The Atlantic*, September 12, 2014. https://www.theatlantic.com/technology/archive/2014/09/the-first-picturephone-for-video-chatting-was-a-colossal-failure/380093/.

[3] Knolle, S. 2016. "The Rising Popularity of Podcasts." *Editor and Publisher* 149(1): 63. http://connection.ebscohost.com/c/articles/112903578/rising-popularity-podcasts.

Chapter 13

Presentation Situations

Objectives

After this chapter you will be able to:

- Understand the various demands of presentation situations (toasts, poster sessions, elevator pitches).
- Discuss the differences and similarities between presentation situations.
- Prepare for a variety of presentation situations.

At the 2018 Golden Globes, Oprah Winfrey was honored with the Cecil B. DeMille Award, a annual award given by the Hollywood Foreign Press to recognize a lifetime of achievement in the entertainment industry. Oprah's award made history as she was the first African American woman to receive the honor. The Hollywood Foreign Press President, Meher Tatna explained why Oprah was selected, "As a global media leader, philanthropist, producer and actress, she has created an unparalleled connection with people around the world, making her one of the most respected and admired figures today." During her acceptance speech, rather than talking about her myriad of accomplishments, Oprah spent her time thanking those who had helped her succeed including her longtime partner Stedman, director Steven Spielberg who cast her in The Color Purple, and her best friend Gayle. From there she talked about the significance of her winning the award as a black woman, recalling watching Sidney Poitier be the first African American man to win the Best Actor Oscar in 1982 stand up to give his speech. Seeing someone who looked more like her being recognized at such a high level encouraged her to consider what she might be able to do. This lead her to talk about the young girls around the world who could be watching her at this moment and might believe that they too could achieve great things.

In addition to expressing gratitude and describing how much the award meant to her, Oprah also took the opportunity to shine light on the pressing issue of sexual harassment and assault faced by women in not just the entertainment industry but in all areas of life. She voiced her support for Time's Up, a movement started in Hollywood to bring attention to the issue of sexual harassment and assault, and declared her hope that the young girls watching would grow up in a time when they would be respected and that their stories would be believed.

Her acceptance speech struck a chord with the audience both in the theater and those watching at home. She received several standing ovations while she was speaking, and her speech was widely shared on all forms of social media. It was so powerful, in fact, that it spurred widespread speculation that Oprah might be running for President in 2020.[1,2]

Let's Talk
1. Do you think that Oprah took any risks by bringing up the issue of sexual harassment and assault in her acceptance speech?
2. How did Oprah turn the focus away from herself during her speech?

Introduction

From toasts to speeches of introduction—presentational speaking will play a role in your life. Throughout this book we have been looking at the basics of how to plan, construct, and deliver informative and persuasive presentations. In this chapter, we are going to describe some of the unique situations and contexts in which you may find yourself addressing a group. We will also be adding in a third category of presentations: presentations whose purpose is to entertain. In this chapter, we will cover several common presentation situations that you may encounter in academic, professional, and personal situations.

Many of these types of speaking situations can occur in multiple contexts. For instance, you may be asked to give a team presentation in both academic and professional settings, or you may be called to give a toast at a business or personal event. Because of this, you always need to consider the situation and who your audience is. Based on this preliminary analysis, you will want to adapt your message and delivery style. A toast that you give at a friend's graduation dinner may be different in terms of tone than a toast you would offer to a colleague at their retirement dinner. With that said, this chapter will provide a broad overview of the many and varied ways presentation speaking is incorporated in your everyday life.

Poster Presentations

Poster sessions are a type of presentation that take place at conferences where a presenter stands in front of a visual aid (often a poster) and shares their research/project/concept with conference or meeting attendees as they walk around the space. Chapter 9 provided information on how to most effectively create and design a research poster. In this chapter, we will focus on how to present that poster to others. Poster presentations are a very common way that those in the STEM disciplines share their research. A poster presentation is unique because rather than addressing a group of attendees all at once, the presenter talks to individuals who attend the session and come over to look at the poster. Rather than a one-sided presentation, poster presenters will generally give a short overview of the project and then will engage with attendees in an open dialogue.

The structure of poster sessions allows for informal discussions about the research and tend to be more conversational in nature as they encourage one-on-one or small group discussions to emerge. However, with the flexibility of this type of presentation situation, speakers must be prepared to answer questions and engage in dialogue with conference-goers.[3] Even though it is more informal, there are still important things to consider. Knowing how best to present can also help you feel more comfortable in this more personal situation.

> You need to be sure that your nonverbal communication is open and welcoming.

The first step to starting your poster presentation is setting up your poster in the provided space. It is always a good idea to check with the venue to know how much space you will have and if they will provide materials such as push pins or tape to hang your poster or if you need to bring your own. When hanging your poster, be sure that it is centered and level.

Once you have displayed your poster, you are ready to begin interacting with session attendees. The goal of a poster session is to have people come and look at your poster and listen to you talk about your research or project. You want people to feel comfortable and encouraged to come look at your poster, so you need to be sure that your nonverbal communication is open and welcoming. If you look bored, angry, and generally like you do not want to talk, people will likely avoid approaching you. Instead, you should stand to the side of your poster, being sure that you are not blocking it with your body.

After someone approaches, you can begin summarizing your research, pointing to any charts, graphs, or visual elements that are relevant. After you discuss the first half of your poster, you should walk to the other side rather than standing and trying to stretch and reach to point out any important elements on the second half. You will want to keep your description of your project brief so that the viewers have time to ask questions. The more that this part feels like a conversation, the more you and your audience will get out of the experience.[4]

Lightening Talk

A **lightning talk** is a brief presentation that is usually part of a larger panel of speakers about a central theme. These have become more popular recently as alternatives to traditional individual presentations at conferences, meetings, seminars, and workshops. For example, there may be a panel about trends in digital currency (e.g., Bitcoin) where five presenters each speak for three minutes about their perspective, experience, or research related to the topic. An advantage of a lightening talk is that the audience is able to take in a lot of information in a short period of time.

When preparing for a lightening talk, the most important thing you need to consider is the time limit. Because your time is limited, you need to be focused and succinct. You might have a lot to say about a topic, but in this situation, you must determine what the most important and useful information is for your audience. You should have one or two talking points, and you need to talk about those points is a succinct and concise manner. Be sure to practice your presentation prior to your presentation, so you can be sure that you are conveying the information in your allotted time.

Elevator Pitch

Elevator pitches are brief, 30- to 60-second persuasive speeches. There are two basic types of elevator pitches. The first is when you are trying to sell or generate interest about yourself. The second is when you are trying to sell or generate interest about your organization or your product. The term "elevator pitch" comes from the idea of being in an elevator with someone and having only the time it takes the elevator to get from the first to top floor to deliver your message. You do not need to be in an elevator to deliver an elevator pitch. Networking events, career fairs, or potential client meetings are all times that having a solid elevator pitch can be useful.

An elevator pitch is a great way to be able to introduce yourself to potential employers or other business contacts. If you have ever been to a job or career fair, recruiters often start with the basic question, "so tell me a little about yourself." This is your opportunity to highlight your skills and capabilities using your brief 30-second pitch. (1) Provide an overview of your background (who you are and what you do), and (2) discuss how you would be a match for a specific company or position (what is your goal?). You want to include information and details that will make you stand out. Highlighting relevant experience, education, or training are all ways to accomplish this. These presentation situations do not necessarily have to take place in a formal situation but can happen anywhere and anytime. You never know when you may be introduced to someone who could provide a job opportunity, so it is best to be prepared with a succinct spiel about yourself and your background.[5]

An elevator pitch is also a useful tool to promote your organization, product, or service. An elevator pitch is a great way to get potential customers, investors, employees, and partners interested in what you have to offer. During your elevator pitch, you need to provide the listener with an overview of what your organization or product does, and describe the unique benefits or your organization or product. The ultimate goal of the elevator pitch is for the listener to want to know more. Adding in a question or connecting your work to the needs and work of the listener is a great way to continue the conversation.

Tips for Preparing an Elevator Pitch

- Know what you want. In other words, be able to clearly articulate your goal.
- Write out your main points.
- Time it. Add and cut content as needed.
- Refine your talking points.
- Be flexible. You should have a stock opening about you and your background, but make sure to tailor the second half to your audience.

- Do not use jargon.
- Practice in front of a friend or family member. It is always helpful to get outside perspectives.
- Update your elevator pitch as needed. Your goals and experience will change over time. Your organization's services or products may change over time as well.[6]

> **Draft your Personal Elevator Pitch**
> Take a couple of minutes to write a draft of your personal elevator pitch. Make sure you have a clear goal (e.g., to get an internship within the actuary industry), include relevant background information (e.g., your education, projects you have worked on), and make a connection between your skills and the goal (e.g., what would you bring to the internship position?).

Briefing

Another situation where you may be called upon to make a short presentation to a group is when you are asked to give a briefing or status update. **Briefings** are short, informal presentations that are often given in the workplace. They can serve as a time when you provide an update on a project, explain information about a topic that you are knowledgeable about, or share a new organizational policy. At a monthly staff meeting, you may be asked to give an update on this month's sales figures or if your team is working on developing a new prototype, letting the group know where your team is in the process. Effective oral briefings should be "presented in a way that allows an audience to understand and apply critical information."[7]

There are two key things to keep in mind if you are tasked with providing a briefing. The first is to be prepared with all of the information and data you need. If you need to report on numbers such as costs or hours worked, have those figures with you so you can provide those you are updating with everything they need. The important thing is to be as brief as you can while giving all of the needed information. Briefings should be brief. Do not include details or information that is not essential or important for the group to know. Stay focused on the information you need to convey. You always want to be respectful of everyone's time. This also means that you should be prepared and know what your talking points are going to be.

Tips for Preparing Briefings

- Know your audience—this will help you decide what information to include and which content to cut.
    - If the team does not need background on what your project is, do not spend time rehashing the details.
- Clearly state the purpose of the briefing.
    - For example, if you are trying to encourage your organization to adopt MFA, then you will state this goal upfront.
- Organize your main points.
    - In continuing the MFA example, a speaker may have two main points: (1) the benefits of MFA in maintaining online security and (2) how MFA can be applied to the organization.
- Make sure to summarize your main points and restate your goal as you conclude the briefing.[8]

Speech of Introduction

Speeches of introduction are presentations that introduce a speaker to a given audience. You may be asked to introduce a new colleague during a staff meeting or will need to introduce a keynote speaker at a professional conference. These types of presentation situations call the speaker to summarize the experience and list relevant credentials of the person who is being introduced.

Take, for example, preparing an introduction of a new co-worker that you hired during a staff meeting. What will you say? That depends on your job, but you will want to provide the new employee's educational and past work background. You will also want to share the strengths the person will bring to their new job. If you are introducing a speaker in addition to providing some background information and qualifications of the speaker, you will want to give a preview of what the speaker will be talking about. This will help the audience prepare for the upcoming talk.

Tips for Preparing Speeches of Introduction

- Focus on the person being introduced.
- Know what the speaker will be talking about and weave it into your introduction.
- Highlight the speaker's background on the topic at hand.
- Be brief ... speeches of introduction should last no more than a few minutes.[9]

Toast

Another common situation you may encounter is being asked to give a toast. Imagine you are at your best friend's wedding. You have been asked to give a toast. What do you say? Where do you start? Many people find themselves in a situation where they have to make a toast—whether it is to celebrate a wedding, engagement, birthday, or promotion. A **toast** is an informal speech that honors or praises someone and/or their accomplishments. It is celebratory in mood and should be focused on the person who the toast is about.

You may have been at an occasion where the toast was less than successful. The toast might have gone on for too long, there may have been jokes you did not understand, or the person giving the toast might have been boring and uninteresting. When you are charged with giving a toast, remember that while your purpose is to honor the person or people being toasted, you also need to keep the rest of the crowd in mind. Rarely will you be able to captivate their attention for 10 to 15 minutes. A good toast should be just a few minutes long. You also want to avoid including too many inside jokes that many in the crowd will not understand. Finally, be sure that your toast ends with a final thought so the audience knows the toast has ended and then ask the group to join in raising a glass to the honoree.

Organizing a Toast

As you are writing your toast, you will want to organize it into three sections.
1. The hook
   - This is where you pull the audience into your speech.
   - Make sure to stay focused on the person you are toasting.
     - A good practice is to not start by saying I, me, or my.
2. The body
   - Rely on stories.
   - Make sure the stories are appropriate for the audience and the context.
   - If you are unsure of the appropriateness of a story, ask.
3. The conclusion
   - Have a definitive end to the toast. Thank the host, offer congratulations, and raise your glass, which marks the end of the toast.

Additional Things to Consider

When giving a toast, remember who the stars actually are. You are not the center of the story. The focus should be on the honorees, whether that is a bride and groom, graduate, or retiree. Good toasts are hard to deliver so you want to prepare well in advance. According to the *New York Times*, it takes months to prepare an effective toast. You do not want to drink alcohol before delivering your toast. It is hard enough to deliver a good toast, so if you are little bit tipsy, it makes it even more difficult. In terms of the content of your toast, you want to tell one nice story about the honoree. When choosing the story make sure you avoid clichés and it highlights the honoree. Private jokes and embarrassing anecdotes are not appropriate. Within the story, you want to identify who you are and your relationship to the honoree. It is also important to practice good delivery. Speak slowly and loud enough for everyone to hear.[10]

Acceptance Speech

Another celebratory speaking situation that you may encounter is an **award acceptance speech.** You may have to accept an award for you or on behalf of someone else, so it is important to know how to handle these types of communicative situations. The overarching goal of an award acceptance speech is to show gratitude. This is the time to thank those giving the award as well as those who helped you achieve the honor. If you have won an award at work for being a top contributor, you will want to thank those on your team and support staff, for example. You can also talk about what the honor means to you.

It can also serve as a platform to make a statement about a topic related to the award. At the beginning of the chapter, you read about how Oprah used her acceptance speech to bring attention to the serious issue of sexual harassment and assault. Another example is Patricia Arquette's speech when she won the 2015 Oscar for best supporting actress for her role in *Boyhood*. During her allotted time, she talked about the pay gap between men and women in the United States.[11]

Tips for Preparing an Award Acceptance Speech

- Let your personality show in terms of your emotions, who you choose to thank, and what you choose to talk about.
- Be excited.
- Be gracious and modest.
- Practice.
- Keep your comments short.
  - Think about the music coming on at the Oscars and drowning out an award winner's comments.

The previous presentations have all been presentations that you would deliver as an individual. In this next section, we will look at some of the unique factors involved in presenting with a group of speakers.[12]

Presenting with a Group

Team presentations are a common occurrence in academic and professional settings. You will be asked to work in groups and communicate about your experience and projects, so it is important to know how to do well in this type of presentational situation.

One of the biggest mistakes of team presentations is that they appear disjointed or like several mini-presentations. Team presentations should be cohesive. While it may be tempting to split up the assignment/project, it will make for a better outcome if you work together. Have group members lead sections, but make sure each group member is included in each section/aspect so the presentation does not turn into five mini-projects, but one, cohesive project that accomplishes a given goal.

Some key elements that will help your team presentation appear cohesive are the introduction, your visual aids, the transitions between speakers, and the conclusion. A group presentation should have one overarching introduction. During the intro in addition to providing the audience with an overview of the topic, you will want to introduce the team members if the audience is not familiar with your team. During the introductions, you can let the audience know what each team member will be discussing.

Another important element of a group presentation is providing clear transitions between speakers. This helps the presentation to flow and orients the audience when a new speaker is talking. An easy way to do this is to use a directional transition where you summarize what you just spoke about and preview what the next speaker will be discussing. For example, "Now that I have covered the market research, I will turn it over to Mark who will discuss the design phase."

Just as you want to have a cohesive introduction, you also want to have one cohesive conclusion. While individual speakers may summarize these sections as they speak, a general conclusion is a place where you can bring all of the different components of the presentation together. Given that group presentations are often longer and contain a lot of information, the conclusion is especially important. Review all of the key components of the presentation. If your presentation is persuasive, remember to end with a strong call to action.

If you are using visual aids during your presentation, you need to be sure that their design and style are consistent throughout the presentation. Even subtle differences in the way that a slide is presented, such as changing fonts or using a slightly different color scheme in charts and graphs, can take away from the sense of unity in a presentation. As a team, determine the basic template of what you want your slides to look like. It can be helpful to assign a person with compiling the visuals and checking them for consistency.

Tips for Preparing a Group Presentations

- Introduce the team members and preview their contributions to the project
- Use names as you transition from one point and speaker to the next.
  - For example, you may say, "now that I have talked about what multi-factor authentication is, Jade will share the security benefits of adapting this technology."
- Move so that the person speaking is in a front and center position.
  - Practice transitions so that you don't bump into one another.
  - Also, consider who is running the visual aids.

- Do not let a speaker stand behind a computer or podium.
  - Consider using a clicker that can be passed from speaker to speaker or have one person responsible for advancing the presentational aids.
- Make sure the people who are not speaking are being attentive (e.g., not looking at notecards, staring off into space, or having a side conversation).
- Practice as a team. While it is good for each individual to review his or her part, unique factors involved in presenting with a group of speakers.[13]

Question and Answer Session

Another communication situation you need to be prepared for is a **question and answer session.** Often, after a presentation, there is a time when people will want to ask questions. These questions may ask you to clarify information, or they may be asking for more information. In some situations, the questions will be intended to challenge the information you presented. It is important to know how to effectively handle this portion of a presentation. You might deliver an excellent presentation, but if you struggle to respond to the questions, you can easily turn off your audience or lead them to question your credibility.

When you are going into a situation where the audience will be asking questions, you will want to take some time to anticipate what some of those questions might be. If your presentation is persuasive, consider what counterarguments to your proposal might be, and think ahead about how you will respond to those arguments. At the beginning of the Q & A session, you will want to set the rules and parameters for the audience. Let the audience know how they can ask questions. Do they need to raise their hands, get in a line near a microphone, or wait for a moderator to come to them? When someone asks a question, the first thing you need to do is acknowledge the question and be sure that you understand it. If you are presenting to a larger audience, it is a good idea to repeat back the question so everyone knows what was asked. If you do not understand the question, instead of forging ahead and trying to answer, take the time to seek clarification. You can ask the person to repeat the question, tell them you are not sure what they are asking, or tell them what you think they are asking and confirm this is correct.

Once you understand the question, you want to answer as completely as you can while being succinct and direct. It is okay to take a brief pause to collect your thoughts and mentally prepare for how you respond. If you are in a situation where you do not know the answer to the question, acknowledge this to your audience. It is unethical to pretend to know an answer or to make up information to answer a question. Thank your audience member for the question and let him or her know that this is something you need to look into. If you have an audience member who starts to dominate the Q & A session by asking multiple follow up questions or starts to advance their own option rather than asking a question, you will want to take control of the situation. One strategy is to tell the questioner that you want to give others in attendance the opportunity to ask questions. You can also tell the person that you would be happy to discuss the matter after the presentation but want to be respectful of the rest of the audience's time.

Another situation that can arise during a Q & A session that you need to be prepared for is if the audience does not initially ask any questions. Sometimes the audience needs some time to formulate their questions, or audience members may be uncomfortable being the first to speak. A good strategy for handling this situation is starting off by posing and answering your own question. Saying something such as "a common question people ask" or "you may be wondering" is a great way to get the discussion started.

Sometimes audiences may be reluctant to ask questions if your topic is particularly sensitive or difficult. Allowing audience members to write down questions is a way to ease their discomfort.

If the question and answer session is following a group presentation, there are additional things you need to consider. It is important for your group to continue to appear cohesive and organized when responding to questions. If several group members jump in at the same time to answer or group members talk over one another, it creates confusion and makes your team seem less professional. It can be helpful to designate one team member as the moderator who takes questions from the audience and then indicates which team member will respond.

You may find yourself in a situation where a team member gives the wrong answer to a question or includes incorrect information in their response. You may wonder what to do when this happens. You do not want your team and team member to look bad, but you also do not want your audience to have incorrect information. A good way to handle this is to add on to your teammates response with the correct information. You can say something along the lines of, "In addition to what Mei said …" Overall, the most important thing going into a Q & A session with a team is to have a plan for how your group approach the situation.

Chapter Summary

In this chapter, we covered several types of situations where you may need to speak in front of a group including individual and group presentations. With any presentation you deliver, it is always important to consider the situation and audience and adapt the message accordingly.

Case Study Conclusion

When Oprah chose to address the issue of sexual harassment in her acceptance speech, she was addressing an issue that was being widely discussed at the time. Given that she knew that many attendees in the audience were also supporting the Time's Up movement, it was not a huge risk for her to bring up the social issue in her speech. Oprah also demonstrated grace and humility during her speech by not focusing on her own accomplishments but instead acknowledging those who have supported and inspired her. In turning the attention away from herself to broader social issues, her speech became a powerful message that viewers found encouraging and inspirational.

References

[1] Hill, L. 2018. "Oprah at the Golden Globes: Is She Running for President? She Should, They Say." *LATimes.*

[2] "Read the Full Transcript of Oprah Winfrey's Speech That Fired up the Golden Globes." *Los Angeles Times,* January 7, 2018. http://www.latimes.com/entertainment/la-et-golden-globes-2018-live-updates-here-s-the-full-transcript-of-oprah-s-1515383639-htmlstory.html.

[3] Lang, B. 2015. "Patricia Arquette's Comments Draw Praise, Unleash Controversy." *Variety,* February 23, 2015. http://variety.com/2015/film/news/patricia-arquette-comments-oscars-2015-controversy-1201439814/.

[4] Carter, M. 2013. *Designing Science Presentations* (1st ed.). Amsterdam, Netherlands: Elsevier.

[5] Collamer, N. 2013. "The Perfect Elevator Pitch to Land a Job." *Forbes,* February 4, 2013. https://www.forbes.com/sites/nextavenue/2013/02/04/the-perfect-elevator-pitch-to-land-a-job/#1089c77f1b1d.

[6] Collamer.

[7] Toastmasters International. 2017. "Delivering Technical Briefings." *Toastmasters International.* https://www.toastmasters.org/resources/public-speaking-tips/delivering-technical-briefings.

[8] Collamer.

[9] Zappala. 2016. "Introduction Construction: How to Make a Good Impression—through Planning and Practice." *Toastmasters International.* https://www.toastmasters.org/magazine/magazine-issues/2016/oct2016/introduction.

10. Bell, S. 2016. "7 Tips for Avoiding a Wedding Toast Disaster." *New York Times*, June 7, 2016. https://www.nytimes.com/2016/06/12/fashion/weddings/7-tips-for-avoiding-a-wedding-toast-disaster.html.

11. Lang, B. 2015. "Patricia Arquette's Comments Draw Praise, Unleash Controversy." *Variety*, February 23, 2015. http://variety.com/2015/film/news/patricia-arquette-comments-oscars-2015-controversy-1201439814/.

12. Toastmasters International. 2018. "Accepting Awards." *Toastmasters International*. https://www.toastmasters.org/resources/public-speaking-tips/accepting-awards.

13. McArthur, J. A. 2011. "10 Tips for Improving Group Presentations." https://jamcarthur.com/2011/11/01/10-tips-for-improving-group-presentations/.